About Island Press

Island Press is the only nonprofit organization in the United States whose principal purpose is the publication of books on environmental issues and natural resource management. We provide solutions-oriented information to professionals, public officials, business and community leaders, and concerned citizens who are shaping responses to environmental problems.

In 2004, Island Press celebrates its twentieth anniversary as the leading provider of timely and practical books that take a multidisciplinary approach to critical environmental concerns. Our growing list of titles reflects our commitment to bringing the best of an expanding body of literature to the environmental community throughout North America and the world.

Support for Island Press is provided by The Nathan Cummings Foundation, Geraldine R. Dodge Foundation, Doris Duke Charitable Foundation, Educational Foundation of America, The Charles Engelhard Foundation, The Ford Foundation, The George Gund Foundation, The Vira I. Heinz Endowment, The William and Flora Hewlett Foundation, Henry Luce Foundation, The John D. and Catherine T. MacArthur Foundation, The Andrew W. Mellon Foundation, The Moriah Fund, The Curtis and Edith Munson Foundation, National Fish and Wildlife Foundation, The New-Land Foundation, Oak Foundation, The Overbrook Foundation, The David and Lucile Packard Foundation, The Pew Charitable Trusts, The Rockefeller Foundation, The Winslow Foundation, and other generous donors.

The opinions expressed in this book are those of the authors and do not necessarily reflect the views of these foundations.

Transportation &

Sustainable Campus Communities

Will Toor | Spenser W. Havlick

Transportation &

Sustainable Campus

Communities
ISSUES, EXAMPLES,
SOLUTIONS

ISLAND PRESS

WASHINGTON • COVELO • LONDON

Library of Congress Cataloging-in-Publication data.

Toor, Will
    Transportation and sustainable campus communities: issues, examples, solutions / Will
Toor, Spenser Havlick.
      p.   cm.
Includes bibliographical references and index.
    ISBN 1-55963-922-9 (cloth : alk. paper)   ISBN 1-55963-656-4 (pbk. : alk. paper)
    1. College students—Transportation—United States. 2. Campus parking—United
States. 3. Local transit—United States—Planning. I. Havlick, Spenser Woodworth. II. Title.
    LB2864.T66 2004
    378.1'9872—dc22   2003024793

British Cataloguing-in-Publication data available.

Printed on recycled, acid-free paper ✿

Design by Henk van Assen with Amanda Bowers and Sarah Gifford

Manufactured in the United States of America
10 9 8 7 6 5 4 3 2 1

Contents

List of Photos, Figures, Tables, and Boxes

TABLES

BOXES

Acknowledgments

This book is the result of our longstanding concern about transportation impacts on college campuses. It has evolved out of our involvement in community service, teaching, and research. A precursor publication, *Finding a New Way: Campus Transportation in the 21st Century* by Will and our fellow city council member Françoise Poinsatte, was a springboard for this work.

We would like first to thank our student research assistant, Kate Mangione, who conducted invaluable research and contributed greatly to the writing of Chapters 7, 8, and 9. Two other student interns, Leanne Sweeney and Charles Bloom, conducted many campus interviews and were helpful in reading early drafts.

We would like to thank Daniel Hess, a professor in the Department of Urban and Regional Planning at the State University of New York–Buffalo, and Jeffrey Tumlin, a principal with Nelson/Nygaard Associates, for their helpful critiques of our draft prospectus.

Special appreciation goes to the students in our spring 2002 senior planning seminar and spring 2002 environmental studies senior seminar for conducting hundreds of campus interviews.

We wish to thank a few key individuals whose insights over the years have helped shape our approach to transportation planning: Jim Charlier of Charlier Associates; John Daggett, City of Fort Collins transportation planner; Todd Litman of the Victoria Transport Policy Institute; Peter Newman for his personal inspiration to us and for his work which has made a difference all over the world; Donald Shoup for his keen insights on the economics of parking; and Tracy Winfree, City of Boulder transportation director. Adam Krom and Brian Mohr stand out as two of our students who taught us as much about transportation as we taught them.

While we visited many campuses and interviewed dozens of individuals, we offer special thanks to the following people: Bob Baker of the University of Minnesota; Ed Beimborn at the University of Wisconsin–Milwaukee; Allan Byam of the University of Massachusetts–Amherst; David Cook, Jim Baily, and Dwayne Nuzum at the University of Colorado–Boulder; Liz Davey and Renee Gardner of Tulane University; Deborah Freed of the University of North Carolina–Chapel Hill; Robert Hawkins and Kathleen Miller of the University of Pittsburgh; Landon Hilliard of the Boulder Valley School District; Barbara Laurenson of Nelson/Nygaard Associates; David Lieb at Cornell University; Gordon Lovegrove and Steve Balyi of the University of British Columbia; Nancy McKiddy and Bob Giordano at the University of Montana; Ian Napier of the Australian Pedestrian Council; Arthur Orsini of **off ramp**, Larry Pageler and Wes Scott at the University of California–Santa Cruz; Robert Penniman of the CATMA in Burlington, Vermont; Steven Pesci ,Tom Kelly, and Julie Newman at the University of New Hampshire; Carl Puffenbarger at James Madison University; Scott Rutherford at the University of Washington; Brian Shaw of Emory University; David Takemoto-Weerts and Jack Harris at the University of California–Davis; James Wagner of the University of California–Santa Barbara, Ken Willit and Phil Smith with the City of Missoula, Montana; and Robert Wonnett of the University of Colorado–Colorado Springs. David Havlick contributed useful comments and provided data for case studies of the University of North Carolina and the University of Montana, where he had teaching assignments.

Staff members at the University of Colorado Environmental Center and the University of Colorado Department of Design and Planning have been most supportive of our work as we used their talents and facilities. Kim Kelly of the College of Architecture and Planning staff at the University of Colorado provided yeoman service by typing and reviewing manuscript editions. Her keen interest in the subject and her punctual turnaround of chapter drafts helped to keep us on task and on deadline. Ben Everson assisted with graphics and photographs.

We want to give special thanks to our Island Press editor, Heather Boyer, who provided superb suggestions for orderly flow of chapters, editorial critique, and fertile guidance as the manuscript developed. James Nuzum of Island Press advised us on graphic layout and preparation of photographs and figures. Sherrie Voss Matthews carried out an extremely helpful task as copyeditor. We would like to thank Cecilia González, our production editor.

We acknowledge financial support from the Colorado Office of Energy Conservation and the University of Colorado Outreach Program.

No work of this magnitude could be completed without the unselfish support of our spouses and children. Mariella, Nikolaus, and Theresa (born during our final chapters) and Val, Scott, Jenny, and David showed great patience.

Introduction

Why Does Transportation Matter?

Any university that is attempting to make the transition toward sustainability must confront the issue of transportation. The daily movement of people back and forth to campus in automobiles burning fossil fuels is one of the largest impacts a typical educational institution imposes on the life support systems of the planet. In addition, the travel patterns that students learn while in college are likely to influence their future travel choices. The personal automobile has become the dominant mode of travel in the United States, with more than 95 percent of personal trips taking place by car. Vehicle miles traveled grew from 1 trillion miles annually in 1970 to 2.6 trillion miles in 1998 (Bureau of Transportation Statistics 2000). This growth in individual automobile use has profound environmental implications. Transportation accounts for over two thirds of the U.S. consumption of petroleum. Of this, more than 50 percent is used for personal vehicles, making U.S. citizens the most profligate petroleum users on the globe. The average U.S. citizen consumes five times as much energy for transportation as a resident of a wealthy Asian country, 1.65 times as much as Canadians and Australians, and 2.5 times as much as Europeans (Newman and Kenworthy 1999, pp. 69–71). One note on the focus of this book—because the transportation infrastructure, urban densities, and transportation culture are so different in Europe and Asia, we do not focus on those areas. The analysis in this book will be most directly applicable to campus communities in the United States, Canada, and Australia.

Despite improvements to automobile technology that have been driven by the Clean Air Act, automobiles continue to be a large source of air pollution. The American Lung Association's *State of the Air Report: 2003* (American Lung Association 2003) concludes that more than 142 million

Americans are breathing in unhealthy amounts of ozone pollution, which has been linked to lung and heart disease. Highway vehicles emit 26 percent of all volatile organic compounds and 32 percent of nitrogen oxides—the precursors to ozone formation. They are also responsible for more than 60 percent of nationwide emissions of carbon monoxide (Benfield and Replogle 2002). In addition, there is increasing evidence of health effects associated with "toxic tailpipe emissions" in the immediate vicinity of high volume roadways. Benzene, butadiene, and diesel exhaust appear to be the major culprits, and can lead to elevated cancer levels for residents near major roads (South Coast Air Quality Management District 1999).

Transportation energy use also is responsible for a substantial portion of greenhouse gas emissions. Overall, transportation accounts for 32 percent of U.S. carbon dioxide emissions, with motor vehicles accounting for the bulk of this, about 25 percent. Transportation is also the fastest-growing source of carbon emissions. While there has been some increase in vehicle efficiency since 1970 (approximately a 17 percent increase)—which would tend to reduce carbon emissions—the large growth in the U.S. vehicle fleet, and in per capita vehicles miles traveled, has led to an increase in carbon emissions since 1970 of more than 50 percent (Benfield and Replogle 2002; Mackenzie 1997). Other impacts include the damages associated with oil drilling and oil spills, and the nonpoint source water pollution, such as runoff from roads and parking lots.

Transportation in University Communities

Throughout North America, college and university campuses have experienced growth in numbers of students, staff, and faculty over the last forty years. In addition, as with the broader population, per capita automobile use and ownership have increased significantly to the point that almost every urban campus faces serious impacts from car traffic and parking shortages. Thus, at the same time that the car has had major impacts on the local and global environment, it also has had a major negative impact on the quality of life in campus communities. Therefore, efforts to tame car traffic can have twin benefits: helping the environment while improving the livability of the campus. In fact, there are also substantial fiscal benefits that campuses can realize.

During the last decade, a number of major North American universities have begun grappling with how to provide access to the campus while maintaining quality of life and environmental values. It has been a difficult and fascinating process, which has led to some fundamental changes in the way many schools approach transportation. Multiple factors—including lack of land for new parking lots, the high costs of building parking structures, pressure from surrounding communities, and the desire to preserve air quality and campus green spaces—are leading many institutions toward a new vision based upon expanded transit access, better bicycle and pedestrian facilities, and financial incentives for students, faculty, and staff to drive less (Poinsatte and Toor 1999; Miller 2001; Daggett and Gutkowski 2002; Toor and Havlick 2002; Balsas 2003; Toor 2003). This is a stark contrast to the traditional approach to campus transportation planning, which tended to assume that the primary solution to increased demand is to build new parking. The new vision goes under the general rubric of *transportation demand management*, or TDM.

Perhaps the most important single driving force behind these new approaches is the economics of parking when cheap land is no longer available for surface parking lots. The transition from surface parking to parking structures can increase the cost of parking by an order of magnitude and require substantial capital outlays. Those campuses with the most robust transportation programs have typically been motivated more by cost containment than by environmental concerns—simply put, it was *cheaper* for them to invest in transportation alternatives than it was to build more parking.

Another important factor is pressure on campuses from surrounding communities to reduce negative off-campus transportation impacts. Parking and traffic impacts off of the campus are perhaps the most widespread source of "town-gown" conflict. These conflicts can be mitigated by strategies that reduce the use of automobiles for access to campus. Several educational institutions have signed agreements with the surrounding community to cap the number of automobile trips to the campus in return for approval of further campus growth.

Demand management techniques used by educational institutions include the provision of transit passes to students and employees that allow free access to bus and rail transit (Brown et al. 2001); developing high frequency and late-night transit services (Poinsatte and Toor 1998); raising parking rates to reduce demand (Wilson and Shoup 1990); using so-called "parking cash-out" to pay employees not to drive (Shoup 1997); banning first- or second-year students from bringing cars to campus; expanding student and employee housing on or near campus to reduce trip lengths; creating employee vanpools; providing a guaranteed emergency ride home for employees who participate in transit pass or carpool programs; allowing compressed work weeks and telecommuting; providing access to shared vehicles for some trips through nonprofit or commercial "carshare" programs or on-campus car rentals; marketing alternative modes; and improving infrastructure and programs to encourage walking and bicycling (Toor and Havlick 2002; Poinsatte and Toor 2001; Litman 2002). We will provide details on these strategies in later chapters.

Because universities tend to have high densities of employment of residents on or adjacent to campus, they are well-suited to policies focused on greater use of walking, bicycling, and transit than is the norm in the United States. A number of universities and surrounding communities have been able to achieve transportation modal splits that are closer to European numbers than the American norm. For example, Boulder, Colorado, has seen a sixfold increase in transit use by university students during the 1990s (Toor 2002). During this time students also increased their bicycle use (from 20 percent of all trips to 31 percent) and reduced the percentage of trips taken in single occupant vehicles from 49 percent to 36 percent (Caldwell and Parker 2001). During this period the city and the university invested heavily in transit passes, high-frequency transit service, and improved bicycle infrastructure, while the university-parking inventory remained essentially static. There are a number of universities where less than 50 percent of trips to campus are by car, with at least one as low as 23 percent (Balsas 2003). For comparison, nationally more than 90 percent of all work commute trips are by car (U.S. Department of Transportation 1995)— so there is clearly something very different going on in some campus communities!

These examples have implications beyond the campus communities.

Universities are a place where visionary thinking and real world institutional decision making meet, allowing new ideas to be developed and tested. In many ways they serve as social change laboratories for the rest of society. In addition, the approaches to transportation that students learn in college are likely to influence their future transportation choices. For many students, their college experience may be their first real experience with pedestrian- and bicycle-friendly design, or with accessible transit. This experience will influence their future choices as individual commuters, voters, and leaders.

The Economics of Campus Parking

The traditional response to demands for parking by campus constituents, or complaints about off-campus spillover, has been to expand the campus parking supply. For growing schools that do not have land available for surface parking, this presents a financial challenge.

Many schools do not have additional land that can be devoted to surface parking lots. In fact, new construction often uses up land that used to be devoted to surface parking. The supply of surface parking decreases as institutions convert parking lots into other uses, such as new research buildings, dormitories, stadiums, and theaters, while the new uses increase parking demand. The campus is then faced with either acquiring new land—a very expensive proposition at urban campuses, and often impossible—or constructing parking structures over existing surface lots. The capital cost of construction is quite high—generally in the range of $15,000 to $30,000 per *net new* parking space (Shoup 1995; Cook 1999). The high end of this range comes when structures are built on top of surface lots, and existing spaces are lost, so that the net number of new spaces may be substantially lower than the total number of spaces built. Thus for 1,000 spaces a campus would be looking at $15 million–$30 million in capital costs.

Recovering this from users would require monthly parking fees of $100 or more—much higher than is typically charged or is politically acceptable to the campus community. Either the university must use general fund dollars to subsidize the cost, or the costs are spread across users who park in surface lots, and the surface parkers subsidize the structures. This second

0.1
The University of Arizona's newest parking structure cost nearly $17 million to build. Additional maintenance and operational costs are significant and are often overlooked.
Photo by Spenser Havlick

strategy requires that the bulk of parking be in surface lots, as the cost/person increases rapidly as the percentage of structured parking increases. Even if the money can be recovered from user fees, construction of parking structures still requires the use of the limited capacity that most institutions have to borrow money for capital construction, putting these parking structure costs in direct competition with the construction of new academic and research buildings. Are there are other approaches to managing transportation demand that are less expensive? In most cases where land constraints lead to the use of structured parking, the answer is yes.

Consider the practice of providing transit passes to the campus community. In a typical case, the institution will contract with a transit agency to allow students, employees, or both to ride the transit system without paying a fare. This will lead to an increase in transit use, and will cause some people to shift from driving to campus to riding transit. This will both free up some parking spaces directly and will have an indirect political impact. When constituents complain about lack of parking, the school will now be able to respond that they provide the pass program as an attractive alternative. In any area with an existing transit system that has unused capacity, a transit pass program may be a viable option.

There are more than 50 universities with more than 800,000 students and employees that offer transit passes. Student ridership increased between 71 percent and 200 percent during the inaugural year of these programs (Brown et al. 2001). Typically, students vote to increase their fees in order to allow any student with a valid university ID to ride local or regional routes fare free, while faculty and staff transit passes are either paid by the university through general funds or out of parking revenues or may be optional fees paid by individual employees. Students and employees benefit from inexpensive transportation; the university benefits from decreased parking supply costs, improved community relations due to the reduction in off campus traffic, and a greener image.

The faculty/staff bus pass program at the University of Colorado provides an instructive example of reduced parking supply costs. This program allows each permanent faculty or staff member who is eligible for benefits to ride local and regional buses and light rail by showing his or her university ID. Because some employees have reduced the number of times they drive to campus, or stopped driving to campus altogether, due to the availability of free transit, a total of 350 parking spaces are freed up. The annual cost of the bus pass program is $393,400, so it costs $1,125 per parking space left open. For comparison, the annual debt service to provide one additional parking space is $2,723. Thus, it is 2.5 times as expensive to provide one additional parking space compared to reducing demand by one space. The net annual savings to campus, compared to providing 350 new spaces, is thus $560,000.

Next, consider the simplest financial incentive—raising the price of parking. There are extensive empirical data that show that parking pricing is one of the most significant determinants of travel behavior (U.S. EPA 1998). The elasticity of demand will depend upon the alternatives that are available. Even in cases where there is no transit serving a workplace, price increases have been shown to reduce single-occupant commuting and increase carpooling. When Cornell University raised the price of parking in 1991 as part of a comprehensive demand management approach, the effect was to reduce single occupant vehicle trips by 26 percent, with most of the shift to carpooling (Cornell 1996). A number of campuses give substantial reductions in the cost of a parking permit for carpools. At the University of Maryland, carpool permits can be 75 percent less expensive than drive-alone permits; at Cornell carpools with three or more people can actually receive rebate payments.

Another important option is the creation of opportunities for occasional parking. If the only way to have a secure parking spot on campus is to buy an annual or semester pass, people may buy passes to assure access when they need it. This then creates an incentive to use their prepaid permit. At least one institution has eliminated permits and instead sells daily coupons. Some schools offer occasional parker programs, allowing users to purchase coupons to park on campus a limited number of times per semester. A number of campuses require users to give up their parking permits as a condition of receiving discounted carpool parking, transit passes, or cash benefits, but then give these users occasional parking privileges.

A variant of the carpool approach is giving students or employees access to shared vehicles. At the Massachusetts Institute of Technology, for example, students have access to vehicles through the company Zipcar.

Students pay a membership fee and then are able to reserve cars through the phone or Internet. Cars are located in off-street parking lots in the campus vicinity. Stanford University contracts with Enterprise Rent-A-Car to allow students easy access to short-term rentals as an alternative to car ownership. At the University of Washington, students and employees can join Flexcar, a membership-based carsharing program.

Because of the political difficulty involved in raising parking rates, some institutions have taken an alternate approach: paying employees not to drive. The campus makes a monthly cash payment to any employee who chooses not to purchase a parking permit. The cost difference between having a parking permit and not having one is then the sum of the cost of purchasing a permit and the cash payment offered to those who do not purchase a permit. Stanford University has pioneered this program with their Clean Air Cash program.

In general, the most cost-effective scenario involves some combination of investment in new parking and in transportation alternatives. This may require that parking rates be raised not only to pay the cost of providing any new parking that is constructed, but also to pay for a range of transportation alternatives.

Taking Bicycles Seriously

Bicycles are the most efficient form of transportation, with the lowest energy input and lowest output of pollutants and greenhouse gases. Active transportation—bicycling and walking—also can contribute to the health of the campus population. Campus populations are well-suited to bicycle use. One study of 23 research universities found that 64 percent of students lived within one mile of campus, and 84 percent lived within five miles (Daggett and Gutkowski 2002). If appropriate bicycle infrastructure is provided, bicycles are very competitive for trips of this length. The basic investments necessary are to provide safe and pleasant routes to and through campus, and adequate bicycle parking. These are relatively inexpensive: The cost of one bicycle parking space (about $100) is less than 1 percent of the cost of one new automobile parking space. Some campuses have invested in additional features such as covered bicycle parking, grade separated

0.2

Bike parking uses land
more efficiently and is
more cost-effective than
car parking lots.

Photo by Francoise Poinsatte

crossings for bike paths, bicycle signal heads at signalized intersections,
full-service "bike stations" with secure parking and repair service available,
free bicycle checkout for students and employees, and even zero-interest
loans for bicycle purchases by students (Poinsatte and Toor 1999; University of Montana 2002). The impact can be significant. The University of
California–Santa Barbara and Davis campuses have achieved student nonmotorized mode shares of more than 50 percent. There is room for a significant increase in bicycling at many campuses for a very modest investment.

The Land Use-Transportation Connection

It has become a truism in planning circles that one cannot separate land use
and transportation planning. This is just as true for institutions of higher
education as it is for cities. Some of the key planning decisions that affect
transportation are the amount of student housing provided on campus; the
amount (if any) of faculty and staff housing provided; and the degree to
which activities are spread across satellite campuses. From the other side,
the transportation policies and infrastructure at a campus will largely

determine the appearance and feel of the campus. Decisions about parking will affect the amount of green space, the amount of impervious surface, and the amount of land available for buildings.

For instance, the new master plan at the University of Maryland will increase the amount of green space on campus, decrease the amount of impervious surface, and make the campus more pedestrian friendly while at the same time allowing more academic and support facilities to be built (University of Maryland 2002). They propose to meet these seemingly contradictory goals—by eliminating much of the existing surface parking, reducing car travel through campus, and moving people by clean fuel shuttles and by bicycle. Their transportation plans are clearly influenced by the desired character of the campus.

Student housing is a key determinant of transportation. When students live on campus, their daily transport needs are likely to be largely met through walking, biking, and campus shuttles, with personal cars being used primarily for weekend travel. At schools where first- and second-year students who live on campus are restricted from bringing cars, this effect will be even more pronounced. By contrast, students living off campus will be more likely to drive to school. Many campuses, including Stanford University, the University of Maryland–College Park, and the University of Colorado–Boulder, are planning or have built new student housing partially to meet their transportation goals.

Town-Gown Relations

If a university generates traffic and overflow parking in surrounding neighborhoods, it probably is also generating community relations problems. Many times, residents' complaints about noise, safety, pollution, and the inconvenience of finding parking in front of their own houses lead to serious conflicts between the municipality and the university or college. This flashpoint for town-gown conflict is perhaps as important as disputes over student housing and off-campus student behavior in residential neighborhoods.

A demand management approach may be able to reduce this conflict. In fact, cooperative efforts on transportation may help improve strained relations because there is a convergence of interests between the institution's desire to provide cost-effective access to campus and the community's desire to reduce off-campus traffic and parking impacts. These can include joint planning and funding of bicycle, transit, and pedestrian improvements in the campus and surrounding area.

One difficulty is that any TDM strategy that involves managing parking supply and price may simply displace parking demand off-campus. In order to prevent this in commercial districts adjacent to educational institutions, it is common to install parking meters. Some cities also have implemented Residential Parking Permit (RPP) zones in nearby residential streets. RPP programs allow residents to purchase full-time parking permits, often for a nominal fee, while restricting nonresident parking.

Because university populations provide such a good market for transit and bicycle use, local government efforts to expand these services will be more successful if they serve university populations. This is an important point. Unlike car travel, where adding additional travelers degrades the overall service, adding more riders to transit makes it possible to increase frequency and thus improve service for all other travelers. This is why a number of communities have been able to maintain long-term funding commitments to improving transit facilities that serve student populations.

The University of Washington offers an example of a creative approach to a significant conflict over university traffic. In the late 1980s, planners estimated that UW's expansion plans would bring 10,000 more cars a day. The city of Seattle was extremely concerned, and ultimately the university and the city agreed to a master plan that allowed the university to grow—without increasing traffic or parking demand in surrounding neighborhoods (University of Washington 1998, 2002). In response, UW created the "U-PASS" program, with the goals of improving transit, providing more bicycle facilities, and changing the financial incentives around parking. Parking costs were increased from $24/month to $46.50/month, followed by more gradual increases, with much of the additional revenue going to support the alternatives. The net effect: while the campus population grew 7 percent during the 1990s, parking demand fell 22 percent and car trips fell by 17 percent during the a.m. peak, and 5 percent averaged over the day. Stanford University offers a similar example. The general use permit that the university negotiated with Santa Clara County requires the university to cap

0.3
Residential parking permit zones are effective tools to decrease long-term student parking in campus neighborhoods.
Photo by Spenser Havlick

peak-period trips to and from campus (Santa Clara County 2001). Using the set of techniques described earlier, Stanford was able to add 2 million square feet of building space during the 1990s under this permit while holding with no net increase in peak-period traffic; Stanford has recently renegotiated a similar clause in its next General Use Permit.

The Structure of the Book

Chapter 1, Transportation and Sustainability in Campus Communities, discusses the trends in surface transportation in the United States and contrasts these to other developed countries with a brief historical review of the major campus and community impacts of automobile use. It will discuss the trends in transportation policy and recent innovations at educational institutions. We will examine why a number of university communities have been able to achieve levels of bicycling, walking, and transit use that are unusual in the United States. This chapter will discuss the influence of urban design contrasts and the campus's culture on transportation policy.

Chapter 2, The Transportation Demand Management Toolbox, presents an introduction to the toolbox of transportation demand strategies that have been tried at different campuses. This chapter will allow users to assess the strategies that are most likely to be successful and cost-effective at a particular campus.

This chapter also explores a variety of approaches that campuses use for funding transportation. Some funding structures, such as general fund subsidies to parking, promote automobile dependence. Other funding structures promote a more balanced mix. We will examine the use of general funds, surcharges on capital construction, student fees, and other approaches to funding parking and demand management programs.

Chapter 3, Parking: The Growing Dilemma, describes the economics of expanding parking supply in a campus context. Many schools do not have additional land that can be devoted to surface parking lots. In fact, new construction is using up land that used to be devoted to surface parking. The supply of surface parking decreases as institutions convert parking lots into other uses, such as new research buildings, dormitories, stadiums, and theaters. The campus is then faced with either acquiring new land—a very expensive proposition at urban campuses and often impossible—or con-

0.4
This expensive parking facility was built in response to parking shortages at the University of Colorado. Campus parking rates almost tripled to pay for this structure.
Photo by Francoise Poinsatte

structing parking structures over existing surface lots. This chapter will show how to calculate the true cost of expanding parking supply in land-constrained environments. We then examine the cost of shifting drivers to other modes of transportation. Now, any approach that reduces the amount of parking provided on campus might cause spillover parking in surrounding neighborhoods, so strategies such as residential parking permit zones must be considered. We also discuss student-parking restrictions and "green" design to minimize the water quality impacts of parking lots.

Chapter 4, Successful Campus Transit Development, examines how transit pass programs can dramatically increase transit use in university communities. The chapter will address the nuts and bolts of student and employee transit pass programs, and it will offer tips for successful negotiations between the campus and the transit agency. It also will discuss how to reposition transit services to serve the higher education community—and how transit ridership from campus can support improved transit services for the rest of the community.

Chapter 5, Promoting Nonmotorized Transportation, describes steps that educational institutions can take to promote walking and bicycle use by students, faculty, and staff. We address both physical infrastructure and educational and promotional programs.

Chapter 6, Developing a Campus Transportation Plan, examines the appropriate scope of work for a transportation plan. Many campuses have long-range master plans or transportation and parking plans. Getting these plans right is important. To get good answers, you need to ask the right questions. We examine how one can determine what level of investment in parking supply will be cost-effective and the noneconomic considerations that may come into play, including preserving campus green space and reducing off-site traffic impacts.

Chapter 7, Campus Case Studies, will present eight innovative campuses across North America. The sample was chosen not as a comprehensive list, but rather as a balanced representation of locations and sizes. Each one is pursuing interesting TDM programs, from small towns in rural settings to major urban areas.

Chapter 8, Greening the Campus Fleet, discusses the use of alternative fuels and low emissions vehicles for both light- and heavy-duty vehicles

0.5
At many campuses
high-frequency transit
and good bicycle
infrastructure
work together.

Photo by Spenser Havlick

used by campus departments. We discuss the costs and benefits of different vehicle technologies. We also will discuss incentives campuses can develop to encourage greener vehicle choices by individual members of the campus community.

Chapter 9, Transportation Demand Management for Elementary and Secondary Schools, shows some of the approaches that have been tried to reduce automobile use by high school students, including the use of school transportation coordinators, parking restrictions, free transit for youth, and efforts to promote cultural changes.

Chapter 10, Conclusions, reminds the reader that this book becomes a "work in progress." As more schools reduce car-related problems, cities and suburbs may discover that TDM measures, increased parking fees, and other car-taming measures employed by universities have applications beyond the campus. Sustainable transportation practices at colleges may promote life-long use of transit and nonmotorized modes of transportation among graduates and other observers.

References

American Lung Association. 2003. *State of the Air Report 2003,* found at
www.lungusa.org/air2003.

Balsas, C. 2003. Sustainable Transportation Planning on College Campuses, *Transport Policy*
10:35–49.

Benfield, F., and M. Replogle. 2002. The Roads Most Traveled: Sustainable Transportation
in America—or Not. *Environmental Law Review* 32:633–10647, found at
www.environmentaldefense.org/documents/2064_ELR_transportation.pdf.

Brown, J., D. Hess, and D. Shoup. 2001. Unlimited Access, *Transportation* 28(3):233–267.
See also www.sppsr.ucla.edu/its/ua for profiles and contact information on university
transit pass programs.

Bureau of Transportation Statistics. 2000. *National Transportation Statistics.* U.S. Department
of Transportation.

Caldwell, E., and D. Parker. 2001. *Modal Shift in the Boulder Valley: 1990 to 2000,* City of Boulder Audit and Evaluation Division, Boulder, CO.

Campus Ecology Web site. 2002. *Transportation Projects,* found at www.nwf.org/
campusecology/ListProjects.cfm?id=10. National Wildlife Federation, Washington, DC.

Cook, D. 1999. The Economics of Parking Garages and the Alternatives to Them. In *Proceedings
of Finding a New Way* conference, University of Colorado Environmental Center, Boulder, CO.

Cornell University Office of Transportation Services. 1996. *Commuting Solutions: Summary of
Transportation Demand Management Program.* Cornell University, Ithaca, NY.

Daggett, J., and R. Gutkowski. 2002. *University Transportation Survey: Transportation in University Communities,* found at fcgov.com/uts.pdf. City of Fort Collins and Colorado State
University, Fort Collins, CO.

Litman, T. 2002. Campus Transport Management Trip Reduction Programs on College, University and Research Campuses. In the *Online TDM Encyclopedia.* Victoria Transport Policy
Institute, found at www.vtpi.org/tdm/tdm5.htm.

Mackenzie, J. 1997. Driving the Road to Sustainable Ground Transportation. In *Frontiers of
Sustainability,* Island Press, Washington, DC.

Miller, J. 2001. *Transportation on College and University Campuses: A Synthesis of Transit Practices.* National Academy Press, Washington, DC.

Newman, P., and J. Kenworthy. 1999. *Sustainability and Cities: Overcoming Automobile Dependence.* Island Press, Washington, DC.

Poinsatte, F., and W. Toor. 1999. *Finding a New Way: Campus Transportation for the Twenty-
first Century,* found at www.Colorado.EDU/ecenter. University of Colorado Environmental
Center, Boulder, CO.

Santa Clara County. 2001. *Stanford University General Use Permit,* found at www.sccplan-
ning.org/planning/content/PropInfoDev/PropInfoDev_Stanford_CommPlan.jsp.

Shoup, D. 1995. *How Much Does a Parking Space Cost?* University of California at Los Angeles,
Institute of Transportation Policy.

Shoup, D. 1997. Evaluating the Effects of Cashing Out Employer Paid Parking: Eight Case
Studies. *Transport Policy* 4:201–216.

South Coast Air Quality Management District. 1999. *Multiple Air Toxics Exposure Study in the South Coast Air Basin:* MATES II. Draft Final Report, Diamond Bar, CA.

Toor, W. 2002. Keynote lecture on sustainable transportation, Missoula Transportation Demand Management Summit, found at www.Colorado.EDU/ecenter/news/publications/will_toor/mim_presentation.html.

Toor, W. 2003. The Road Less Traveled: Sustainable Transportation for Campuses. *Planning for Higher Education* 31(3):131–141.

Toor, W. and S. Havlick. 2002. *Finding a New Way: Campus Transportation Slideshow,* found at www.Colorado.EDU/ecenter/news/publications/new_way_slideshow.html. University of Colorado, Boulder, CO.

University of Maryland. 2002. *Campus Master Plan,* found at www.inform.umd.edu/CampusInfo/MasterPlan/index.html.

University of Montana. 2002. Office of Transportation, found at www.umt.edu/asum/ot.

University of Washington, *Agreement with City of Seattle,* found at www.washington.edu/community/cuagree.html, 1998.

University of Washington. 2002. Master *Plan 2002–2012,* found at www.washington.edu/community/cmp/cmp.html.

U.S. Department of Energy. 2002. *Clean Cities Success Stories—University of California at Davis,* found at www.ccities.doe.gov/success/ucdavis.shtml.

U.S. Department of Energy. 2002. Clean Cities Success Stories, found at www.ccities.doe.gov/success/ucdavis.shtml.

U.S. Department of Transportation. 1995. *National Personal Transportation Study.*

Willson, R. and D. Shoup. 1990. Parking Subsidies and Travel Choices: Assessing the Evidence. *Transportation* 17:141–157.

Chapter 1

CHAPTER 1

Transportation and Sustainability in Campus Communities

The historic or traditional American college campus was designed around the pedestrian, and walking was the primary transportation mode for most students. Up until the 1940s most students lived on campus and arrived by bus, train, or trolley.

In the earliest years of many colleges and universities, the first buildings were located just beyond the bustling commercial center of the "host" town or city. The institutions of higher learning were often separated from the town by woods, a stream, a meadow, or some natural buffer. Among thousands of examples we could cite are Colgate University (1819) at the southern edge of Hamilton, New York, or Beloit College (1846) up on the hill above the Rock River and above downtown Beloit, Wisconsin. Old Main is the original University of Colorado (1876) edifice and it was situated several blocks south of Boulder Creek and on a predominant hill overlooking downtown Boulder, Colorado. Western Washington State University's picturesque campus (1933) began somewhat isolated from and to the south of Bellingham, Washington. Today most of these schools and thousands of other campuses are surrounded by urban development. In some cases—such as the University of Chicago, Carnegie Mellon, the Massachusetts Institute of Technology, San Jose State University, Wayne State University, or Georgetown University—not only has there been an "engulfment" of urbanization but also there have been substantial increases of population density in close proximity to the typical urban campus. These two forces, the urban swallowing of the campus and the densification of the contiguous neighborhoods, set the stage for land-use problems. Many school administrators believe the institution needs to grow in order to survive or stay competitive with other schools while the town struggles with added housing demands and traffic congestion and overspill into the community (Gurwitt 2003).

1.5
(ABOVE)
The cost of adding parking by building structures can exceed $30,000 per net new space.

Photo by Francoise Poinsatte

The University of Michigan demonstrates a typical transformation from a pedestrian-oriented campus plan to one that became saturated with automobile trips. From the 1880s until 1920, the landscaped corridor of the central campus was a pedestrian place. In the 1930s and 1940s parking for the infrequent automobile was provided. In the period between 1960 and 1990 the once peaceful strolling mall was modified to accommodate car parking. In recent years some car parking has been eliminated and replaced by flower gardens and seating for students and visitors.

The number of students who own cars has increased over time. Today there is a common and rather widespread problem of automobile overspill beyond campus parking facilities onto the neighborhoods surrounding the campus. In many communities, housing in close proximity to a campus has become a premium. As student-housing scarcity occurs, middle- and low-income students resort to housing that is farther from campus and somewhat more affordable. This tends to increase automobile travel. As campus parking facilities fill each day, and as parking rates rise, student car commuters search for parking in neighborhoods already heavily populated by students—most of whom have a car and have used the public and private car parking areas for their auto storage needs.

Short-term car parking, with a car space "turning over" four to six times a day, tends to change the livability of a neighborhood by increasing the noise, litter, vandalism, and general degradation of the residential environment that come from the increased number of student vehicles. The car storage overspill is a documented nuisance, and blight has now become a trademark of most large university neighborhoods where student enrollment outpaces the town's ability to absorb the greater number of cars that are brought to school by increasing numbers of students.

We have contacted 150 campus planners and parking management officials at university and college campuses around the country. (Please see the Appendix for a list of respondents and institutions contacted.) In our survey of nearly 8 percent of the 3,300 colleges and universities, only six reported that they had no parking problems on campus or in nearby university neighborhoods. The University of North Carolina–Charlotte reported they have 2,000 empty car spaces per day and Warren Wilson College in Asheville told our research team that "they have more spaces than cars." No freshman cars are permitted at Warren Wilson (on the basis of educational priorities), which has 800 students and 375 faculty and staff. This is certainly the exception rather than the rule in our survey of colleges and universities. The overwhelming number of responding schools report "severe to critical" parking overspills into their communities. It should be no surprise when the average student-staff-faculty population ratio to available car parking spaces is approximately 4:1, according to our study of institutions of higher education.

There are at least three schools of thought on how the student auto overabundance can be managed. One approach is to increase the supply of car storage and parking areas (University of Arizona Parking and Transportation Services 2003). The costs of this approach vary from city to city and campus to campus. A second position is for the academic institution to rely on the free market system to meet increasing demand. This approach is where the institution relies on private facilities and outside parking providers. Some say this is the status quo, a do-nothing stance. The third

1.6
The University of
California–Santa Cruz
provides an example
of a comprehensive
demand management
approach to campus
transportation. The
campus provides a bike
trailer and van to assist
bike commuters up
steep roads on inbound
trips—a unique
TDM tool.
Courtesy of University of
California–Santa Cruz

technique can be called the demand management approach. Instead of increasing the supply of parking the university would explore ways in which the demand for parking could be reduced (Shoup 1997).

Later in the book examples of transportation demand management (TDM) will be discussed in more detail, but it should be noted here that effective parking demand management, which reduces neighborhood overspill, is composed of multiple tools for specific town and campus conditions. The toolkit usually contains specialized parking permits, various forms of bus service and bus shuttles, and differential parking prices related to distance from campus. Other components in a TDM toolkit could include effective bike paths, storage lockers and other biking facilities, and special incentives for vanpool and carpool parking that are "close in." Some schools are experimenting with free bikes, such as those that are seen scattered around campus at the University of Florida–Gainesville.

No one parking demand management tool works all by itself, nor is one parking reduction plan appropriate for every campus. Each institution and

community should craft an array of parking management technologies that fit the needs of the student body and faculty. Campuses that are primarily residential-based have different parking and traffic challenges from a commuter college or junior college, which tend to be more automobile dependent more hours of the day and evening. Universities with a medical center and medical schools as a part of their central campus have different peak demand periods than a liberal arts college with 80 percent or higher residential enrollment.

Factors That Influence Campus Transportation Policies

There are seven major factors that influence the transportation policy and practices on university and college campuses. These factors play different roles of importance at different educational institutions, but they are all at work to one degree or another.

BOX 1.1 | **TRAVEL DEMAND MANAGEMENT AT THE UNIVERSITY OF CALIFORNIA–SANTA CRUZ**

Wes Scott, director of Transportation and Parking Services (TAPS) at the University of California–Santa Cruz, has become a champion of traffic demand management (TDM) practices. The Santa Cruz campus is nestled amidst a redwood forest with a campus population of 17,000, but with only 5,000 parking spaces. Scott has implemented an array of TDM practices as an alternative to cutting down redwoods for car lots and as an economically wise decision.

The UC–Santa Cruz TDM tools include carpools that carry 300 people per day, vanpools transporting 100 per day, a transit pass system that moves 525 students each day, and a differential pricing system for parking permits. The TAPS parking permit for close-in parking costs $684 per year and the remote lots cost $384 annually. Freshmen and sophomores

1. The physical layout of the campus as driven by campus growth, the campus master plan, and aesthetic considerations. Aesthetics and the value of campus green spaces influence parking and transportation programs.

2. The philosophy about transportation priorities as determined by the governing body (regents, trustees, etc.) or student initiatives and implemented by university administration.

3. Resources available, both staff and funding, to create efficient campus transportation options.

4. The physical transportation infrastructure in the surrounding region. Urban campuses differ from suburban and rural campuses.

5. Residential campuses differ from commuter campuses.

6. The trend of more students and employees living farther from campus in order to achieve rent or homeownership savings.

7. The cost of parking.

In a university that has doubled or tripled its student population in the past forty years in a densely built up urban area, three options exist. The administration could call for a cap on growth, or increased density, or it could require a satellite or sister campus. The University of Michigan–Ann Arbor is a model for using the satellite campus to accommodate growth. Their North Campus is intended to accommodate new growth, research

are not permitted to have cars on campus. Scott reports, "We stack vehicles in the aisles of remote parking lots and have created 400 new 'virtual' parking places." Like many other progressive campuses, Santa Cruz has a comprehensive Web page that displays all the alternative mode options, parking regulations, and penalties. Because there is a buffer zone between the scenic campus and the city of Santa Cruz, there is not an aggravated condition of campus car overspill.

Biking is heavily promoted in the Santa Cruz TDM portfolio and bike paths are abundant on the campus and in the town. To make the bicycle a favored mode, Scott's TAPS operation has created a bike shuttle service. Cyclists load their bikes on a trailer, jump on the van, and are taken to related drop off points on the Santa Cruz campus. One hundred faculty, staff, and students use this bike shuttle service daily.

1.9

(ABOVE LEFT)

The University of
California–Santa
Barbara is among the
most bike-friendly
campuses in America.
Well-designed
infrastructure improves
safety for cyclists and
pedestrians.

Courtesy of James Wagner

1.10

(ABOVE RIGHT)

The University of
California–Berkeley bike
service center provides
an extra incentive for
students and faculty
to bike to campus,
purchase parts, get
repairs, and rent or
store bikes.

Photo by Spenser Havlick

facilities, and academic buildings. Portland State University, Arizona State University, Wayne State University, and University of Wisconsin–Milwaukee have all opted to increase density. These campuses tend to reduce dependency on the auto by providing improved bicycle access, safe pedestrian facilities, and shuttle bus service.

The University of Washington–Seattle is an example of a school committed to land-use and transportation sustainability practices. Because of improved alternate mode facilities and decreased auto dependency, and "despite ten years of population growth, University of Washington's peak hour traffic levels today remain below 1990 levels. Of the campus population, 75 percent now arrive on campus using an alternative to driving alone. We have avoided building 3,600 new parking spaces saving as much as $100 million in construction costs" (University of Washington Transportation Office 2002).

A second important factor that influences transportation choices and policy is the philosophy of transportation priorities held by student leadership and the governing body of the institution. If a campus student council or other student leadership group such as a president's scholar class or an environmental center demonstrates the need for more efficient mobility, the faculty and administration can be encouraged to support changes. If a chancellor or president also favors alternate modes, this may be seen by the college or university staff as an invitation to be creative, more car-free, and inclined to use land more efficiently. If the trustees, students, or administration are fearful of reduced admission applications due to car restrictions on freshmen or car-reduction practices such as high parking fees and high parking fines, the institution may try to accommodate more cars by adding more parking, may provide more parking permits, and may not fund alternative modes of transportation.

In most cases the governing board of a college or university does not send out a directive on transportation behavior. Changes toward sustainable transportation policies and practices correlate with a well-organized and visionary campus transportation department or office. In some cases such as the University of California–Davis, and more recently the University of Colorado–Boulder, the hierarchy of transportation priorities has been stipulated in a transportation plan with the pedestrian ranked first, followed by bicyclists, buses, and lastly, automobiles. However actual implementation may differ from this hierarchy with auto facilities such as car parking getting a much larger piece of the budget pie than other modes.

The initiative for the pedestrian-bicycle-bus hierarchy usually originates in the campus planning and transportation offices or in discussions with student leadership. If there is an active student government or environmental organization, the student leadership can be mobilized to assist the staff in designing and implementing pedestrian and bicycle facilities. For example, Colorado State University in Fort Collins is one of several large schools that have a bicycle service center at the student union. With a centrally located "bike station," services such as bike repairs, bike rentals, and bike parts are easily available to the student body. The University of California–Berkeley has their bike service center inside the BART (Bay Area Rapid Transit) station, which is contiguous to the UC Berkeley campus. In addition to sales and minor repairs, very secure bike storage is available while the students are in class.

1.11
Several campuses, including Portland State University, use trolley or rail service to augment commuting options.
Courtesy of Tri-Met

For transit, pedestrian, and bicycle modes to be provided at adequate levels, the administration must believe in the importance of these non-car options and the financial resources must be pledged to provide them. Undergraduate students who are typically on a campus four to five years cannot bear the full responsibility of implementing a reduced auto policy. Normally the first- and second-year student is overwhelmed making educational, social, and financial adjustments to college life. Perhaps in the junior year elective courses will be taken in transportation planning, environmental impact assessment, resources management, or urban design. The student explores the related literature and good examples of cities with low car use. It may be then that the student is inspired to seek an elected office on the student council. If elected, the "transportation candidate" has less than one-and-a-half years to influence a campus master plan that has a ten- to twenty-year blueprint for the campus. Our research shows that the most comprehensive alternate-mode programs are on campuses that have good student–staff partnerships and a full-time transportation coordinator, as is the case at the University of Arizona and University of Washington.

Once the transportation master plan for a campus has been approved the support of the student body becomes very important. Most student governing bodies require an election or referendum in order to increase student fees for, let us say, a student bus pass. A bike service center, improved bicycle racks, nighttime safety lights, and emergency phones for walking safety may all require a vote of the student body if a student fee increase is required. Dollar amounts for fees to provide a semester-long bus pass and other transportation upgrades range from about $10 to $30 per semester. It averages about $15, but is considerably higher at some schools. In some cases the transportation "amenities" are folded into general student fees. In other cases some funding for transit, bike, or pedestrian facilities comes from parking permits, parking fines, and from general funds (as is the case with a portion from general fund for the University of Colorado faculty/staff bus pass).

No college or university campus is an island. The degree to which the college community uses alternate modes of transportation is influenced by the availability of transportation options other than an automobile. If the campus town or city has an inadequate or inefficient transit system, students will normally use this as an excuse for needing a car at college. If the campus has an excellent bicycle network but there is not connectivity with town bike paths, students will be reluctant to bike to town for recreation, shopping, or other errands. This is the complaint of students from Lewis and Clark University at the southern edge of Portland, Oregon. Portland State University, on the other hand, is located near the central business district of Portland and has access directly to a new trolley line and connections to the Portland light rail system known as MAX.

Students and staff cannot be expected to make significant shifts toward alternate modes of transportation if bike paths, transit routes with

1.12
Caltrain in the San
Francisco Bay Area offers
commuters a designated
car in which to store
bicycles.
Courtesy of Caltrain

frequent headway (time between bus arrivals), and safe pedestrian routes are not available in the community and larger region. The University of Miami in Coral Gables, Florida, is easily accessible by rail service and linked by the Hurricane Bus Shuttle to the campus. Stanford University has excellent regional transportation connections with heavy rail commuter service (Caltrain) from San Francisco and light rail from San Jose and cities in the Bay Area to the south of Palo Alto. To further lure non-car users, Stanford and Palo Alto have provided a bicycle service center for repairs, rentals, and storage in the passenger rail station east of the Stanford campus. One of the coaches on Caltrain has been converted to handle primarily bicycles similar to the custom of European railroads that have had special bicycle carriages on passenger trains for more than twenty-five years.

Information technology also has begun to play a role in reducing car trips. Coursework by correspondence has taken on a new meaning with the widespread use of the Internet on campuses. In recent years courses have been taught where both the student and the instructor stay at home. Tests and assignments are coordinated by e-mail and examination answers and

1.13
Caltrain allows the
commuter to board
right along with
his/her bicycle.
Courtesy of Caltrain

term papers are returned to the professor electronically. A student and teacher may never see each other during the semester except for the hyper-media transmission on the Internet that streams the image of the instructor live to the student's computer screen. In any case, no auto trip is taken to the campus for that class.

Do we want the trend of heavy reliance on the automobile to be destined as a permanent feature of the American university campus? Will the sea of asphalt parking lots and high-rise parking structures obliterate the tranquil ambience of the academic ivory towers of the past? In Chapter 2, The Transportation Demand Management Toolbox, we present strategies for reducing car use and car impact. The campus sustainability movement may provide an impetus away from the current dominance of the student automobile culture.

Today sustainability has become a major theme in many campus-planning policies (Keniry 2003). Colleges and universities that have shrinking budgets are seeking ways to make financial and other resources last longer. The practice of sustainability seeks to use resources more effectively without diminishing their supply for future generations. Recycling of paper, glass, metals, and plastics by towns and colleges has become widespread (Eagan and Keniry 1998).

In the twenty-first century, energy efficiency and conservation are goals of campus facility managers. It is becoming common to restore and rehabilitate old campus buildings instead of demolishing them (Browning 2003). Xeriscaping on campus, community garden plots, and water-efficient appliances in dormitory and classroom facilities are outcomes of a campus sustainability policy (Sowell et al. 2003). Perhaps the most difficult practice to change is the fifty-year trend of automobile dependency on American campuses. Will student body and university administrative leadership rise to the challenge of student car dependency on the campuses of America? This remains to be seen. The chapter that follows will shed light on this debate and discuss possibilities of reducing auto use on and near campuses.

Colleges and universities of the future can be expected to draw larger numbers of students, including nontraditional students and members of the larger community to the campus. Film festivals, athletic events, theater and music presentation, business workshops, lecture series on world affairs will continue to create campus destination trips. Townspeople who come to the campus will appreciate the tranquility and beauty that a pedestrian-dominant campus provides.

For institutions of higher education to carry on their historical functions as repositories of knowledge and centers of culture and learning in a community, wise transportation management should be part of the formula for their continued sustainability, success, and models of livability.

References

Browning, W.D. 2003. Successful Strategies for Planning a Green Building. *Journal of the Society for College and University Planning* 31(3):111–119.

Eagan, D.J., and J. Keniry. 1998. Green Investment, Green Return: How Practical Conservation Practices Save Millions on America's Campuses. National Wildlife Federation, Reston, VA.

Gurwitt, R. 2003. A Delicate Balance: Can Charm and Small-Town Values of Hanover Survive the Ambitious Expansion of the College? *Dartmouth Alumni Magazine* (Jan.–Feb.):26–33.

Keniry, J. 2003. Environmental Management Systems: A Framework for Planning Green Campuses. *Journal of the Society for College and University Planning* 31(3):62–69.

Shoup, D. 1997. Evaluating the Effects of Cashing Out Employer Paid Parking: Eight Case Studies. *Transport Policy* 4:201–216.

Sowell, A., A. Eichel, L. Alevantis, and M. Lovegreen. 2003. Building Better Buildings: Sustainable Building Activities in California Higher Education Systems. *Journal of the Society for College and University Planning* 31(3):120–129.

University of Arizona Parking and Transportation Services. 2003. University of Arizona Parking and Transportation Services Report, found at http://www.parking.arizona.edu.

University of Washington Transportation Office. 2002. University of Washington Transportation Office Annual Report, found at http://www.washington.edu/community/cmp/cmp.html.2002

Chapter 2

The Transportation Demand Management Toolbox

The reduction of numbers of vehicles, or vehicle trips and vehicle miles driven, is the goal of transportation demand management (TDM). TDM is a collection of tools, approaches, and strategies to encourage single-occupant drivers to use other means of transportation. These strategies can include parking management, the use of financial incentives, improved transit access, improved access for nonmotorized modes, and promotion and marketing efforts. If a campus community is successful in implementing a variety of TDM ideas, the quality of life on and in the vicinity of a campus should be improved. Some increased car parking and other auto infrastructure improvements, such as lane widening, turning lanes, and signalization, may be necessary in addition to TDM tools, but TDM is often a more sustainable and cost-effective approach than simply increasing the supply of auto facilities in order to accommodate increases in student and support staff populations.

Recent studies have shown that moving from an auto dependent campus policy to one that favors biking, walking, transit, and other TDM approaches may face opposition (Tolley 1996) and many challenges (Balsas 2003). Changes at several campuses are under way as car-related costs rise and awareness of TDM tools increases (Creighton 1998). Car-based transportation has many hidden costs (Balsas 2001) and obligatory parking is a major expenditure on most campuses (Shoup 1997; Dober 2000). Colleges are unique proving grounds for testing TDM ideas, which may help to reshape the broader society's transportation preferences and patterns (Balsas 2003; Travelsmart Australia 2003). The campus experience in the world of higher education also may hold useful lessons that can be applied to the "corporate campuses" where an increasing share of economic activity takes place.

We present the TDM "toolbox" with the following sections in the paragraphs below. These tools are common practice among colleges and universities that have pioneered in TDM efforts. Each category may have different applications to various campuses across North America. It is our hope that many of these tools will find new applications where they have not been utilized in the past. In this chapter we give a brief introduction to these TDM tools; those that we believe are most important are developed in much greater detail in Chapters 3 through 6. In this chapter we give more detail in those areas that are not covered in later chapters. A comprehensive resource for readers wishing to find more information on other aspects of TDM is the *Online TDM Encyclopedia* maintained by the Victoria Transport Policy Institute (Victoria Transport Policy Institute 2003).

Economic Incentives to Reduce Automobile Use

Most students possess little knowledge about the full cost of operating a motor vehicle. In fact the life cycle costs of car use are essentially unknown to the total population. Factors that cloud the true costs of vehicle operation include large federal, state, and local subsidies to highway construction and operations. While some of these costs are paid through user fees (gas taxes and tolls), significant portions are paid by other sources, such as local or state sales taxes. A variety of studies have indicated total annual subsidies to drivers in the United States ranging from $184 billion to $997 billion, equivalent to a subsidy of $1.50 to $7.55 per gallon of gas (Glickman 2001). These subsidies are deeply embedded in our economic system in a way that near future changes appear unrealistic. In addition, many of the costs that drivers pay are essentially fixed costs, rather than costs that vary with the amount of driving. Simply changing some of these to variable costs can have a significant impact on travel behavior.

One of the most powerful or effective economic TDM tools is to increase the cost of parking (see Chapter 3). As the price of parking increases, the demand for that parking is reduced. Of course, a campus parking authority that raises parking rates must have reliable alternative modes of transportation available to attract motorists to use them. One economic incentive to keep cars away from a central campus is the widespread use of higher-priced parking permits in lots close to a campus. University of Vermont,

University of Michigan, and others sell no parking permits to students who live less than one-half mile from campus and, like many other schools, have reduced permit fees for lots at greater distances from the main campus.

Programs where students or employees are paid not to drive are relatively new. Their long-term effectiveness has not been documented, but early results are promising. Stanford University has a program to pay $160 per year for those who do not bring a car to campus. A variant is a transportation allowance program, where employees are given an allowance and can then choose whether to use this for parking or pocket it and get to work another way. In 2002, the City of Boulder, Colorado, created a program where employees can earn up to $250 per year for promising not to drive alone to work in the congested central business district.

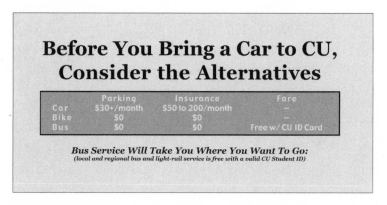

Before You Bring a Car to CU, Consider the Alternatives

	Parking	Insurance	Fare
Car	$30+/month	$50 to 200/month	—
Bike	$0	$0	—
Bus	$0	$0	Free w/ CU ID Card

Bus Service Will Take You Where You Want To Go:
(local and regional bus and light-rail service is free with a valid CU Student ID)

FIG. 2.1
Some campuses have sent mailings to newly admitted students (and their parents) urging them to leave their cars at home due to the costs of driving. (Courtesy of University of Colorado Environmental Center)

Another economic incentive to reduce auto use on a campus is for the administration of a university to communicate with prospective or current parents what cost savings are available to the college student if a vehicle is not brought to campus. Letters are usually sent from the admissions office, and in some cases, from the college or university president. The depreciation of a student-owned car on campus is substantial but the financial drain is much greater when the average annual total costs to a student is nearly $6,000 per year for car ownership. Gasoline, insurance, maintenance, tires—

including repair parts replacements—parking permit costs, and unexpected fines vary in every student situation but are often higher than expected.

John Crawford of the University of Utah's Parking and Transportation Services expressed this view about TDM financial incentives, "We found it's cheaper to pay folks not to park rather than build new parking. Furthermore you gain things that are harder to quantify: clean air, less congestion, a better quality of life, and good relations with neighbors. We're convinced we've done a good thing with this."

Parking Management

The price and supply of parking have significant impacts on travel behavior. A comprehensive approach to managing the parking supply is a very important part of a TDM strategy. In general, it is unlikely that any of the other strategies will be highly effective if parking management is not tackled.

There are several elements. First is the overall supply of parking. This acts as a constraint on the total volume of vehicle traffic that can access the campus. If the supply is held below the demand, then the result is either a shift to offsite parking or a shift to other modes of travel. Because the administration has central control over the parking availability on campus, it is relatively straightforward (albeit sometimes politically difficult) to set a cap on the parking supply. The University of Washington provides an example: They have set a cap at the number of parking spaces that existed in 1990.

Another approach available to campuses is restrictions on what categories of students may bring cars to campus. At residential universities it is not uncommon to ban first-year and second-year students from bringing a car to campus. Some schools also restrict other students from getting parking permits if they live close to the campus.

Another approach is to change parking permit costs from fixed costs to variable costs. This can be done by charging based on the actual number of days a permit holder parks on campus, rather than through an annual or semester permit at a fixed cost. A related concept is giving some guaranteed parking to employees or students who choose not to park on campus on a regular basis. This can make the difference that allows an individual to be comfortable commuting regularly by another mode, if they know that they can still park if they occasionally need to drive to campus.

2.1

Boulder's Ecopass
provides unlimited
access to popular
transit options for
University of Colorado
faculty, staff, and
students.

Photo by Spenser Havlick

The location of parking also will make a difference. More of the campus can be made available for other important core functions of the university if parking is centralized in a few parking structures or is located in peripheral lots. Both of these approaches mean that most users cannot simply park in front of the building they are accessing. Because of this, if they can ride a bike or a transit route right to the building, these other modes may gain a travel time advantage over the automobile, encouraging a shift to these modes. Chapter 3 will examine financial incentives and parking management.

Transit Pass Programs

Campus transit pass programs are a very popular and important component of the TDM toolbox. This is not to be confused with the common inter- and intra-campus bus shuttle services that move students from dorms to classrooms. The typical unlimited access transit pass program targets the

TABLE 2.1

POSSIBLE TDM STRATEGIES BASED ON THE USE OF FINANCIAL INCENTIVES AND PARKING MANAGEMENT THAT MAY BE SUITABLE FOR CAMPUS APPLICATIONS. (MODIFIED WITH PERMISSION FROM THE CITY OF BOULDER: *BOULDER TDM: STRATEGIES AND PROGRAM OPTIONS,* LSA ASSOCIATES, RAY MOE, PRINCIPAL, AND SHELLEY BRUNO, GRAPHICS SPECIALIST, AND CITY OF BOULDER TRANSPORTATION DEPARTMENT, TRACY WINFREE, DIRECTOR, RANDALL RUTSCH, PROJECT MANAGER, JUNE 2002.)

Strategy	Description	Opportunities	Limitations	Effectiveness	Cost to Implement
Transportation allowance	A transportation allowance is provided to commuters, for use on whatever modal options they choose. Typically, allowances are used in conjunction with parking pricing and other modal strategies.	A transportation allowance is very effective at "leveling the playing field" between parking and alternatives. The opportunity to save money and avoid out-of-pocket parking costs is appealing to many travelers. Employers in Washington and California have seen a shift in alternative modes by over 30 percent.	Spillover parking will occur unless the policy is accompanied by neighborhood parking restrictions. The allowance will work best where alternatives are readily available.	High (mode shift); High (VMT reduction)*	**Low** if policy is structured to be relatively cost-neutral. **High** if costs can not be recovered through higher parking fees.
Carsharing	Carsharing involves a pooled fleet of vehicles that are available for limited tasks by either members of a car-share program (similar to a timeshare), or, for a per-use fee.	Carsharing is similar to guaranteed ride home, in that it makes using alternatives easier for travelers. Carsharing can reduce the need for vehicle ownership, which in time, also reduces vehicular use in general.	Carsharing has limited application in the United States, and thus, it is difficult to project the potential effects. Furthermore, cost recovery over time becomes an issue, especially administration and maintenance.	Medium (mode share); High (VMT reduction)	**High.** However, costs may be partially recovered by membership and user fees.
Commuter club	Similar in functions to "airline miles," a commuter club provides either points or cash-based incentives to commuters who use alternative modes of transportation.	A commuter club provides tangible incentives and recognition to those who use alternative modes. Southern California and Aspen have successfully implemented commuter clubs that maintain very high alternative mode shares from month to month.	Developing a commuter club program has some financial and administrative expenses associated with it. As with other TDM promotions, a commuter club will only be as effective as the convenience of available alternatives.	Medium (mode share); Medium (VMT reduction)	**Medium**
Free transit passes	Implemented as either student or employee unlimited access transit pass program.	Unlimited access transit passes provide travelers with a motivation to use transit. They have been successful in encouraging high transit ridership in many college towns.	To be effective, adequate transit service must be available.	High (mode share); High (VMT reduction)	**High**

Strategy	Description	Opportunities	Limitations	Effectiveness	Cost to Implement
Free bicycle accessories	Providing bicycle accessories to commuters, such as headlamps and helmets, can improve the safety of bicyclists and serve to encourage greater use of bicycle commuting.	Providing accessories can alleviate the safety concern of bicyclists. Promotes use of bicycling as viable alternative.	Equity concerns are most apparent, including the specific vendors and outlets, so as not to compete with Boulder's retail base. Furthermore, free accessories may only serve to reward those who are already bicycling.	Marginal (mode share); Marginal (VMT reduction)	Low
Guaranteed ride home	A guaranteed ride home (GRH) program provides a free taxi ride home to those who fall ill, have an emergency, or are left stranded by a carpool.	As cited by most commuters, having a guaranteed way to avoid being "stuck at the office" is a desirable incentive. GRH allows for employees to always have a ride home, regardless of the emergency or situation. Interestingly, GRH is rarely abused nationwide.	The main limitation is ensuring an appropriate commute trip reduction program is implemented for GRH to be effective. Employers may also hesitate to provide GRH due to costs and liability; however, costs are usually low and GRH is included in ECO pass and/or RideArrangers participation.	Medium (mode share); Low (VMT reduction)	Low
Parking cash out	Allows employees the opportunity to choose a parking space or receive cash equivalent of the space. Works best when parking spaces are unbundled from leases.	Similar to transportation allowances, parking cash out is very effective at "leveling the playing field" between parking and alternatives. The opportunity to save money and avoid out-of-pocket parking costs is appealing to many travelers. Parking cash out can reduce SOV commuting by up to 25%, if alternatives are readily available.	Potential problem is that employees may claim to commute by alternative modes but actually drive by themselves and park off-site, creating spillover parking problems. Overcoming various institutional and political barriers may be difficult.	Medium (mode share); Medium (VMT reduction)	**Low** if structured so that costs can be recovered through higher parking fees. **High** if costs cannot be recovered.
Taxation incentives	Provide and/or promote the availability of tax benefits for the use of alternatives. Currently, federal tax law permits pre-tax allocation of certain alternative transportation expenses.	Commuter choice benefits offer up to $100 per month for transit or vanpool expenses and up to $180 per month for parking. Commuter choice initiatives have shown to be effective with employees nationwide.	The commuter choice programs and regulations are sometimes difficult to declare pre-tax expenditures on payroll. As such, implementation by small and medium sized employers will be limited.	Medium (mode share); Medium (VMT reduction)	**Neutral.** Employers may actually save money on reduced payroll taxes.

Strategy	Description	Opportunities	Limitations	Effectiveness	Cost to Implement
Vanpool empty seat subsidy	As vanpools lose riders over time, such as when someone changes jobs, it is important to ensure other riders maintain a consistent user fee. The empty seat subsidy covers the cost of the lost rider in the van until a new rider can be found to replace that individual, or at least for a minimum period of time.	The empty seat subsidy ensures that the SOT for other users will not increase for users who continue in the vanpool. Vanpooling tends to have the lowest cost per passenger-mile of any motorized mode of transportation, since it makes use of a vehicle seat that would otherwise be empty.	To be effective, the empty seat subsidy should expire, in order to provide incentive for actually finding a replacement rider. This will require an efficient matching system.	Low (mode share); Medium (VMT reduction)	**Low** cost (typically $100 per month per empty seat).
Vanpool subsidy	Subsidizing the monthly cost for using a vanpool greatly increases the cost-savings incentive for participating in a vanpool. A typical subsidy is 30% to 50% the per-seat cost.	Provides financial incentive to first-time users of vanpool to allow a "trial" periods. The trial period allows the user to be able to directly compare personal cost savings by not driving versus the eventual cost for use of the van.	Requires efficient matching system to be effective.	Low (mode share); Medium (VMT reduction)	**Medium**
Bike checkout program	A bike checkout program provides a set of bicycles for student or employee use. These bicycles are associated with either an individual or a department, for tracking and maintenance purposes.	Greater flexibility for those who do not use SOV as their preferred commute method and provided an alternative for short-distance errands.	Program requires administration to ensure safety and security of bicycles is maintained.	Low (mode share); Low (VMT reduction)	**Medium**
Parking fees	Parking fees can be set for cost-recovery, or, variable based upon time of day and length of parking.	Parking fees are effective in providing a disincentive for traveling alone to work. If convenient alternatives are available, a shift of up to 25% to alternative modes is possible as a result of parking pricing.	Spillover traffic will be a concern, unless an aggressive parking permit program is pursued. Furthermore, the "sting" effect of parking charges wears off over time, reducing long-term effectiveness.	High (mode share); High (VMT reduction)	**Neutral.** Fees are used to recover cost of parking facilities and enforcement.

Strategy	Description	Opportunities	Limitations	Effectiveness	Cost to Implement
Clustered parking	Clustered parking (including parking structures) reduces pedestrian distance between buildings and improves ambient quality for pedestrians.	Creates safer, more attractive pedestrian friendly environment behind buildings and encourages clustering of buildings. Safer environments have been proven to attract greater numbers of pedestrians and cyclists.	Campus master plan may need to be rewritten to support these parking practices.	Low (mode share); Low (VMT reduction)	**High** cost for parking structure construction; cost may be recovered from users.
Incidental use parking	Incidental use parking spaces are those that are dedicated for use by an "irregular" driver--such as transit rider or carpooler who must drive to work on occasion.	Incidental use parking spaces are very effective in managed or priced parking lots. One downtown Denver employer increased transit use by over 10% by providing a free parking space for occasional use to transit riders (as an added incentive similar to GRH).	Incidental use parking has limited effectiveness without parking pricing of some kind.	Medium (mode share); Low (VMT reduction)	**Neutral**
Parking management	Parking management strategies utilizes a variety of factors to balance the availability of parking with the availability of modal alternatives. Residential and commercial parking permits, parking pricing, shared use parking, time restriction, and other strategies are included in general parking management.	Limits the availability of free and subsidized parking. As with transportation allowances, parking management levels the playing field, thereby allowing greater use of alternatives, as they are perceived to be more convenient.	Parking that is difficult to find, inadequate, inconvenient, or expensive will frustrate users and can contribute to spillover parking problems in other areas.	Medium (mode share); Medium (VMT reduction)	**Medium**
Parking maximums	The establishment of parking supply maximums ensures that a campus does not oversupply parking, thereby creating an imbalance between modal options. Parking maximums are sometimes jointly negotiated between a campus and municipality or county.	Cities across the United States have used maximums to varying levels of success in reducing SOV traffic. Campuses are well suited to this approach since supply of parking is controlled by campus administration.	Often, parking maximums do not have immediate results. Even established sites with excellent transit service can be overrun with vehicles demanding parking.	Low (mode share); Low (VMT reduction)	**Neutral**

Strategy	Description	Opportunities	Limitations	Effectiveness	Cost to Implement
Preferential parking	Preferential parking programs provide parking spaces for carpoolers and van-poolers near the front entrances. These reserved spaces typically require a hang tag or other identifica-tion mechanism for use.	Provides incentives for those in carpools and vanpools to have the most desired parking spaces. Preferential parking has been successfully imple-mented at employ-ers nationwide, and at many campuses.	Parking that is difficult to find, inadequate, inconve-nient, or expensive will frustrate users and can contribute to spillover parking problems in other areas.	Low (mode share); Low (VMT reduction)	**Low** cost (parking signs and hang tags run less than $100 per space)
Unbundled parking leases	Separating parking from building leases provides an oppor-tunity to offer a transportation allowance or other cost-neutral promo-tion of alternatives, without incurring any additional cost for "wasted" parking.	Unbundling parking prices from building leases allows for the opportunity to pur-sue transportation allowances or park-ing cash-out. This is an important issue for university housing.	Spillover parking need to be addressed on sur-rounding streets. Without parking cash-out or trans-portation allowances unbundling leases will not accomplish SOV or VMT reduc-tion goals.	Low (modal share); Low (VMT reduction)	**Neutral**, depending upon cost-recovery plan.

*Mode share refers to the percentage of trips shifted out of single occupant vehicles; VMT reduction refers to the reduction in vehicle miles traveled. Thus, shifting longer trips out of cars will have a larger effect on VMT than shorter trips.

student and college employee who lives beyond easy walking or biking dis-tance. The user of unlimited access programs depends on city or regional transportation systems that give the pass holders free access to light- and heavy-passenger rail service, ferries, buses, and so on, without need of the private automobile. Normally a university identification card serves as the seamless transit pass upon which annual validation can be indicated.

In addition, there are many other steps a campus community can take to increase transit use by students and employees. In order for individuals to choose transit, it needs to go where they want to go when they want to go, and the travel time must be reasonably competitive with driving. In many areas in the United States, public transit service is either nonexistent or so poor that it is only used by transit-dependent populations who have no other choice. Many university communities are leading the way in devel-oping transit systems that have simple routes, high frequencies, and a friendly feel. Chapter 4 will examine transit pass programs and other ways to make transit more effective for campus communities.

Transit-oriented
Strategies for Consideration

BASIC
Transit-oriented TDM Packaging

Information	Facilities	Support	Incentives
Transit Riders' Guide		Transit to Work Day	Taxation Incentives
Transit Marketing		Flexible Work Hours	Discounted Transit
Transit Maps/Routes			Passes
Employee Orientation			Pre-tax Benefit for
Special Events			Faculty/Staff
Transit Promotion			

MEDIUM
Transit-oriented TDM Packaging

Information	Facilities	Support	Incentives
Information Kiosks	Bikes on Buses Promotion	Special Events	Student Transit Pass
Online Transit Routing	Incidental Use Parking	Guaranteed Ride Home	
		Employee Transportation	
		Coordinators	
		Residence Hall	
		Transportation	
		Coordinators	

HIGH
Transit-oriented TDM Packaging

Information	Facilities	Support	Incentives
Enhanced Marketing	Transit Friendly Site Design	Promotions and	Transportation
Realtime Transit	Bus/HOV Priority System	Campaigns	Allowance
Information	Transit Mall on Campus	Visitor Trip	Parking Cash Out
	Campus Transit Center	Management	Unlimited Access
		On Site Amenities	Employee Transit Pass
		Commuter Store	Parking Permit Rate
			Increase

*Each successive category includes the
previous categories' strategies

FIG. 2.2
This illustrates some possible packages of transit-oriented TDM strategies. (Modified with permission from the City of Boulder: *Boulder TDM: Strategies and Program Options*, LSA Associates, Ray Moe, principal, and Shelley Bruno, graphics specialist, and City of Boulder Transportation Department, Tracy Winfree, director, Randall Rutsch, project manager, June 2002.)

2.2

(ABOVE LEFT)

Separation of
pedestrian and bicycle
paths increases safety
and encourages greater
use by cyclists and
pedestrians at the
University of Colorado.

Photo by Francoise Poinsatte

2.3

(ABOVE RIGHT)

Stanford's bike service
center near the campus
and a Caltrain station
provides repairs,
storage, and bike parts
for bike-train
commuters to campus.

Photo by Spenser Havlick

Promoting Bicycle Use

Another important ingredient of the TDM toolbox is the opportunity for college students to use a bicycle as a primary mode of transportation instead of an automobile. Because many students live within a few miles of their classes, and because they are often young and physically active, bicycles can play a much larger role in a campus transportation system than is common in the broader community in the United States. To move many students from potential bicycle commuters to actual bicycle commuters several important requirements must be met.

Both the university and community must be involved to ensure safe, reasonably easy, and direct connections between the school and residence of the off-campus students. Bicycle paths or bike lanes are important for bike commuter safety and for reduced travel time. Bike paths are routes that are separated from roadways and can be multiuse for pedestrians, in-line skaters, and so forth, or the paths can be restricted bikeways for bikes only. Bike lanes are usually striped routes near or on the shoulder of the roadway. Off-road paths that enjoy maximum use often parallel roadways or follow stream corridors or water features such as the Anacostia River, Jefferson Memorial Tidal Basin, and C&O Canal tow path in the District of Columbia.

Another incentive for bicycle commuters in a TDM program is safe, protected bicycle storage when the student is in class or the employee is at work. The design of bicycle racks on campuses needs to keep pace with changes in the frame, tire configuration, and style of commonly used commuter bicycles.

Allowing commuters to bring their bikes on the bus can enhance both bicycle use and transit use. This gives them access to transit for the long part of their trips, and great flexibility at the two ends of the transit ride. In hundreds of universities from Duke in Durham, North Carolina, to Simon Fraser and the University of British Columbia in Vancouver, bike racks have been installed on city and regional buses, which can accommodate at least two bikes on the front rack and several more in the baggage compartments of larger regional buses. Students at the Colorado Mountain College campuses in Summit County can place four bicycles on the front bike rack of the Summit County Stage, which is a free transit service in the Dillon, Breckenridge, Frisco, and Silverthorne areas of Colorado.

Repairs, tune-ups, and periodic adjustments that are required by bicycles are made more convenient to college students if a bicycle service center is located on or near a campus. It is important to add this facility to our toolbox. Without a convenient bike shop or campus bike station, a broken chain link or flat tire may go unattended and be used as an excuse to revert to automobile commuting. Staff from a local bike shop operated most of the university bike service centers we found. Bike parts, repairs, helmets, lights, bells, and bicycle storage and rentals are common retail items and services.

Creating a Pedestrian-Friendly Campus

Everyone is a pedestrian during some part of the journey to campus. The motorist walks from a parking place. The cyclist walks from the bike rack, and the transit rider walks from the bus stop to class or to an office. But the most healthy and most environmentally benign commute to and from a campus is as a pedestrian.

For walking to be a convenient option the sidewalk or pathway should be a direct route, safe at all times, well-marked and well-maintained at all seasons. Whenever possible priority of passage should be given to the pedestrian over vehicles, bicyclists, and in-line skaters.

College students who live on campus or less than twenty minutes (walking time) or approximately one mile from a campus should be

Bicycle-oriented Strategies for Consideration

BASIC Bicycle-oriented TDM Packaging

Information

Bicycle Riders' Guide
Bicycle Promotion
Bike to Work Day/Week
Bicycle Marketing
Bicycle Maps/Routes
Orientation
Special Events

Facilities

Bicycle Rack Requirement
Bicycle Racks at Shelters

Support

Bicycle Users Group
Bike Safety Programs

Incentives

Bicycle Accessories

MEDIUM Bicycle-oriented TDM Packaging

Information

Information Kiosks
Online Bike Routing

Facilities

Bike Station
Bike Lockers at Shelters
Enhanced Bike Signage
Bikes on Buses Promotion
Dedicated Bike Paths and
    Lanes Accessing Campus

Support

Special Events
Guaranteed Ride Home
Employee Transportation
    Coordinators

Incentives

Commuter Club

HIGH Bicycle-oriented TDM Packaging

Information

Enhanced Marketing

Facilities

Bike-Friendly Site Design
Shower/Locker Onsite
    Requirements
Pedestrian/Bike
    Campus Core

Support

Bicycle Promotions
    and Campaigns
Commuter Store

Incentives

Transportation
    Allowances
Taxation Incentives
Bike Loan Program
Parking Cash Out or
    Increased Parking
    Rates

*Each successive category includes the previous categories' strategies

FIG. 2.3
This illustrates some possible packages of bicycle-oriented TDM strategies. (Modified with permission from the City of Boulder: *Boulder TDM: Strategies and Program Options*, LSA Associates, Ray Moe, principal, and Shelley Bruno, graphics specialist, and City of Boulder Transportation Department, Tracy Winfree, director, Randall Rutsch, project manager, June 2002.)

candidates for the pedestrian mode. Health incentives may not be persua-
sive enough to lure a student out of a car commute habit to a walking habit.
But if the college and town cooperate to provide maximum safety in the
form of emergency phones, excellent lighting, foot patrol police (or officers
on bikes), night escort service, night safety shuttles, and pedestrian priority
street crossings or underpasses, then more students, faculty, and staff
will be inclined to walk. The University of California–Berkeley is reported to
have 51 percent of its students walking as a primary mode. When local
laws are enforced to give pedestrians the right-of-way (such as in Victoria,
British Columbia, Canada), more people within the mile radius of a campus will walk. Cities in Michigan, California, Washington, Minnesota, and
Colorado have installed flashing yellow strobe lights to warn motorists
to stop for pedestrians in a crosswalk in the pavement and at shoulder level.
Striping in a parallel or zebra configuration alerts motorists of a pedestrian
crossing. In many states speeding fines are doubled for violations in school
zones where college students tend to be oblivious to auto traffic.

Special provisions should be in place for pedestrians with disabilities.
Curb cuts, color-coded walkways, audible crossing signals, and sidewalks

2.5
This traffic gate prevents cars from entering the University of Arizona campus and allows access by bicyclists.
Photo by Spenser Havlick

uncluttered with bicycles or construction activities, and removal of illegally parked cars should be rigorously enforced designs and practices.

Pedestrian-friendly and expeditious routes to campus should be a primary goal of the TDM toolbox. Once the pedestrian has arrived on the campus, the final stages of the trip should be a network of well-maintained hard surfaces where pedestrians continue to have priority right-of-way over cyclists, university vehicles including contractor equipment, and private autos. During construction events, smooth, well-lit, well-maintained pedestrian detours should be provided for pedestrians (and cyclists). Chapter 5 will give more detail on strategies to promote both walking and cycling.

Promotion of Carpools and Vanpools

Promotion of carpools and vanpools is one of the more established TDM tools that encourage commuters to shift demand away from personal car trips. Ridesharing (car and van pools) can optimize travel to campus with journeys at a more efficient time, route, or place.

Carpooling implies two or more people in a car whose passengers

Walking-oriented
Strategies for Consideration

BASIC
Walking-oriented TDM Packaging

Information	Facilities	Support	Incentives
Walking Guide	Pedestrian Corridors	Walking Support Group	Discounts at Retailers
Walking Promotion	Wide Sidewalks	Walking Safety Seminars	
Walk to School Day	Adequate Signalization		
Walking Marketing			
Walking Maps/Routes			
Commuter Orientation			
Special Events			

MEDIUM
Walking-oriented TDM Packaging

Information	Facilities	Support	Incentives
	Enhanced Signage	Special Events	Commuter Club
	Illuminated Sidewalks	Guaranteed Ride Home	
	Retrofit Sidewalks	Employee Transportation Coordinators	
		Flexible Work Hours	

HIGH
Walking-oriented TDM Packaging

Information	Facilities	Support	Incentives
Enhanced marketing	Shower/Locker Onsite	Targeted Campaigns	Transportation Allowances
	Access Management	Commuter Store	Parking Cash Out
	Clustered Parking		Taxation Incentives
	Pedestrian Under/ Overpasses		
	Student and Staff Housing on Campus		
	Pedestrian/Bike Campus Core		

*Each successive category includes the previous categories' strategies

FIG. 2.4
This illustrates some possible packages of pedestrian-oriented TDM strategies. (Modified with permission from the City of Boulder: *Boulder TDM: Strategies and Program Options*, LSA Associates, Ray Moe, principal, and Shelley Bruno, graphics specialist, and City of Boulder Transportation Department, Tracy Winfree, director, Randall Rutsch, project manager, June 2002.)

share a common origin and common route and destination. Carpools usually involve individuals who live in the same neighborhood and work at or near a destination shared by all. One person may drive every day with passengers paying for the cost of parking and/or gasoline. Some carpoolers cover the cost of fuel and parking but do not charge the driver on the assumption the vehicle owner has annual costs of depreciation, maintenance, and insurance. In other carpools participants rotate driving responsibilities each day or week. Vanpools are distinguished by the use of larger vehicles, generally a van that is not owned by the participants in the pool. The university may own the van and charge a rental fee to the users.

Rideshare programs can have a significant impact under some circumstances. The combination of financial incentives to rideshare, combined with paid parking, can lead to up to 20 percent of employees choosing this option (Pratt 1999). Another factor that can create incentives for carpool use is the presence of high-occupancy vehicle lanes on congested roads that serve campus commuters. Carpools and vanpools are also most likely to be used for trips that are not well served by transit. In rural areas or small towns that typically have less transit service, carpooling may be very important. At Cornell University in Ithaca, New York, for example, carpooling went from 5 percent of trips to 15 percent of trips to campus in the early 1990s after financial incentives were adopted.

Special advantages to school-related carpools include their flexibility or easy adjustment to changing class schedules, holidays, illness, or a rider's peace of mind due to daily reliability. Because the participating students or faculty know each other and the number of riders is small, changes in

BOX 2.1   **CARPOOL REQUIREMENTS AT SEATTLE CENTRAL COMMUNITY COLLEGE. CARPOOL INCENTIVES CAN BE A VERY APPROPRIATE TOOL AT COMMUNITY COLLEGES.**
Seattle Central Community College is located in the heart of downtown Seattle, Washington. The college provides no campus housing for its 10,000 students. The campus has only 550 parking spaces. However, Seattle Central has taken an unusual step to maximize the number of students that their parking spaces serve: every student wanting to purchase a parking permit that allows access in the morning hours *must* purchase a carpool pass, requiring two or more people per vehicle.

pick-up or drop-off times can be made quickly; in fact, in many cases adjustments are made on the same day of travel.

Participants of ridesharing are often arranged by using a campus Web site or calling a carpool or vanpool number. In some cases a map of the commute service area is posted on a campus with phone numbers of participants. Ride arranging for faculty and university staff is less problematic than with students due to the employee's more structured hours and work schedule.

Carpools that operate for participants who are on an 8:00 a.m. to 5:00 p.m. daily schedule are normally inconvenienced by morning and evening peak travel periods. To offset the hassle of the carpool commute at rush hours, several incentives can be implemented. There can be a reduced parking permit rate for carpool vehicles. There should be preferential close-in parking for carpoolers and a guaranteed ride home program during the day if an emergency arises at home. One approach a number of institutions have taken is to reserve a set of desirable spaces for carpool parking until a set time, often 9:30 a.m. This allows carpoolers access to these spaces, but avoids the problem of prime spaces sitting unused all day if there are not enough carpoolers to fill them.

At the University of Washington, employees who need cars during the day for meetings and trips may borrow one from the university car pool fleet. Obviously the guaranteed ride home options are available on a limited basis to avoid abuse. Other carpool benefits could include gift certificates for excellent participation, HOV priorities on multilane roadways and at traffic signals, and coupons for reductions at college and universities events such as concerts, athletic events, and theater productions. Significant costs-savings to the educational institution made possible by carpoolers could be applied, in part, to these and other benefits for those who rideshare on a regular basis. At the University of Utah–Salt Lake City carpool parking permits are discounted 50 percent off the regular cost.

Carpooling tends to be most attractive to university commuters who live at least ten miles from campus or whose trip takes at least thirty minutes.

Vanpooling is a larger scale of ridesharing than carpooling in that it usually involves six or more people sharing a ride in a van or other large-

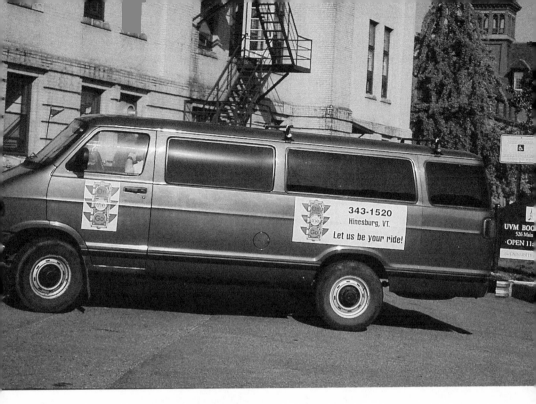

2.6
The University of
Vermont, like many
schools, uses vanpools
to reduce parking
demand on campus.
Photo by Spenser Havlick

capacity vehicle. Vanpools have been successful where commute distances from residence to campus are greater than twenty-five miles and where transit service is absent. Colleges and universities that own and operate vans tend to serve employee commuters more than students.

Several types of cost sharing are available. Some schools lease vans or own them outright, other institutions have public–private partnerships with a regional transit provider, and some vanpools function under an owner-operator plan. Some are supported by subsidies from student tuition, departmental payments, or cost sharing by the other public agencies. The U.S. Forest Service or U.S. Geological Survey may co-partner with a college forestry department or a geology department in order to obtain a van for multiple uses, including students, faculty, and field research staff. In some areas, public agencies and nonprofit or private groups have encouraged the use of owner-operated vanpools by offering low-interest loans, arranging for the purchase of vehicles at wholesale prices, and working with operators to obtain better insurance and maintenance rates. Universities that operate vans for vanpooling or multi-passenger field trips seldom have vehicles sitting idle in their motor pool fleet.

Vanpools that serve only the campus employees need to offer the same "amenities" mentioned for carpoolers: on-line ride matching, the guaranteed ride home, subsidized travel costs, convenient drop-off and pick-up points, and preferential parking locations such as sheltered or covered parking versus outlying, exposed parking spaces. At Yale University, the principal driver is not required to pay the usual monthly fee and has unlimited use of the vehicle on weekends and evenings. At the University of Washington, all van drivers get free U-Passes. The time of travel, however, is of greatest importance and must be equivalent to, or faster than, the travel time of the single-occupant student car. The portal-to-portal time calculation begins when an individual leaves the door of his or her residence and arrives at the door of the commute destination. The priority parking place or a drop-off close to the destination could save the vanpooler ten to fifteen minutes (portal to portal) over the typical single-occupancy vehicle driver who parks in an outlying surface lot. Despite these incentives, vanpools seldom carry a large percentage of the campus population, but they can be an important option for employees who live far from campus, in areas not well served by transit.

Carshare and Campus Car Rental Programs

These are programs designed to serve students or staff who do not own vehicles and those who choose not to bring an automobile to campus because of environmental or financial reasons. The idea is to give occasional access to a vehicle through a rental program. This provides participants with some of the benefits of private car ownership, without the associated fixed costs of owning a car. The institution benefits because it does not have to provide parking for a large number of individual vehicles. And, because users have to plan their use ahead of time and pay a cost proportional to their use, there is a strong incentive to minimize vehicle use.

Carsharing began in Europe and has begun to be adopted in the United States (Sperling et al. 2000). There are both for-profit carsharing companies and nonprofit carsharing cooperatives. Typically, members will be charged

TABLE 2.2

Organization	Web Site	Year Established	Membership (as of 2002)	Number of Vehicles
CommunAuto (Quebec)	www.comunauto.com	1995	750	40
AutoShare (Toronto)	www.autoshare.com	1998	225	15
Cooperative Auto Network (Vancouver, British Columbia)	www.cooperativeauto.net	1997	450	24
Victoria Car Share (Victoria, British Columbia)	www.victoriacarshare.ca	1997	40	4
Flexcar	www.flexcar.com	1999	350	12
Zipcar	www.zipcar.com	2000	650	37
City Carshare	www.sfcarshare.org	2001	250+	4+

an annual membership fee and will then be charged a fee for each hour a vehicle is checked out and each mile that is driven. For example, several universities in Boston contract with Zipcar, a private carshare company. As of 2002, students paid a $30 membership fee, and a user fee of $5 to $8 per hour. This clearly would not be financially sensible for someone who will be using a car on a daily basis, but may make sense for the occasional driver; for example, for a student who does not need a car during the week, but needs one for an occasional weekend trip out of town. In general, carsharing makes financial sense for users who drive less than 6,000 miles per year. This may be a very good fit for students who live on campus and are able to walk or bike to school, many of whom use campus parking lots primarily as long-term storage for cars they use only occasionally.

A variant of the carshare approach is the provision of an on-campus car rental option. Under this model, the campus contracts with a private car rental agency to provide rental services to students. Students then have convenient access to car rentals that can be picked up on campus. The rental company gets high visibility among a large group of potential users. A rental program of this type could be a good application for campus residence halls that provide no or very limited parking. It also opens up the possibility of marketing the purchase of a given number of days of rental access to students' parents, as an alternative to allowing their child to bring a car to school. One difficulty with this approach is negotiating an affordable approach to insurance for students who are under the age of 25. Stanford University developed a rental car program of this type, offered to students who are 18 years or older, with the caveat that students must be covered by their own personal insurance. Another variant is where a sorority or fraternity or other campus organization purchases a vehicle with shared ownership. Students or employees that possess a motor vehicle license make reservations in advance for limited use.

Reduction of Demand through Campus Land Use

Thoughtful campus land-use planning can foster travel patterns that enable a reduced number of trips and miles driven. Older colleges and universities in North America tended to be pedestrian-oriented, compact, and easily accessible without an automobile. As a campus population increases and expands into nearby neighborhoods, conflicts arise over parking, conversion of family homes into student rental units, and more traffic congestion. The design of a campus with special attention given to compact land use can mitigate many of the negative impacts of excessive car use and in some cases negate the need for a student automobile on campus at all.

A campus land-use plan that acknowledges the value of a walkable or bikeable campus tends to reduce the distance a student must travel between essential functions. Classrooms and libraries and other academic buildings should be clustered in convenient proximity to each other as is the case at the University of Chicago, Dartmouth College, Lewis and Clark University, University of North Carolina, University of Iowa, and most of the small- or middle-sized liberal arts colleges of North America.

Refinements in a campus master plan to reduce auto trips can reduce trips away from a campus if several basic services are provided on campus. For example at the University of Utah specific land uses have been set aside for five child care centers, an ATM, a fitness center, a post office, and a credit union. The specific reason for these facilities was to reduce extra trips off campus.

The University of Iowa has developed a Pedestrian-Oriented Campus Plan that will minimize the intrusion of vehicles into the campus and keep

Ridesharing-oriented
Strategies for Consideration

BASIC
Ridesharing-oriented TDM Packaging

Information	Facilities	Support	Incentives
Guide to Vanpooling	Preferential Vanpool	Online Ridematching	Empty Seat Subsidy
Carpool/Vanpool	Parking Locations	Zip Code Meetings	for Vanpools
Promotion		Guaranteed Ride Home	Pre-tax Payments
Marketing		Registration Surveys	
Commuter Orientation			
Special Events			

MEDIUM
Ridesharing-oriented TDM Packaging

Information	Facilities	Support	Incentives
	TDM Friendly Site Design	Special Events	First Time Ride
	Incidental Use Parking	Employee Transportation	Incentive
		Coordinators	Prize and Promotional
		Flexible Work Hours	Events
			Vanpool Subsidy
			Commuter Club
			Preferential Parking
			Rates for Carpools

HIGH
Ridesharing-oriented TDM Packaging

Information	Facilities	Support	Incentives
Enhanced marketing	HOV Priority System	Pay-As-You-Go	Transportation
Promotions &	Parking Management	Insurance	Allowances
Campaigns	Parking Maximum Ratios	Commuter Store	Van & Car Loan
	Car Sharing		Program
			For-profit Vanpools
			Parking Cash Out or
			Increased Parking
			Rates

*Each successive category includes the
previous categories' strategies

FIG. 2.5
This illustrates some possible packages of rideshare and carshare oriented TDM strategies. (Modified with permission from the City of Boulder: *Boulder TDM: Strategies and Program Options*, LSA Associates, Ray Moe, principal, and Shelley Bruno, graphics specialist, and City of Boulder Transportation Department, Tracy Winfree, director, Randall Rutsch, project manager, June 2002.)

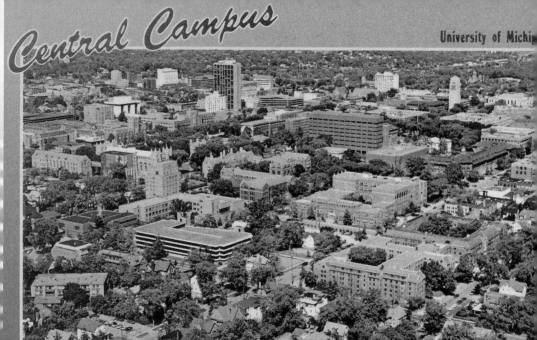

2.7
This University of
Michigan postcard
highlights the compact
nature of the campus.
Courtesy of University of
Michigan Bentley Library

general vehicular circulation to the periphery of the campus. Whenever student, staff, or faculty housing is located on or near a campus, vehicle trips to and from that campus tend to be reduced. Whenever a campus master plan has established a hierarchy of travel modes with walking and bicycling as the two highest priorities, one can be confident that over time, efficient land-use patterns will continue. Densities will increase. More people will be seen walking and cycling. The vitality and vibrancy of a campus will be greater when more students are living on campus and are able to get to all of their activities by walking, by wheelchair, or by biking. There will be a stark contrast between the fully walkable, residential campus and one where students commute home at the end of the day and on the weekends, leaving an empty ivory tower behind.

Several large universities in the Big Ten Conference, Big Twelve Conference, and Pacific Coast Conference have been forced to revise their campus master plans and locate residential units or research facilities—in some cases, their medical complex—on a satellite campus several miles from the main campus. This multicampus land use mandates an internal bus shuttle system that may have to operate 15 to 18 hours per day, at very high costs per rider.

One of the factors in a campus land-use and facilities plan that creates controversy in the host community is often the siting of major athletic facilities such as a football stadium or basketball arena. Those complexes can attract between 10,000 and 100,000 extra car trips per event to a campus. If the sports complex is on the campus the additional auto trips can and do cause infrequent, yet vexing, problems of parking and traffic congestion that do not lend themselves easily to TDM solutions.

Telecommuting

The ideal component of a campus land-use plan would be an educational function that requires no new land, essentially no physical space, no parking, and no transit requirements. This TDM option exists in the form of telecommuting. It has the advantage over flextime, which staggers arrival and departure times over a longer period of the morning and evening rush hours, because the auto infrastructure is not used at all. Flexible schedules may ease the peak demand travel period but they may hinder or make carpools and vanpools infeasible.

Telecommuting enables students to participate in classes electronically. Telecommuting can take the form of an interactive, real-time, online exchange between an instructor and students in their respective places of residence. Or special video conferencing studios on a campus enable the students to see and hear the instructor at a distant location. The Internet can be used by an instructor to teach a class where the students receive the course assignments on a home computer (via e-mail), complete their homework, and send the finished work back to the professor electronically. Papers can be assigned, returned to the teacher, corrected, and returned via e-mail to the student with neither party using any transportation or using any parking space, assuming the faculty member transmits the assignments, reads, and corrects the paper from his or her place of residence instead of making trips to campus. This distance learning or the virtual classroom gives optimum flexibility to faculty and students inasmuch as work can be assigned at any time—even without the student being present at the computer. And the returned work can be shipped electronically back to the faculty member at any time of day or night, at or before the assigned time the work is due.

Telecommuting has application to university research and administrative staffs that are able to complete work at home independently from other colleagues. Telecommuting students and college employees may experience increased productivity, less strain, and more task satisfaction as a result of less inconvenience and reduced stress and fatigue from no travel several days a week. Parking spaces are unneeded by the telecommuter. A vehicle, if still needed, is used less and thus incurs lower operating costs, produces less air pollution, and increases the capacity of the traditional transportation infrastructure. The equipment required for basic telecommuting is a computer, telephone, and in some situations a printer and fax machine. The potential for reduction of auto trips to campus is considerable, especially if instructors and students in large undergraduate classes find this technology advantageous over daily traffic-jammed auto trips and steadily increasing parking rates.

Telecommuting and related TDM practices, such as video conferencing and video phones, were pioneered in business and industry in Asia and Europe, and are now becoming widespread in North America. The future will determine whether the electronic exchange of course work and academic administrative tasks will become widespread on American campuses. We predict it will. It may be one of the most innovative nonuses of land the campus has ever seen. It could be a popular TDM tool in the future.

Marketing

One important aspect of TDM programs is marketing. Traditional transportation planners may be more focused on engineering solutions, but marketing is a much more integral part of the TDM approach. This is particularly true at a college campus where a large portion of the population turns over every four years. Because a TDM strategy has the goal of changing transportation behavior, it is important both to offer a range of transportation choices and to make sure that people are aware of these choices and have an incentive to try them. Because many people have the habit of commuting by car and may never have tried an alternative, a marketing approach that gets them to try out their available choices, even for a short period, may lead to long-term change if they like what they find. As Todd Litman puts it, "TDM marketing programs can help overcome inertia in travel habits"(Litman 2003).

There are a number of indications that marketing makes a real difference. One study indicated that marketing programs could reduce automobile driving by 6 to 14 percent; another indicated that a marketing program will increase the effectiveness of other TDM program elements by an additional 3 percent mode shift (Litman 2003). These are significant shifts, on a par with those created by other, often expensive or controversial, TDM strategies.

There are multiple elements of an effective marketing strategy. Marketing can start in the admissions materials that the campus sends out to prospective students and communication with admitted students and their parents. The most effective approaches will include multiple mediums, including as much direct person-to-person communication as is feasible. Techniques used at some institutions include annual transportation fairs, bike-to-school days, commuter contests, peer support groups for transit riders or cyclists, alternative transportation guides, campus displays, and even e-mails to students and employees giving personalized transportation options based on their home addresses. One common thread in all of these approaches—they require resources. Any TDM program should make sure to budget personnel and funds for marketing efforts.

Funding Campus Transportation Demand Management Programs

Any TDM strategy will require funding and staffing. There are a variety of sources that the campus may be able to use. We will briefly summarize the options that are in use by different campuses.

- *Student fees* are one option. These are widely used to pay all or a portion of the cost of student transit pass programs. They are also occasionally used to pay for other transportation programs. For example, the University of Montana student transportation fee also pays for their bicycle programs; at Florida State University, the fee pays for transit and for parking; and the University of California–Santa

TABLE 2.3
POSSIBLE MARKETING-ORIENTED TDM STRATEGIES THAT MAY BE SUITABLE FOR CAMPUS APPLICATIONS. (MODIFIED WITH PERMISSION FROM THE CITY OF BOULDER: BOULDER TDM: STRATEGIES AND PROGRAM OPTIONS, LSA ASSOCIATES, RAY MOE, PRINCIPAL, AND SHELLEY BRUNO, GRAPHICS SPECIALIST, AND CITY OF BOULDER TRANSPORTATION DEPARTMENT, TRACY WINFREE, DIRECTOR, RANDALL RUTSCH, PROJECT MANAGER, JUNE 2002.)

Strategy	Description	Opportunities	Limitations	Effectiveness	Cost to Implement
Bicycling promotion	General promotion and marketing activities oriented toward encouraging commuters to bicycle. Marketing messages can include health and cost savings, convenience, and other benefits.	Locations along multimodal corridors hold the potential for enhanced bicycle share. Promotion will aid the use of the facilities. Some campuses have developed very high bicycle mode share.	Bicycle commuting declines during the winter in many climates. Unless marketed with Bike-n-Ride, the market for bicyclists may be limited.	Medium (modal shift); Low (VMT reduction)	Low
Bicycle riders' guide	Develop a specific guide for a particular worksite that includes bicycle routes, locker and rack locations, and other information pertinent to the bicycle commuter. General campus information can be included on a cut-and-paste basis in order to save costs.	Assisting bicyclists with accessing their specific worksites, including where/how to park their bicycle and prepare for the workday has been proven to be more effective than promotion alone.	General limitations of bicycling promotion apply. Students will not change their behavior simply by publishing a guide at the worksite; it will require word-of-mouth promotion, preferably by a transportation coordinator.	Low (modal shift); Low (VMT reduction)	Low
Bicycle users' group	Organizations of bicyclists and bicycle commuters tend to increase the sustainability of bicycle commuting over time.	User groups help encourage each other to bicycle more often, especially when combined with a social interaction (such as a bike station café).	Those inclined toward a users' group are most likely already bicycling on a somewhat regular basis. As such, the program only affects how often the users bicycle, not typically the encouragement of new riders.	Marginal (modal shift); Low (VMT reduction)	Low
Bike station	Bike stations provide secure and covered parking for bicyclists. Most effective in dense concentrations of worksites or classrooms, bike stations can serve as an encouragement to commute by bicycle.	Bike stations have been used to encourage the development of new safety (from theft) and complementary services (such as showers, lockers, and other services offered by bike stations).	Total modal shift is limited. Additional limitations of bicycling promotion, and bicycle users' group apply. Competition with local bike shops.	Low–Medium (modal shift); Low (VMT reduction)	Medium

Strategy	Description	Opportunities	Limitations	Effectiveness	Cost to Implement
Bike to work day (week)	A bike to work day promotion provides many commuters with a "first-time" experience with bicycling to work. A small proportion of these commuters, every year, become habitual bicycle commuters.	Allowing a day where commuters can be introduced to the ease of bicycle commuting is a great way to change commuting modes. It has been found in the Denver area that more than 25% of new BTWD participants will continue to bicycle to work after the event.	Bike to work day usually only occurs once a year, and building a sponsor and promotions list can be taxing. Furthermore, BTWD participants tend to fall back to using SOV after a couple of months.	Medium (mode share); Low (VMT reduction)	**Medium** cost. Bike to work day is a high-profile event.
Carpool promotion	General promotion and marketing activities oriented toward encouraging commuters to carpool. Marketing messages can include cost savings, stress reduction, socialization, convenience, environmental reasons, and other benefits.	Promotion and marketing is extremely important in introducing and educating people in the benefits of carpools. When partnered with ridematching events, carpooling can help provide for trips that are poorly served by transit.	Carpool participation declines over time if marketing programs are not continued.	Low (mode shift); (VMT reduction)	**Low**
General marketing	Comprehensive marketing of all modal options, and how to best make use of them, is a key component to TDM promotion. Marketing materials can include flyers, brochures, posters, and targeted e-mail messages.	Marketing is more effective when it emphasizes the positive benefits commuters will achieve from using alternative modes, including exercise and financial incentives. Marketing that supports other TDM strategies that improve transportation choice or provide tangible incentives have been proven to show significant long-term impacts on travel behavior.	The travel impacts of TDM programs that rely only on marketing tend to decline over time as participants lose interest. TDM also faces competition from all other marketing messages. Strategies may be more effective with personalized information and face to face contact.	Medium (mode share); Low (VMT reduction)	**Medium** cost, depending upon specific campaigns.

Strategy	Description	Opportunities	Limitations	Effectiveness	Cost to Implement
Transit promotion	General promotion and marketing activities oriented toward encouraging commuters to use bus and rail alternatives. Activities can include: bus route maps, brochures, posters, how-to classes, and free-ride days; campus transit fairs; and information at student and employee orientation.	With promotion of services to regional travelers, commuters may better connect how to use regional transit and community transit to access worksites.	As with general marketing programs, transit promotion faces competition from all other marketing messages. If the promotion misses its target market or carries an uninteresting or confusing message, it will be ineffective.	High (mode share); Medium (VMT reduction)	Medium
Transit rider's guide	A rider's guide oriented to new bus riders can help overcome any predispositions against riding the bus due to a lack of information. Items can include how to read a bus schedule, where to wait for the bus, how to use online information, and how to use the bikes-on-buses racks.	Similar to a bicycle user's guide, the transit user's guide provides potential users with information on how to use the bus system. Research has shown that "not know what to do" is the number two reason (besides convenience) why people state they do not ride the bus.	A transit rider's guide will have limited appeal and effectiveness. Information overload becomes a concern. Employees will not change their behavior simply by publishing a guide at the worksite; it will require word-of-mouth promotion, preferably by an employee transportation coordinator.	Low (modal shift); Low (VMT reduction)	Low
Vanpool promotion	General promotion and marketing activities oriented toward encouraging commuters to vanpool. Marketing messages can include cost savings, stress reduction, socialization, convenience, environmental reasons, and other benefits.	Commuters in vanpools usually have longer commutes than other modal alternatives, which dramatically reduces VMT. Vanpools also tend to have the lowest cost per passenger mile of any motorized mode of transport.	The more people who register the more effective the program is, due to declining cost-to-scale. If few people participate, promotional efforts will be ineffective. The program should serve an entire geographic region to be successful.	Low (mode share); High (VMT reduction)	Low. This assumes promotional only.
Advanced traveler information systems	ATIS implementations offer commuters advanced information on the availability of alternatives. Specific examples of ATIS include kiosks at bus shelters informing patrons when the next bus will arrive, and online ridematching.	ATIS systems have had success in encouraging new transit riders by providing up-to-date information on bus travel times. As found in Washington, DC, ATIS helped allay transit riders' fears and generated greater repeat travelers.	ATIS can be expensive to implement, especially if monitors are provided at all bus shelters. ATIS will be best suited only for multimodal corridors, with limited effectiveness off of high-frequency transit corridors.	Medium (mode share); Medium (VMT reduction)	High

Strategy	Description	Opportunities	Limitations	Effectiveness	Cost to Implement
Bikes on buses promotion	Bicycles serve the "last mile" connection between community or regional bus service, and, the worksite or school. Promoting this connection often satisfies the convenience factor associated by many commuters with using the bus.	Bike storage on transit vehicles helps encourage new riders, especially if promoted with bicycle parking at the worksite. In Vancouver, a survey found that 30% of new riders were attracted specifically to bikes-on-buses.	Although bicycling helps extend the market area for transit users, it is still limited to students and/or residences that are well connected and served by multimodal corridors.	Medium (mode share); Medium (VMT reduction)	**Low** cost. This assumes only promotion costs, not the actual provision of bicycle storage.
Student or employee transportation coordinators	Employers dedicate a representative and/or liaison to all students and employees informing them of commute alternatives and the availability of services or incentives at the worksite.	A strong student or employee transportation coordinator is the difference between the "maximum" effectiveness of TDM and the "minimum" effectiveness.	ETCs can be costly to maintain for small or medium-sized employers.	Medium (mode share); Medium (VMT reduction)	**Low** to **Medium**

Barbara has a student fee allocated to bicycle programs. Student fees usually require a vote of the student body; at some schools this vote must be re-ratified every few years. An advantage of the student fee approach is that, because new money is generated, the TDM funding is not in direct competition with other programs, and it tends to be relatively secure long-term funding. However, it is not an appropriate funding source for programs that do not directly serve the student body, such as faculty/staff transit pass programs or TDM efforts targeting campus visitors. The use of student fees is discussed in greater detail in Chapter 4.

- *Parking revenues* are a natural source of funding for transportation programs. There is a clear nexus between parking and transportation, and increasing parking charges has the side benefit of decreasing demand for driving. Parking revenues can be a very significant and stable source of funding. For example, the University of Washington invests more than $4 million per year of parking revenues into their TDM program. The major disadvantage of this source is the political difficulty that may be associated with using parking revenues or raising parking fees for other purposes than building more parking. In addition, if the institution is investing in expensive parking structures, any use of parking revenues for other purposes will need to be carefully evaluated to make sure that the parking fund will be able to support debt payments on the structures.

- A variant is the use of *parking fines*. This can still generate substantial revenue and may be politically easier than the use of parking permit or meter revenues. In California, parking fines are widely used to fund the TDM programs at public universities. However, if the campus starts from a system where parking fines have traditionally gone to subsidize the parking system, reducing the cost of permits and meters, there may be political resistance to raising rates when the subsidy is removed.

- Some schools charge a *transportation impact fee* to new capital projects on campus. This is analogous to the impact fees charged by many municipalities. The concept is that new building projects must pay some portion of the costs of providing parking and other transportation infrastructure to serve demand generated by the building. A variant of this is to charge a fee per parking space for new building projects that are built on parking lots and reduce the supply of parking. Both of these approaches are appropriate for generating capital funds, but would probably not be a wise source for ongoing operating funds.

- *Campus general fund revenues* also may be used. This simply means that the campus allocates a share of its core operating revenues (tuition and/or public support) to transportation programs. This is simple in concept, but may be difficult in practice due to the intense competition for these funds. Because the core mission of higher education is research and teaching, auxiliary services such as transportation tend to lose out in the competition for these funds.

- *Auxiliary departments may be taxed* to support transportation programs. At many institutions departments such as housing, intercollegiate athletics, and parking are self-supporting auxiliaries, which are required to cover their budget through self-generated revenues. Some campuses charge a "tax" on auxiliary departments to pay for the campus administrative system and infrastructure that the auxiliaries use. A portion of this can be channeled to transportation services. Some schools also charge auxiliary departments a separate transportation fee as a "head tax" per employee to support employee transit pass programs.

- *User fees* may be able to provide some services. For example, bicycle registration fees may be able to provide partial funding for bicycle programs. Some transit pass programs are at least partially funded through optional fees paid by the users.

- *Federal enhancements funds* are available for capital investments in transportation infrastructure. Under federal transportation legislation, 10 percent of federal surface treatment funds are set aside for transportation enhancements as of 2003. These funds are distributed to the state transportation department and are generally then allocated by regional transportation planning agencies. They are available for improvements such as bicycle and pedestrian path improvements and grade separated interchanges serving bicycle and pedestrians. A local government must apply for the funds, but a university or college can partner with the local government to invest in improvements serving their students or employees. There is a 20 percent local match requirement, which can be jointly provided by the school and the local government.

- *Federal Congestion Mitigation and Air Quality (CMAQ)* funds are available for projects that help support clean air objectives in areas that do not meet federal air quality standards. Eligible projects include transit improvements, TDM programs, conversion of fleets to cleaner fuels, and roadway improvements that support clean air (such as dedicated transit bypass lanes at congested intersections). As with enhancements, a local government must apply for the funds and there is a 20 percent local funding match required. CMAQ funds have been widely used to provide for campus transit improvements. The University of Minnesota was able to use CMAQ funds as seed money for starting a transit pass program; the University of Colorado has used the fund for the first two years of funding for a new high-frequency transit route serving the campus. This is also a good source of funds for campus transit centers, dedicated transit lanes, and other similar capital projects. In general, CMAQ funds are not available for ongoing operational funding.

- *Local and regional partnerships* may provide funding for transportation programs that also serve the policy goals of the surrounding region. For example, it is relatively common for a campus and the surrounding city to share resources for bicycle or pedestrian improvements that serve both the campus and the city. In some cases, the campus may be able to donate right-of-way for an improvement, such as a new bike path, while the city provides the funding for construction. In some cases, partnerships between the local government, a transit agency, and the university provide joint funding for operating transit routes.

- *Public/private partnerships* may be a way to fund the management of a TDM program. In a number of areas a variety of private companies and public agencies have come together to form nonprofit organizations known as transportation management associations (TMAs). These groups can advocate for specific policies, directly administer programs, and market TDM activities. For example, the University of Vermont has teamed up with the city of Burlington and several health care providers to form the Campus Area TMA.

Administrative Structures

At many schools, there is no dedicated transportation office. Instead, there is a parking services office responsible for providing parking, and there may be a separate parking operation for the residence halls. As TDM programs are instituted, this may present an administrative challenge, with no department or position feeling that it is their responsibility to implement these programs. In order to maintain an effective TDM program, it will be important to create administrative structures and staff positions to support the program. There are many different structural possibilities; we will review a few that are in wide use.

At a number of schools, the student government has grown to have a significant role in TDM. This is commonly an outgrowth of student decisions to provide funding for transportation programs. There are many schools where students have established dedicated fees to pay for student transit passes, and a smaller number of schools that provide student funding for operating transit systems and bicycle programs. Control of programs tends to follow funding, so in many of these cases the students have established offices to oversee these programs. Typically the office will be staffed by professional employees who report to the student government or a student board. Under these circumstances, decisions about parking and about general roadway and bicycle infrastructure are usually housed within the campus parking or facilities departments. This can lead to a creative interplay, which helps advance new programs; however, it can also lead to conflicts among departments, and to decisions that affect all modes of transportation being made in isolation.

Another approach is the evolution of parking departments into broader roles. This is often accompanied by a name change, to parking and transit services or parking and transportation. In California, most public universities have a transportation and parking services (TAPS) department, funded primarily by parking fees and fines, which has overall responsibility for all areas of transportation from bicycles to cars. This has the advantage of assuring a higher degree of coordinated planning.

Some schools have a shared administrative structure with other government or private entities. For example, Emory University in Atlanta joined several prominent organizations to form the Clifton Corridor Transportation Management Association (CCTMA). The executive director of the CCTMA is also the Emory director of alternative transportation. CCTMA contracts Emory to work on transportation solutions for the corridor. Alternative transportation improvements for the university tend to serve the needs of the corridor and vice versa.

Whatever administrative structure is chosen, there are a number of staff roles that may be needed as a TDM program grows, which are not likely to be present in a traditional parking department. Depending on the size of the program, one person may fill all these roles or there may be multiple people filling a single role. These roles include:

- *Transit pass administrator.* Because the transit pass program is often a centerpiece of TDM efforts, this is a critical position. Someone needs to be responsible for negotiating the contracts with the transit agency or agencies, addressing the logistics of pass distribution and validation, tracking ridership, and engaging in service planning for transit modifications to better serve the campus community.
- *Bicycle/pedestrian coordinator.* Unless someone has responsibility for these areas, it is very easy for bicycle and pedestrian programs and infrastructure to fall through the cracks. A comprehensive program that improves and maintains paths, parking, and other infrastructure, and promotes walking and bike riding, requires dedicated staffing. The most successful programs do have dedicated coordinators.
- *Parking management.* Because managing the supply and pricing of parking is so central to the success of TDM programs, it is important that there be a close link between parking planning and overall transportation efforts. This role can be played by a planner or director of parking services, or perhaps by someone in the campus planning office, but requires a broader background in TDM than many parking staff now have.
- *Marketing/outreach coordinator.* Because marketing is such an important part of TDM efforts, and because this is not typically a core skill for parking or transportation staff, it is important to assure that there is dedicated outreach staffing with the appropriate experience in marketing to students, faculty and staff, and campus visitors.

Conclusions

This chapter has outlined some of the strategies that a campus community can use to manage their transportation system to achieve mobility, wisely use campus funds, and protect quality of life and the environment. There is no one recipe for a successful program, but each strategy must be evaluated in the context of the existing physical infrastructure, funding opportunities, campus and community culture, and political constraints and opportunities. The next three chapters will examine three of the most important strategies—parking management, transit incentives, and promoting bicycling and walking—in more depth. Chapter 6 will then discuss how to put all of this together and evaluate the appropriate mixture of parking and TDM strategies.

References

Balsas, C. 2001. Cities, Cars, and Sustainability. *Urban Affairs Review* 36(3):429–432.

Balsas, C. 2003. Sustainable Transportation Planning on College Campuses. *Transport Policy* 10:35–49.

Creighton, S. 1998. *Greening the Ivory Tower.* Massachusetts Institute of Technology Press, Cambridge, MA.

Dober, R. 2000. *Campus Landscape.* Wiley, New York, NY.

Glickman, M. 2001. *Beyond Gas Taxes: Linking Driving Fees to Externalities.* Redefining Progress, found at www.rprogress.org, March, p. 2.

Litman, T. 2003. TDM Marketing: Information and Encouragement Programs. *Online TDM Encyclopedia,* found at www.vtpi.org/tdm/tdm23.htm.

Poinsatte, F., and W. Toor. 2001. *Finding a New Way: Campus Transportation for the 21st Century,* 2nd ed. University of Colorado Press, Boulder, CO.

Pratt, R. 1999. *Traveler Response to Transportation System Changes, Interim Handbook,* TCRP Web Document 12, found at www4.nationalacademies.org/trb/crp.nsf/all+projects/tcrp+b-12, DOT-FH-11-9579.

Shoup, D. 1997. The High Cost of Free Parking. *Journal of Planning Education and Research* 17(1):3–20.

Sperling, D., S. Shaheen, and C. Wagner. 2000. *Carsharing and Mobility Services: An Updated Overview,* CalStart, found at www.calstart.org/resources/papers/car_sharing.html.

Tolley, R. 1996. Green Campuses: Cutting the Environmental Cost of Commuting. *Journal of Transport Geography* 4(3):213–217.

Travelsmart Australia. 2003. Universities Travelsmart Resources Kit, found at www.travelsmart.gov.au/universities/index.html.

Victoria Transport Policy Institute. 2003. *Online TDM Encyclopedia,* found at www.vtpi.org/tdm.

Chapter 3

Parking: The Growing Dilemma

A university is a diverse community held together
by common complaints about parking.
   —**Clark Kerr**, former chancellor of the University of California

This chapter examines the economics of expanding parking supply in a campus context. Many educational institutions do not have additional land that can be devoted to surface parking lots. The supply of surface parking decreases as institutions convert parking lots into other uses, such as new research buildings, dormitories, stadiums, and theaters. At the same time, the additional buildings generate new vehicle trips to campus. In order to provide sufficient parking, the campus is then faced with either acquiring new land—a very expensive proposition at many urban and suburban campuses, and often impossible—or constructing parking structures over existing surface lots.

In this chapter we show how to calculate the cost of expanding parking supply in land-constrained environments and examine the cost of shifting drivers to other modes of transportation. Finally, any approach that reduces the amount of parking provided on campus might cause spillover parking in surrounding neighborhoods, so we consider strategies such as residential parking permit zones to alleviate parking problems.

How Much Does Parking Cost?

Because so many automobile trips in the United States begin and end at "free" parking spaces, many drivers have the perception that parking truly is free. But there are real costs associated with providing parking, either in surface parking lots or in parking structures. There are, of course, many different ways to pay for parking. At many educational institutions, the parking department is organized as an auxiliary service, which must generate sufficient revenue to cover the costs of constructing, maintaining, and operating the parking system. This revenue comes from the sale of parking permits, from parking meters and other short-term parking charges, and in some cases from parking fines. At other schools, general funds may be used to pay some portion of the costs of providing parking. In either case, it is important to understand all of the costs involved.

The Cost of Surface Parking

At campuses where land is plentiful, most of the parking supply generally consists of surface parking lots. The price to add a new space varies depending on the price of the land underneath it. The old real estate adage, "location, location, location!" is very apt when considering the costs of parking expansion. Land prices vary greatly depending on whether the expansion takes place in a rural community college, a fast-growing suburban university, or a core area urban campus. An acre of land close in to the west side of the University of Colorado campus in Boulder can cost as much as $1 million/acre, but on the east side around the research park land costs about $350,000/acre. For some California schools land prices may approach $2 million/acre. Though there is no easy general response to the question of land value, university planners should determine the land costs at their individual university or college and figure it into the equation when calculating total costs. Note that at urban campuses there is often no raw land available near the campus, so the cost of "land" is really the cost to purchase existing buildings and tear them down to get access to the underlying land. In fact, campuses sometimes do this, both to create building sites for campus buildings and to create parking lots.

Typically, a surface parking lot will require about 350 square feet per space, or 124 spaces/acre. Table 3.1 shows the land cost for a new parking space for a range of land values.

Note that an assessment of the cost of parking should include land value even if the school already owns the land. There is an opportunity cost to using the land for parking rather than for another use such as an academic building, housing for students or faculty, or recreational or green space. In a campus within a land-constrained environment, using limited land for parking means either sacrificing another of these uses or going out into the market and purchasing additional land. This is an important point, and one that is often missed.

A common argument made is that surface lots are only a temporary

TABLE 3.1
THE LAND VALUE PER PARKING SPACE FOR DIFFERENT LAND VALUES.

Land Cost per Acre	Land Cost per Surface Space
$350,000	$2,825
$700,000	$5,645
$1,000,000	$8,065
$1,500,000	$12,100

A typical surface parking lot will accommodate 124 cars per acre.

use, holding land that will eventually be used for building pads. One planner describes this as "weed abatement on future building sites." Therefore, there is no opportunity cost associated with using a site for surface parking. To test this concept, consider the following thought experiment. Propose allowing university land to be used for a ten-year period by an outside company; presumably, the answer would be that, even if the use could be allowed, the company will be expected to pay rent for the land. A fair pricing of parking should do the same. Now, even at campuses where parking is a self-supporting auxiliary, the land is generally treated as free because it is already owned by the educational institution—in practice, the only time that land price is included is when an institution has to rent off-campus parking spaces. This means that in general the land price does not affect the actual fee that parkers pay, and thus does not have a feedback effect on demand. However, for purposes of campus decision making, it is still important to understand the market value of the land.

This is particularly important given just how much land is devoted to the automobile at many educational institutions. A 1991 survey of campuses (Van Dyke 1991) found that the percentage of the campus devoted to parking varied from a low of 8 percent to a high of 45 percent.

The construction costs also must be factored in. While this cost will vary depending on the local construction market and the site geology, a reasonable order of magnitude estimate is $3,000 per space. There are also a number of ongoing costs—maintenance of the lots, parking administration, and parking enforcement.

Let's look at one example of the full cost of surface parking from the University of Colorado. The total cost of surface parking at the University of

Colorado–Boulder main campus in this example is more than $83/month. What if we don't include the land cost? Then we would simply remove the land cost from the table, reducing the total to $28/month. This is a reasonable estimate for the cost of surface parking for campuses where land is very cheap. In this type of cheap land environment, it is actually quite common for campuses to absorb the costs of operating surface lots within their general fund and make parking free to the users. There is then no financial incentive to reduce automobile use.

TABLE 3.2
THE TOTAL COST OF SURFACE PARKING IN THIS EXAMPLE FROM THE UNIVERSITY OF COLORADO INCLUDES THE COST OF THE LAND, CONSTRUCTION, MAINTENANCE, AND ADMINISTRATION AND ENFORCEMENT. (COURTESY OF DAVID COOK, PARKING AND TRANSPORTATION SERVICES, UNIVERSITY OF COLORADO)

Type of Expense	Capital Costs	Annual Cost
Land cost	$1,000,000 acre = $8,064/space	$660/year
Construction cost	$3,000/space	$245/year
Maintenance		$30/year
Administration and enforcement		$60/year
Total cost		$995/year; or $83/month

The Cost of Parking Structures

In a common scenario, a parking structure will be built upon an existing surface lot. To calculate the net cost per new space, there are two subtleties: One must subtract the number of existing spaces out of the total in order to only count new spaces, and one *should* count the land value as zero, because there is no additional land cost to adding a second or third level to an existing parking lot. The number of new spaces is lower than one might expect, because the structural supports and the access ramps can take up a significant portion of the space, so it can take a three-level parking structure in order to double the number of spaces on a surface lot.

If there is raw land available for the structure, then the cost per net new space created will be lower because there will not be existing surface spaces lost. In this case, a full cost per new space should include the land value. However, since educational institutions generally do not include the land value in the cost that consumers must pay, and since the cost of construction will be much higher than the land costs, we will treat land value as zero for the remainder of this discussion.

The capital cost of a parking structure will be determined both by the construction costs in the area and by campus design standards. The cost per space in a parking structure will typically range from $10,000 to $20,000. Underground parking can be considerably more expensive. In addition, if design standards require building wrap-around parking structures to reduce the visual impacts, there will be an increased cost per space. When the structure is built on an existing surface lot, the cost per net new space created is also increased. A 1995 study of parking construction at the University of California–Los Angeles (Shoup 1995) examined the cost of 4,912 spaces added since 1977 and found that the average cost/new space is $23,600, and that the average monthly cost, including operating expenditures, is $124. A 1994 study of Stanford University's Parking Structure III found a capital cost/net new space of $18,235, and a monthly cost of $121 (Siegman 1994). A 1998 study at the University of Colorado–Boulder (Cook 1998) found a monthly cost for structured parking of $197/net new space.

What do these numbers mean? First, adding new parking in areas where structures are the only option is very expensive compared to surface parking. It is striking that, in the examples above, the actual cost to users is much less than the cost to provide the space. For example, a student parking at the University of California–Los Angeles in 1998 would pay $43/month, which means that the university is subsidizing the parker by $81/month. In the Stanford example, in the early 1990s parking permits cost only $20/month. The university subsidy would be $100/month for each new parking space. Either the university must use general fund dollars for this subsidy, or the costs are spread across users who park in surface lots, and the surface parkers subsidize the structures. This second strategy requires that the bulk of parking be in surface lots, as the cost/person increases rapidly as the percentage of structured parking increases. For example, in David Cook's 1998 study of parking at the University of Colorado–Boulder, he calculated the following table, using the assumption that land is treated as having zero value.

TABLE 3.3

ANNUAL COST OF PARKING PER ADDED SPACE AT THE UNIVERSITY OF COLORADO.
THIS TABLE SHOWS THE MONTHLY FEE REQUIRED TO COVER BOND PAYMENTS ON
PARKING STRUCTURES, ASSUMING THAT THE COST IS SPREAD ACROSS ALL USERS,
INCLUDING THOSE PARKING IN SURFACE LOTS. (COURTESY OF DAVID COOK, PARK-
ING AND TRANSPORTATION SERVICES, UNIVERSITY OF COLORADO)

Percent of Structured Parking	Average Monthly Fee Required to Cover Cost of Parking Structure
0%	$13
20%	$29
40%	$89
60%	$124
80%	$160
100%	$197

Table 3.3 illustrates why many schools are looking for new ways to manage their transportation systems and provide better nonautomobile access to campus. If the only way to expand the parking supply is to convert from surface parking to parking structures, a supply-side approach leads to a very unappealing choice for a university parking manager—either provide heavy subsidies from somewhere else in the budget or raise parking fees substantially and deal with the resulting outcry. One caveat to this analysis—if a parking structure is used for short-term parking, it may be easier to charge enough to pay for the structure. At $1/hour, if an average space is occupied for 160 hours/month, it will generate $160/month, which is comparable to the total cost per new space.

Even if the campus politics allow parking fees to be raised this much, there is yet another problem. Many institutions have master plans replete with schemes to add new research facilities, academic buildings, student housing, or athletic facilities. In most cases, they don't have the cash on hand to build these buildings, so they have to borrow money to finance them. Bond rating agencies place a limit upon the amount of debt that can be incurred. If an institution wishes to go over the limit, they become a higher risk, and the interest rate they must pay to borrow goes up. This places an effective cap upon the amount of debt most campuses are able to take on. This means that even if user fees can cover the costs of a new structure, the structure will still be in direct competition with other uses for the campus debt financing capacity. This may make it more attractive to pursue transportation options that do not require incurring as much debt.

When Is It Cheaper to Invest in Alternatives?

Are there any other approaches to managing transportation demand that are less expensive? In most cases where land constraints lead to the use of structured parking, the answer is yes. There are a variety of approaches—among them providing transit passes to employees and students and creating financial incentives not to drive alone—that may be less expensive.

Transit Passes

While we will go into detail on these strategies in future chapters, it is useful to understand the cost comparison at this point. Consider first the practice of providing transit passes to the campus community. In a typical case, the institution will contract with the transit agency to allow students or faculty and staff or both to ride the transit system without paying a fare. This will lead to an increase in transit use and will cause some people to shift from driving to campus to riding transit. This will free up some parking spaces directly and will also have an indirect political impact. When constituents complain about lack of parking, the school will now be able to respond that they provide the pass program as an attractive alternative.

In the United States, federal tax law has traditionally encouraged employers to provide free or subsidized parking to employees, rather than other types of transportation incentives. This is because employer-provided parking is not taxed. Thus, an employer can provide a free parking space worth, for example, $1,000 per year, whereas an employee might have to earn $1,250 or more per year in pretax earnings to pay for that parking. Until recently, by contrast, if an employer offered a transit allowance to employees, this was a taxable benefit. Federal tax law has changed, however, and transit benefits of up to $100/month are tax-free as of 2002.

The faculty/staff bus pass program at the University of Colorado provides an instructive example, showing how a transit pass program can reduce parking supply costs. This program allows each permanent faculty or staff member who is eligible for benefits to ride local and regional buses and light rail by showing a university ID. In 2001, the program cost $1,125 per parking space left open due to the program. For comparison, the annual debt service to provide one additional parking space was $2,723 (Table 3.4).

How do we arrive at the cost per parking space left open? For the University of Colorado, in the year 2001 the total cost of this program was $393,400. This includes the cost of the contract with the Regional Transportation District, the cost of administering the program, and the marketing costs. The university conducts an annual survey to determine how parking behaviors have changed since the advent of the pass program in 1998. The result is that the average number of days each person parks on campus declined from 2.81/week before the advent of the program to 2.47/week in 2001, a decrease of 12 percent. There are 6,250 employees who are eligible for the program, so on an average weekday there are 425 fewer employees parking on campus.

This does not mean that there are 425 fewer physical spaces required. There are two correction factors that must be applied. First, not everyone parks for the entire day, so there is turnover in the same parking space during the day. For the University of Colorado, on the average 1.43 cars will use any given central campus space during one day. The other correction factor that must be applied is the desired occupancy ratio. If occupancy is close to 100 percent, then drivers will have a difficult time finding free spaces. For this reason, campus parking managers generally target some lower occupancy rate. For the University of Colorado, this target is 85 percent. Then, if there are P fewer cars parking each day, a turnover ratio T, and an occupancy target O, the actual number of parking spaces avoided (N) is $N=(P/T \times O)$. In the University of Colorado example, this is $425/(1.43 \times 0.85)$, or 350 spaces. The cost per space avoided is then $393,402/350 = $1,125. Note that this is actually a conservative estimate of the reduced parking demand. Another approach would be to look at the peak parking demand (D)—that is, the percentage of parking permit holders who park during the peak period. Then the number of parking spaces avoided is $N=P \times D/O$. If $D>O$, then $N>P$. This approach would show an even larger benefit to the transit pass program.

The annualized cost/net new space for a two-level parking structure built on an existing surface lot, by comparison, is $2,723 (Cook 2001). The following table shows how the calculation was performed. This actually

TABLE 3.4

COSTS PER NET NEW SPACE FOR A PARKING STRUCTURE AT THE UNIVERSITY OF COLORADO. EVEN IF CONSTRUCTION COSTS ARE RELATIVELY LOW, THE COST PER NET NEW SPACE CREATED BY BUILDING A PARKING STRUCTURE CAN EXCEED $200 PER MONTH. (COURTESY OF DAVID COOK, UNIVERSITY OF COLORADO PARKING AND TRANSPORTATION SERVICES)

Number of spaces in new structure	295
Number of spaces in existing lot	147
Net number of spaces added	148
Cost per space for construction	$12,000
Contingency and bond issue costs	$3,000
Total capital cost per space to build	$15,000
Total capital cost per new space added	$29,898
Projected construction cost	$4,422,871
Cost for interest	$3,605,205
Total cost to build and finance	$8,028,076
Annual debt service payments	$401,403
Annual cost per added space	$2,723

underestimates the cost, as it assumes that a two-level structure can double the number of spaces of the existing lot, whereas in reality fewer spaces will be provided due to the space taken up by ramps and structural supports.

It costs two-and-one-half times as much to accommodate an additional person parking on campus than to shift one person from driving to riding the bus. The total annual savings to the campus from the faculty/staff bus pass program, compared to providing 350 net new parking spaces, is approximately $550,000. Note that the results would be quite different if additional surface parking were available. In this case, the cost of adding one more parking space will be $300 to $950/year, depending on whether land costs are included or not. Even if land costs are included, however, the cost of parking is still somewhat lower than the cost of the transit pass.

Donald Shoup, a planning professor at the University of California–Los Angeles, analyzed the cost of three different programs at UCLA—expansion of the PS4 parking structure, the university vanpool subsidy program, and a pilot transit pass program. His results are shown in Table 3.5 (Shoup 1999).

TABLE 3.5
THE COST PER STUDENT SERVED BY DIFFERENT TRANSPORTATION PROGRAMS AT THE UNIVERSITY OF CALIFORNIA–LOS ANGELES VARIES WIDELY. (COURTESY OF DONALD SHOUP)

Program	Number of Students Served	UCLA's Cost/Student Served	Fees Paid/Student Served	Subsidy/Student Served
Parking structure expansion	1,003	$126/month	$43/month	$83/month
Vanpools	195	$165/month	$100/month	$65/month
Pilot transit pass program	4,001	$29/month	Free	$29/month

In this case, the largest subsidy per person is for the students who use the expanded parking structure. Note that the number of students who use the structure is larger than the number of spaces, reflecting the fact that there is turnover, so that each space is used by more than one person each day. Shoup also determined that the transit pass program reduces permit demand by 1,077 spaces and reduces parking space demand by 798 spaces. The total cost of the transit pass program is $116,029/month, all paid by the university. The cost per parking space avoided is $145/month, or $1,745/year. The total cost of the parking system expansion is $126,378, of which $83,429 is paid by the university, and the remainder by the users. The total cost/parking space provided is $170/month or $2,041/year, of which the university pays $112/month or $1,344.

This example highlights two different ways of looking at the costs of parking. If we are interested in the total cost of each program, including the costs paid by the user and the cost paid by the institution, the transit pass is less expensive, costing $1,745/year for each parking space avoided, compared to $2,041 per year for each parking space provided. If we are interested only in the "subsidy," for the transit pass program the subsidy/parking space avoided is higher than the subsidy per new parking space. If parking revenues pay the costs for both of these programs, then the total cost is the relevant figure for planning purposes.

One caveat to this type of analysis is the potential for saturation of transit pass use. Factors such as where students and employees reside, the quality and availability of transit service to campus, and the price of parking will determine at what level transit use will saturate. Thus, depending on how much growth in parking demand the campus is anticipating, it may not be feasible to shift *all* new demand simply by providing transit passes, even if it is less expensive to shift *one* person to transit. Or, increasing the level of transit use beyond a saturation point may require investment in improved transit service. However, there may be a willingness by the surrounding municipality or transit district to provide some or all of this investment if it also will provide service to the broader community.

Managing Demand through Financial Incentives: Parking Pricing

If parking consumers are demanding more parking than the campus is able to supply, there are several ways that parking can be allocated. At many campuses, there are rationing systems, where parking is allocated based upon status or seniority, by lottery, or by a waiting list system that locks in possession of a parking pass—once you get one, you never give it up. While this approach often has a strong political constituency, it lacks one of the virtues of the market system—there are no price signals to guide consumers. A market-based approach allows prices to rise until the demand for parking matches the supply and allows individual users to decide whether or not to purchase parking.

The simplest financial incentive to reduce parking demand is simply to raise the price of parking. There are extensive empirical data showing that parking pricing is one of the most significant determinants of travel behavior (U.S. EPA 1998). Interestingly, increasing the cost of parking seems to have a greater impact on travel behavior than a similar dollar increase in other components of the total cost of a vehicle trip.

One study examined the impact when a number of employers shifted from offering free parking to charging for parking, at rates ranging from $23 to $58 per month (Willson and Shoup 1990). The results were decreases in the number of cars being driven to the workplace of between 15 and 38 percent. The average was a 0.88 percent decrease in demand per dollar increase in monthly permit cost. This is a measure of the price elasticity of demand.

An analysis at the University of Colorado (Bamberger and Associates 1997) showed a nonlinear elasticity. A fee increase of 25 percent (about $7.25/month) would reduce demand by 4 percent, a 0.55 percent decrease in demand per dollar. However, a 40 percent increase ($11.60/month) would reduce demand by 14 percent, a 1.26 percent decrease per dollar. At the University of Washington in the early 1990s, prices were raised by $18/month, and parking demand dropped by 17 percent. The analysis conducted for the University of Washington 2001 master plan update concluded that a 10 percent increase in price would lead to a 1 to 2 percent decrease in demand.

The elasticity of demand also will depend upon the alternatives that are available. If there are options other than driving, such as good transit access to the campus or good bicycle access, then a price increase is likely to produce a larger shift than if there are few alternatives. However, even in cases where there is no transit serving a workplace, price increases have been shown to reduce single-occupant commuting and increase carpooling. Donald Shoup (1997) has analyzed a set of studies of the impact of financial incentives on employee transportation behavior in areas with good public transportation and areas with little or no public transportation, and found surprising results. In five examples of areas with little or no public transportation the average financial incentive offered not to drive was $49, with a resultant 26 percent decrease in parking demand. In two areas with good public transportation, financial incentives averaging $45 led to a 21 percent reduction in parking demand. This surprising result reflects the fact that there is already a higher percentage of commuters using other modes in the areas with good public transit, so it may be harder to create additional modal shift. However, it also shows that even if there is little availability of transit, increasing the cost of parking can have a significant impact on travel behavior. As an example, when Cornell University raised the price of parking in 1991, the effect was to reduce single-occupant vehicle trips by 26 percent, with most of the shift to carpooling.

Combining the concept of elasticity of demand with the fact that providing additional parking can be very expensive leads to an intriguing scenario: *There are cases where raising parking rates to limit demand may ultimately lead to lower parking rates than a supply-side approach.* This may seem confusing, but the following example illustrates the point.

At the University of Colorado, we have seen that increasing the percentage of structured parking from 20 percent to 40 percent would require parking rates to increase from $29 to $89. If the parking supply is increased by 33 percent, by adding structured parking, the effect would be to increase the percentage of structured parking from (0.2/1) to (0.2 + 0.33)/(1 + 0.33) = 40 percent. So, *parking fees will need to be tripled to increase the parking supply by 33 percent.*

Now, compare this to a strategy that attempts to reduce parking demand by increasing price. Using the elasticity relationship, a price increase of about 55 percent would be expected to reduce demand by 33 percent. This would no doubt be a very politically charged decision, with many campus constituents opposing such a large (55 percent) increase in parking fees. *But the alternative strategy of expanding the parking supply to yield the same increment in available parking spaces would require fee increases nearly six times as large.* This concept will be true in many cases where the only way to increase the parking supply is through structured parking. It will generally not be true at institutions where plentiful land is available for new surface parking lots.

There are a number of other advantages to this approach. First, since no new construction is required, no debt capacity is used. Second, there is net revenue generated. In the scenario where new parking is developed, the new revenue from increased permit fees goes into paying for the new parking, so there is no *net* revenue. In the demand management scenario, however, there is significant new revenue that is generated that can be used for other purposes. This opens up the possibility of investing parking revenues in additional transportation options. A third benefit is the low-risk nature of this decision. Unlike a supply-side approach, which locks in long-term debt and the possibility of default, a demand-side approach incurs no risk and is reversible.

It is also important to realize that parking demand at an educational institution is quite different from parking demand in a retail environment. Decision makers are often reluctant to charge market rates for parking in retail areas because of the fear that this may discourage shoppers from visiting the area. Charging for parking for employees is generally more politically acceptable. In the case of an educational institution, the primary customers are students, who are unlikely to choose their school based upon parking availability. Thus, there is more room for using parking pricing as a demand management strategy in the educational environment.

On the negative side, it is often difficult for parking consumers to accept a price increase that is not linked to an obvious, tangible benefit such as the construction of additional parking facilities. There are a number of ways to respond to this difficulty. First, if you can make a convincing case that increasing parking rates and using this to fund other transportation alternatives will actually lead to lower parking rates than the option of building more parking, this may blunt that argument. Second, it may be important to examine the equity impacts of increases to parking rates. In most cases, car ownership and per capita driving increase with income, while alternate mode use decreases with income. Thus, a policy that increases the charges for parking and invests the new revenue in alternate modes is likely to increase equity. However, lower-income employees or students who drive to campus may find market-rate parking to be a significant financial burden. At some (though not all) campuses, these may be the employees who are most likely to live furthest from campus and in areas least well served by transit, so the equity issues need to be examined carefully.

Another approach is to decouple the variety of types of revenue that are typically collected by a parking system. In general, parking revenue will consist of permit fees, meter revenues or other forms of daily parking charges, and parking fines. One approach some institutions use is to have the permit and meter revenues support the parking system and use the fine revenues to support alternative modes. This can reduce the perception among those paying for parking permits that they are unfairly being forced to pay for someone else's use of other transportation modes.

California actually has a state statute that requires that public universities segregate parking fines and use them to support alternative modes. California Penal Code section 1463.7 directs that parking fines collected at any of the University of California campuses may not be used to purchase land or construct or maintain parking facilities. The funds must be used for "the development, enhancement and operation of alternate methods of transportation for students and employees" and for "the mitigation of the impact of off-campus student and employee parking in university communities." A similar requirement exists for the California State University system.

At the opposite extreme, Florida State University assesses a mandatory transportation fee to all students, which is used both to pay for transit services and to provide free parking to students. Revenues from the fee are used to pay for construction of new parking garages. In this model, there is no financial incentive to use another mode, other than driving and parking on campus.

Another important consideration is how much flexibility is built into the parking permit system. At many campuses, the only way to get access to parking is to purchase a permit that allows you to park on campus every day. This provides an incentive to drive regularly, as car owners have already paid a fixed fee, and each individual trip will have no additional parking fee associated. In addition, if new alternatives are available, parking permit holders may be reluctant to give up their permits if they have occasional parking needs. There are a few possible approaches to this issue. One is to create occasional parking privileges for non–permit holders who participate in campus demand management programs.

A few campus parking authorities are experimenting with new technologies to ease the neighborhood overspill and car traffic problems. The University of Wisconsin–Madison has begun an in-car "pay as you use" device. The meter, which is located inside the car, turns on when you arrive in a paid permit lot and turns off when you leave. The cost of parking is electronically charged to the permit holder. This automatic deduction system has the advantage of charging the user only for the time of the car storage. Presumably it increases turnover, with the electronic meter running and the cost going up. The prudent car owner would not park any longer than necessary, making the same space available for more users. It has the potential to charge higher rates at peak periods (congestion pricing) or rewarding car parkers who have the flexibility of using the "pay as you use" lot at off-peak times. By only charging for actual parking use, the perverse incentives created by monthly or annual passes are eliminated.

Managing Demand through Financial Incentives: Paying People Not to Drive

Because of the political difficulty involved in raising parking rates, some institutions have taken an alternative approach—paying employees not to drive. The concept here is that the campus makes a monthly cash payment to any employee who chooses not to purchase a parking permit. The cost difference between having a parking permit and not having one is then the sum of the cost of purchasing a permit and the cash payment offered to those who do not purchase a permit.

This type of program is known as a "parking cash-out program." An advantage of a cash-out system, compared to simply raising parking rates, is that there will be less opposition from employees. The downside is the cost of the program—composed of the cost of administering the program and the actual value of the employee benefit. It may be possible to couple a cash-out program with an increase to the cost of parking, so that the net cost to the institution is reduced.

The leading U.S. example of an educational institution using this approach is Stanford University, which in the mid-1990s began a program of paying any employee who did not purchase a parking permit during the year $90—which has since grown to $160 (Siegman 1994, 1998; Stanford 2002). This modest financial incentive, known as the "Clean Air Cash" program, convinced many employees to look for other ways to get to campus. Stanford also slowly raised parking rates, increasing them by about 15 percent annually, but still holding them well below the actual cost of providing parking. At the same time Stanford dramatically expanded the alternative ways to get to campus. They invested $4 million in improving bicycle facilities and got 900 more people to shift from cars to bikes—a cost of $4,400 per person, which compares to the $18 million or more Stanford would have had to spend on parking structures for the same number of people. A main road through campus was changed into a bike/transit mall and dramatically increased transit service to campus. This combination of financial incentives to drive less and significant investment in alternatives to driving has allowed Stanford to hold traffic to campus steady during the 1990s, while the university grew substantially, adding more than 2 million square feet of building space.

A cash-out system may be particularly appealing at a campus currently offering free parking. Outside of central business districts, most employees in the United States do not pay for parking. These employees are likely to perceive the cost of parking as zero, and a switch from free parking to pay parking is likely to meet stiff resistance. In this circumstance, a cash-out system can be based on providing employees with a transportation allowance.

Individual employees will then have the choice of keeping the allowance and choosing another way to get to work, or continuing to drive to campus, and paying the allowance back to campus. There will still be no net cost for those who wish to park on campus, but parking will no longer be perceived as free. This approach does not have as large an impact on employee travel behavior as simply charging for parking, but can still have a significant effect. Table 3.6 shows data on commuter response to cash-out and to paid parking in the Los Angeles central business district.

TABLE 3.6
TRAVEL BEHAVIOR RELATED TO WHO PAYS FOR PARKING. WHEN THE INDIVIDUAL DRIVER PAYS THE COST OF PARKING, THE AMOUNT OF DRIVING CAN GO DOWN SUBSTANTIALLY. DATA IS FROM DOWNTOWN LOS ANGELES. (COURTESY OF DONALD SHOUP [SHOUP 1993])

Travel Behavior	Driver Pays for Parking	Cash-Out System	Employer Paid Parking
Solo driver share	48%	55%	69%
Daily vehicle miles traveled per employee	18.1	20.2	24.1

In this case, a cash-out approach achieves 67 percent of the reduction in solo commuting that charging for parking provides. Note that the conversion from free or subsidized parking to a cash-out system will increase equity. Because real institutional resources are required to provide parking, when the parking is free or below a cost recovery rate, there is essentially a transfer of resources from those who either choose not to drive or cannot afford to drive, to those who drive to the campus. A cash-out system ensures that the nondrivers receive the same subsidy. The Victoria Transport Policy Institute's *Online TDM Encyclopedia* offers case studies of a number of parking cash-out programs (Litman 1999).

Restrictions on Student Parking

One other factor that will affect the appropriate mix of parking and alternatives is the campus philosophy on student parking. Some schools have created special limitations on the availability of parking permits to students. Several schools do not issue parking permits to students who live within a short distance of campus. The rationale is that students who live this close to campus will have other options for travel to school than driving. As an example, the University of New Hampshire will not issue parking permits for those that live off campus within one-half mile. They are considering expanding that to three-fourths mile as shuttle service is expanded. The University of Wisconsin–Madison only issues permits to students meet a rather stringent set of criteria: they must live beyond one mile of the city transit system, use their vehicle at least three days per week for employment, or have special or unusual needs (such as medical students with rounds that start before bus service begins). Some campuses manage student parking through long waiting lists for student parking permits and a first-come, first-served policy. At the University of Arizona the waiting list for permits is not weeks, or months, but years.

A significant number of universities and colleges discourage first-year and second-year students from bringing cars to campus by either eliminating or limiting their ability to obtain a parking permit. At residential schools, freshmen generally live on campus, often as a requirement, and thus are much closer to university academic and activity centers. Meals are provided in the residential dining halls or a cafeteria. A small retail business district is usually contiguous to these campuses. Therefore, the first-year student is within convenient walking, biking, or shuttle bus distance of most needs that are not found in a typical campus bookstore or student union. The 2001 University Transportation Survey of twenty-three colleges and universities (Daggett 2001) found that 35 percent of responding colleges had restrictions on freshman or other students bringing cars to campus, while 65 percent had no restrictions.

Most faculty and some administrators believe an automobile is not a crucial factor in the academic success of an undergraduate student. Furthermore, many believe that the absence of student cars in the early semesters of a college educational experience may improve the intellectual enrichment and focus of most students. Wherever this rule is in place, there are exceptions for students with special needs, such as temporary or permanent disabilities, parenthood, and necessary employment far from campus. All parking management offices provide special permits for these and other legitimate exemptions.

Some schools that *do not* issue freshmen parking permits are Bryn

Mawr College, University of New Hampshire, Tulane University, University of Vermont, Warren Wilson College, University of Wisconsin–Madison, and Purdue. Stanford University recently implemented a freshman parking ban, and the Utah State University in Logan (17,000 students) is considering implementing restrictions on freshman cars. Some academically strong institutions have a policy of car permits only for graduate students, juniors, and seniors. The University of California–Santa Cruz, the University of Maryland–College Park, and the University of New Hampshire have no-car policies for freshmen or sophomores. Some of the colleges at Rutgers University do not permit students to have cars on campus until their senior year.

Instituting these types of limitations at institutions that currently allow student parking may be quite controversial. Students are likely to feel that they are being discriminated against, because the restrictions do not apply to faculty or staff. In addition, there may be concerns from the admissions office that parking restrictions may cause some students to choose not to attend the school. On the other hand, there is often strong support for student parking limitations by off-campus neighborhoods.

There also may be a positive reaction from parents. The following quote from Clifford Contreras, the Transportation Alternatives Program director at the University of California–Davis, illustrates this point, "The elimination of freshman parking permits in 2002 freed up six hundred spaces. Positive parent feedback has followed the parking ban, as parents are relieved to not have to worry about where and how their kids are driving around. As the university turns away applicants every year, there was little concern about the effect of the ban upon applicant numbers."

BOX 3.1 | **PARKING RESTRICTIONS FOR FACULTY? LEWIS AND CLARK UNIVERSITY HAS AN INNOVATIVE APPROACH TO FACULTY PARKING.**

One innovative idea that is being implemented at Lewis and Clark College in Portland, Oregon, is a restriction on some faculty parking. Lewis and Clark is facing two issues--high housing prices have had a negative impact on the ability to recruit faculty and a lack of parking on campus. While the campus does have a relatively large amount of open land, they treasure the beauty of their campus and do not want to convert green space to new

Overflow Parking in Neighborhoods:
Managing Off-Campus Parking Impacts

If a university generates traffic and overflow parking in surrounding neighborhoods it is also generating community relations problems. Residents' complaints about noise, safety, pollution, and the inconvenience of finding parking in front of their own houses often lead to serious conflicts between the municipality and the university or college. If free or cheap parking is available nearby, some sort of off-campus parking management program is needed in cases where the educational institution raises parking rates substantially (whether to pay for new parking construction or to pay for transportation alternatives) or if a parking cash-out program is instituted. Otherwise, the effect will be simply to shift parking off campus and into the surrounding neighborhoods.

Across the country, cities are instituting parking management programs in neighborhoods impacted by traffic from schools and major employment centers. In commercial districts adjacent to educational institutions, it is common to install parking meters. Some cities have also implemented residential parking permit (RPP) zones in nearby residential streets. RPP programs allow residents to purchase full-time parking permits often for a nominal fee. As an example, residents in RPP zones in Boulder, Colorado, pay $12/year for each permit. The general public, including students and university employees, may park in the RPP district for a limited posted time. The time period is often restricted to two hours or less during business hours. In some cases, a limited number of commuter permits may be sold in RPP zones. In the Boulder example, commuter permits are sold for $240/year, but only a small number are sold (two per blockface). The idea is to set the

parking. The college has begun acquiring houses in the immediate vicinity of the campus for subsidized faculty housing. The university retains ownership of the underlying land, and sells the structure to a faculty member. There is a catch--faculty members residing in these homes will not have access to a campus parking permit; in fact, the purchase agreement includes a clause that purchasers will not use their cars on campus. Lewis and Clark also owns a number of houses that are available for rent by faculty, graduate students, and professional students. The same automobile restrictions apply to this housing (Sestric 2003).

number of permits issued so as to maintain some parking availability throughout the day. The 2001 University Transportation Survey of twenty-three colleges and universities (Daggett 2001) found that 60 percent of responding institutions had residential parking permit programs in neighborhoods adjacent to the campus.

Note that the surrounding community may institute these RPP programs even in the absence of any transportation policy changes at the educational institution. The effect will be to cause some people who were parking in the surrounding neighborhoods to shift to campus. This may force the institution to expand the parking supply, expand alternative mode access, or use financial incentives to reduce parking demand. In any case, overflow parking is almost always a challenging problem for universities and communities to resolve. Universities need to examine which options will result in the best long-term solutions.

"Green" Parking Designs and University Applications

Most of our discussion has focused on the impacts of parking decisions on campus finances, and on the travel choices made by students and employees. However, parking lots and structures also have site-specific environmental impacts. When installing or updating parking facilities, there are a number of options that can help mitigate run-off from impervious surfaces and protect sensitive areas. "Green" parking lot techniques include minimizing the dimensions of parking lot spaces, utilizing alternative pavers in overflow parking areas, and using "bioretention areas" to treat stormwater (University of Connecticut, 2002; U.S. EPA 2002).

Alternative pavers consist of two broad categories: paving blocks and other surfaces, including gravel, cobbles, wood, brick, natural stone, and mulch. Paving blocks are concrete or plastic grids with gravel or grass inside the holes for infiltration. Porous pavement is a permeable pavement surface with an underlying stone reservoir to temporarily store surface runoff before it infiltrates into the subsoil. Porous asphalt and pervious concrete are manufactured by removing the finer materials and incorporating void spaces to allow infiltration. Grass pavers are concrete interlocking blocks or synthetic fiber–embedded grid systems that stabilize the soil and allow grass to grow in open areas. Cold climate concerns can be mitigated in some instances by attaching a rubber strip to the bottom of a snowplow.

Bioretention sites are landscape features that treat on-site storm-water run-off. The run-off is collected in a shallow depression and filtered through a mulch and soil mixture before returning to the storm drain system. Native vegetation around the area can disguise the depression.

The University of Connecticut installed green parking outside its new Rentschler Field (Garrick and Brown 2002). The parking lot design will reduce run-off, protect the outlying wetland areas, and provide a friendlier surface for tailgaters. This particular installation of turf parking is significant because of its immense size, prominent location, and innovative design. The 40,000-seat football stadium lies in East Hartford, about 20 miles from the main campus in Storrs. The parking lot holds 4,000 cars. Design consultants hired by the University of Connecticut installed Turfgrid, a fiber-reinforced turf system. Turfgrid uses propylene fibers embedded into the topsoil at a depth of 4 to 6 inches. The microfibers stabilize the soil and prevent the grass from crushing under the weight of the vehicles. Once the seed is spread, it takes a full growing season for the root system to interlock with the fibers and provide the necessary strength and integrity to support traffic. Processed aggregate driveways run between the stalls. University of Connecticut pursued this installation for its environmental benefits as well as the low cost. The Orange Bowl in Miami, Florida, also has a large green parking lot outside the stadium.

In the fall of 2002, the University of Rhode Island installed a 1,000-space permeable lot on campus. Another 800-car lot is being built this year. Both lots cost approximately the same as a conventional lot. The primary reasons for the installation were minimizing the run-off impacts to a nearby stream and maintaining recharge to the local groundwater aquifer. The site serves a new convocation center that features events on evenings and weekends. The lot also provides student parking throughout the day and reaches maximum capacity during the school year. These lots feature asphalt with the fine grains removed to allow water infiltration. Crushed rock beneath the asphalt provides temporary storage and infiltration.

Other alternative pavers applications at institutions of higher education include:

- San Jose State University in San Jose, California, installed Grasspave2 in 1995 for a 3,552-square-foot pedestrian mall. The mall was installed to increase student safety and increase the size of the campus core, while maintaining emergency and maintenance vehicle access. Santa Clara University in California completed a similar project in 1996.
- Frostburg State University in Frostburg, Maryland, installed a gravel-paved lot for student parking. The original lot was always a muddy mess and run-off concerns for the nearby stream prevented conventional paving. The lot covers 14,800 square feet and uses white tape marks along a border fence to designate parking spaces, rather than striping.
- The University of South Alabama in Mobile installed 438 parking spaces in 1998 using a combination of Grasspave2 spaces with Gravelpave2 aisles. The reduction of flooding risk was the primary motivation for the medium, because two people had died at the flooded University Boulevard intersection.

Conclusions

In this chapter we have examined the economics of supply-side and demand-side approaches to managing parking at institutions of higher education. We have found that at institutions where the supply of land is constrained such that new parking can only be created by building parking structures, it is often less expensive to reduce demand than to expand supply. Some tools for managing demand include raising the price of parking, "cashing out" parking, and providing transit passes to employees and students. At campuses where there is sufficient land for new surface parking lots, by contrast, the cost of parking is generally less than the cost of many of the options for reducing demand. However, even in these cases the desire to preserve campus green spaces, to limit new traffic generation, and to reduce emissions of air pollutants may shift decision making toward demand management. In all cases, a financial analysis should include the impacts of price increases on parking demand, and a comparison of the cost of demand management with expanding parking supply, in order to determine the most cost-effective approach. Campus values around aesthetics and environmental quality may then be used to shift in one direction or another from the cost-effective mix. We have also seen that any attempt at parking management will likely require cooperation from the surrounding community to constrain off-campus parking by employees and students.

References

American Lung Association. 2003. *State of the Air Report 2003*, found at lungaction.org/reports/stateoftheair2003.html.

Bamberger and Associates. 1997. *CU–Boulder EcoPass Financial Feasibility Analysis*.

Cook, D. 1999. The Economics of Parking Garages and the Alternatives to Them. In *Proceedings of Finding a New Way Conference*, University of Colorado, Boulder.

Cook. 2001. *Comparative Annual Cost Analysis: CU F/S Eco Pass vs. Added Parking Structure*. University of Colorado, Boulder.

Daggett, J., and R. Gutkowski. 2002. *University Transportation Survey: Transportation in University Communities*, found at fcgov.com/uts.pdf. City of Fort Collins and Colorado State University, Fort Collins, CO.

Garrick, N., and K. Brown. 2002. Green Parking Lots at UCONN's New Football Stadium. *Technology Transfer Newsletter* 19(3). Also found at www.cti.uconn.edu/ti/Technology/text_winter2002_ttnews.htm#two.

Litman, T. 1999. *Commuter Financial Incentives: Parking Cash Out, Travel Allowance, Transit and Rideshare Benefits*, found at www.vtpi.org/tdm/tdm8.htm. Victoria Transport Policy Institute, Victoria, British Columbia, Canada.

Sestric, M. 2003. Lewis and Clark University campus planner, personal communication, June.

Shoup, D. 1993. *Cashing Out Employer-Paid Parking*. Access No. 2, University of California Transportation Center.

Shoup, D. 1995. *How Much Does a Parking Space Cost?* University of California–Los Angeles Institute of Transportation Policy.

Shoup, D. 1997a. The High Cost of Free Parking. *Journal of Planning Education and Research* 17:3–20.

Shoup, D. 1997b. Evaluating the Effects of Cashing Out Employer-Paid Parking: Eight Case Studies. *Transport Policy* 4(4):201–216.

Shoup, D. 1999. Expanding Parking Supply: What Are the Tradeoffs? In *Proceedings of Finding a New Way Conference*, University of Colorado, Boulder.

Siegman, P. 1994. *Solving Stanford's Parking Shortage*. Stanford University Department of Economics.

Siegman, P. 1998. *Stanford University's General Use Permit Agreement*. Presentation at Congress for the New Urbanism.

South Coast Air Quality Management District. 1999. *Multiple Air Toxics Exposure Study in the South Coast Air Basin:* MATES II. Draft final report, Diamond Bar, CA.

Stanford University Parking and Transportation Services. 2002. *Incentives Programs*, found at transportation.stanford.edu/incentives_programs/CleanAirCash.shtml.

University of Colorado Environmental Center. 2002. *2002 Update to the Blueprint For a Green Campus*, found at www.Colorado.EDU/ecenter. University of Colorado, Boulder, CO, pp. 18–19.

University of Connecticut Nonpoint Education for Municipal Officials. 2002. *Parking Lots*, found at nemo.uconn.edu/reducing_runoff/parking_lots.htm.

U.S. EPA. 1998. *Technical Methods for Analyzing Pricing Measures to Reduce Transportation Emissions*. U.S. EPA Report No. 231-R-98-006, found at www.epa.gov/clariton/clhtml/pubtitle.html.

U.S. EPA. 2002. *Post-Construction Storm Water Management in New Development and Redevelopment: Green Parking, National Pollutant Discharge Elimination System,* found at http://cfpub.epa.gov/npdes/stormwater/menuofbmps/post_12.cfm.

van Dyke, W. 1991. *Campus Parking and Transportation Planning Issues for the 1990s*. Paper presented at the 26th Annual International Conference, Society for College and University Planners.

Willson, R., and D. Shoup. 1990. Parking Subsidies and Travel Choices: Assessing the Evidence. *Transportation* 17:141–157.

Chapter 4

CHAPTER 4 | # Successful Campus
Transit Development

Because transit pass programs have been such an important part of university TDM strategies, much of this chapter is devoted to an examination of how transit pass programs can dramatically increase transit use in university communities. The chapter will describe a variety of approaches to student and employee transit pass programs, discuss funding options, and offer tips for successful negotiations between the campus and the transit agency. It also will discuss how to develop transit services to serve the higher education community—and how transit ridership from campus can support improved transit services for the rest of the community. Most of our focus will be on transit programs that connect the campus to the surrounding community, rather than on the short-distance shuttles that many institutions run to connect destinations within the campus.

We will focus primarily on bus-based transit. We should also note the role that rail transit can play. The rail costs are so high that few campuses are likely to develop stand-alone rail systems. However, if rail is developed by a larger transit agency, the same factors that make many college campuses ripe for high levels of bus use also make them natural destinations for rail lines. In cities with well-established subway or light-rail systems, campus travelers often heavily use the rail option. Examples include BART to access the University of California–Berkeley campus, or the use of the T in Boston by Harvard and Massachusetts Institute of Technology students. As new light-rail systems are developed, some of the examples of collaborative efforts to place stops on or adjacent to campuses include the University of Utah–Salt Lake City; the Auraria Higher Education center in Denver, Colorado, and the University of Washington–Seattle. Because these capital-intensive rail projects are so dependent on decision making beyond the campus level, and because far fewer areas in the United States have rail systems than bus transit, we will focus on bus transit. However, the same principles that apply to the use of transit passes for bus transit will apply to their use for rail-based systems.

University transit pass programs have become increasingly widespread during the last decade. The first university transit pass program in the United States was started in 1969 at the University of California–San Diego. A handful of additional programs were created in the 1970s and 1980s. Then in the 1990s many more programs began. By 2000 there were thirty-five programs serving more than 825,000 students (Brown et al. 2001).

The basic concept is that a university contracts with the local transit provider to provide fare-free access to some part of the campus community. In some cases the university itself may run the transit system. Most transit pass programs are universal access programs, where every member of the target group (every student or every employee) is covered. A few programs such as the University of Washington's U-PASS program create incentives for individuals to buy in, rather than covering the entire population.

The experience at most universities has been that student transit use increases significantly after the creation of a transit pass program. A survey of thirty-five universities that have student transit pass programs showed that student ridership increased from a low of 70 percent to a high of 200 percent in the first year of the program (Brown et al. 2001). Transit pass programs have been successful both in "college towns" and in large urban areas.

Typically, the university will negotiate a contract with a transit agency, in which the university pays an annual contracted amount. In return, students will have the right to ride all or part of the transit network fare-free by showing a valid university ID. The amount that the university pays per students is much lower than an individual would have to pay to purchase a monthly pass from the transit agency. For example, at the University of California–Berkeley, all students pay a mandatory bus pass fee of $34.20/semester, of which $20 goes to the AC Transit Agency for fare-free access to local and Transbay buses. By comparison, it would cost an individual more than $400 per semester to purchase the same service.

Some institutions also provide transit passes for employees. Typically, the programs start with student passes, often funded by student fees. Then, as faculty and staff see how successful the program is, they begin asking for the same benefit. There is generally not a mechanism for assessing a mandatory fee—faculty and staff cannot vote to require all employees to contribute. Thus the university must find another funding source. The most common sources are general fund dollars and parking or parking fine revenues. Some universities provide transit passes to all students and then offer a partially subsidized transit pass as an option for employees. In the Berkeley example above, employees who choose not to purchase a campus parking permit are eligible for a $10/month transit pass subsidy and are able to use pre-tax wages for this purpose, allowing savings of 12 to 46 percent depending on the employee's tax bracket.

There are many benefits that universities get from transit pass programs. They provide low cost transportation to students, reduce parking demand, provide a benefit for employees, and improve relations with the surrounding community. These benefits accrue both to the individuals who use their passes and to the campus community as a whole. In addition, since students and employees who use transit are likely to have lower incomes than those who drive, transit pass programs have a positive impact on equity. There is also some evidence that offering a transit pass program can help with recruitment and retention of students. At the University of Wisconsin, 15 percent of students surveyed indicated that the U-PASS program had a major impact on their decision to attend the university (Meyer and Beimborn 1996).

For the community, these programs reduce traffic generated by the university, reduce off-campus parking demand (at least near the campus), and can lead to improved transit service for the broader community. Because off-campus transportation impacts are often a flashpoint for "town-gown" conflict, the perception that the campus is tackling the issue can be a real plus in community relations.

For the transit agency, university pass programs can provide increased ridership, a predictable level of revenue, and a constituency that supports expanded transit service. Brown et al. (2001) studied the performance of thirteen transit systems before and after beginning university transit pass programs. What they found were significant positive impacts on perfor-mance: increased total ridership, an increased number of riders per bus, an increase in the total vehicle hours of service, and a decrease in the cost per ride. Another benefit is the ability to retain ridership when fares increase. However, there are a couple of important caveats here. First, if the transit system is already operating at or near capacity, it may be very difficult to serve the additional riders, so the cost of a pass program will be higher. Second, the benefits to a transit agency assume that the agency wants to increase ridership. This may not always be the case. Because public tran-sit agencies in the United States typically get most of their funds from tax support, not from farebox revenue from riders, they can have a financial incentive to reduce ridership. That is, even if increased ridership lowers the total cost/rider and increases the revenue generated/rider, much of the cost of the additional service required will have to come from their tax revenues. If the agency is facing fiscal challenges, or of the agency is trying to focus resources on new capital investments, it may not want to respond to service demands generated by a pass program.

Two Canadian researchers have attempted to quantify the benefits of a campus pass program (Litman and Lovegrove 1999). They conducted an economic analysis in which they monetized the costs and benefits to tran-sit users, students and staff, the university, the transit agency, and society at large, for the U-PASS program at the University of British Columbia. They considered the costs of administering the program, the fee assessed to stu-dents, and the transit subsidies provided by the transit agency. Benefits considered were the savings to students who would otherwise be paying a higher price for transit, and reductions in parking costs, congestion, acci-dent risks, roadway costs, and environmental pollution. Their analysis indi-cated that the benefits of the program are six times greater than the costs. In addition, they note that there are other benefits that they were not able to quantify, including increased equity for transportation users and support for regional land-use goals.

Because of these benefits, the number of schools and transit agencies offering these programs began growing rapidly during the early 1990s. Because transit pass programs are central to so many schools' TDM programs, we will spend some time discussing how to start transit pass programs and some of the issues that need to be addressed to maximize success.

Transit Pass Program Elements

One fundamental issue is whether to create a universal coverage system, in which all members of a given group—students, employees, and so forth—receive the pass, or whether there is a buy-in process. A few schools have

TABLE 4.1

SUMMARY OF COST AND BENEFIT CATEGORIES FOR A TRANSIT PASS PROGRAM AT THE UNIVERSITY OF BRITISH COLUMBIA. (COURTESY OF LITMAN AND LOVEGROVE 1999.)

Impact	Description	Estimate	Distribution
Administrative expenses	Annual TREK program expenses	$500,000/year	UBC
U-Pass fees	Monthly student payment	$20/month	Students
Additional subsidies	Annual subsidies for increased transit service	$4 million/year	UBC/TransLink
Current transit user savings	Monthly savings to students who would purchase a transit fare anyway	$15/month	Current transit users
Mode shift benefits	Net consumer benefits to students who shift modes, based on the "Rule of Half"	Ω of marginal cost savings	U-PASS users
Additional U-Pass benefits to users	Noncommute trips, discounts, recreational use of shower facilities	?	U-PASS Users
UBC parking savings	Avoided parking subsidy per trip	$3.52/trip	UBC
Congestion reduction	Congestion reduction benefit of a reduced peak-period vehicle km	$0.15/km	TransLink
Accident reductions	Reduced external costs per km shifted	$0.04/km	Society
Road and traffic service savings	Reduced external costs per km shifted	$0.02/km	Society
Reduced pollution	Reduced external costs per km shifted	$0.04/km	Society
Equity benefits	Financial benefits to lower-income students	?	Society
Support for transport and land use objectives	Reduced automobile dependency, economies of scale, reduced sprawl	?	Society

The value for those categories with a ? are unknown.

created successful transit pass programs, which do not include all students or all faculty and staff. In this model, students or employees are given the option of buying into a program, which usually offers a constellation of benefits. For example, the U-PASS program at the University of Washington offers students and employees fare-free access to bus and rail service, a guaranteed ride home, free carpool parking, discounted occasional parking, and a certain number of days of free parking on campus for occasional driving needs. For students, a U-PASS was $35 per quarter in 2001; for staff and faculty a U-PASS was $48.96 per quarter. As of the 2000–2001 academic year, 86 percent of students chose to purchase the U-PASS. Part of the success of this example may lie in the fact that the university also has significantly increased parking permit rates, from $72/quarter before the U-PASS program was created, to $178/quarter in 2000–2001 (University of Washington 2001). However, in most cases, colleges have opted to create programs that all students pay for through mandatory fees because this is most likely to attract new transit users. In addition, transit agencies often base their pricing on a model similar to health insurance, where the rates are much lower if an entire population, including individuals who seldom use transit, is "insured," rather than a self-selected group of high transit users.

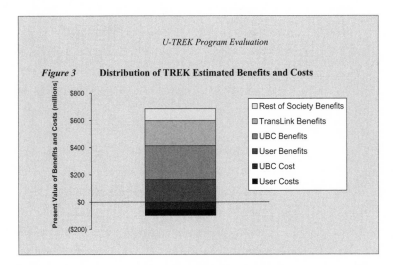

FIG. 4.1
This shows the overall benefits compared to costs for a transit pass program at the University of British Columbia. (Litman and Lovegrove, 1999.)

It is also important to identify potential partners. First is the transit provider. This may be a transit district, a municipality, or even a division of the university. The transit agency may already have extensive experience with large-scale pass programs, or the university pass may be their first entrée into this arena. This prior experience is likely to determine the initial comfort level of the transit provider.

There are a few areas where the transit agency itself takes the lead on creating university pass programs. The leading example of this is the Chicago Transit Authority (CTA) which has created a Schoolpass program with a uniform set of services and pricing that are offered to Chicago area schools. This program was started in 1998, with a focus on increasing transit ridership during off-peak hours. The CTA offers the program at a set price to any school that is willing to enroll all full-time students. As of 2002, twenty-eight colleges and universities with 62,000 students participate in the program. The Port Authority Transit system in Pittsburgh also has established a university pass program that they have actively marketed to Pittsburgh area colleges and universities.

There also may be other potential partners. If the surrounding community perceives a benefit from a university pass program, this may translate into political or financial support for a pass program. As an example, when the student bus pass program at the University of Colorado was started in 1991, the City of Boulder Transportation Department both provided assistance in the negotiations with the transit agency and provided startup funding, which was phased out over a period of five years.

It will be important to collect baseline information. Some questions to answer include:

- What transit service is available to serve campus constituents?
- What is the current student and employee transit ridership?
- Where do students and employees reside?

It also may be useful to survey projected effects of transit passes on ridership. While surveys give much more accurate information when they ask about existing behavior rather than asking speculative questions about how transportation choices will change after a pass is instituted, this can still give some useful information. This baseline information will help to answer two basic questions: How useful will a transit pass program be to the university? and What is the appropriate price for the program?

How Should a Pass Program Be Priced?

While transit agencies have the mission of moving people, and may see transit pass programs as a way of helping to fulfill this mission, generally they will want to ensure that they are not losing money through the creation of a transit pass program. This means that the revenue from the program should equal the farebox revenue that the agency would otherwise be receiving from individual fares, plus the added costs of new service that must be provided to meet the demand created by the program.

Lost revenue is the revenue that the transit agency would be getting from fare-paying customers if the pass program did not exist, and does not receive if the pass program does exist. This is not simply equal to the number of trips by pass-holders multiplied by the individual fare. To demonstrate this, suppose that a survey indicates that prior to the creation of a pass program there are 300,000 trips per year by students, paying $300,000 per year in cash fares. After the pass program begins, suppose there are now 900,000 trips/year. The lost revenue is $300,000, not $900,000, because two thirds of those trips would not have taken place if the pass program did not exist.

How much do those extra trips cost the transit provider, and how should these costs be allocated? These are surprisingly subtle questions to answer. In the United States, many transit systems have significant excess capacity on existing routes. If student pass-holders are primarily filling excess capacity on existing service, the marginal cost/added rider may be very low. This is most likely to be the case if the peak period for student travel is different than the peak travel times for the entire customer base of the transit agency. A system that is operating at capacity, on the other hand, may not be able to accommodate pass riders without spending a lot of money on expanding service.

One piece of information that may be useful in this negotiation is an analysis of the time distribution of student travel. While direct information may be difficult to obtain, the number of students registering for classes at different times of day can serve as a proxy for student trips to campus. At many schools the result is that the time of morning peak travel by college students will be later than the peak for commuters. This means that student travel may be able to fill empty seats during off-peak hours, rather than requiring expensive extra service during the morning peak. There is also a public relations value to the transit agency. Empty seats off the peak may contribute to a public perception of empty big buses clogging the streets. Filling those empty seats with university pass holders can significantly reduce that perception.

The other subtlety is that even if service has to be added, the improved service may benefit the broader community. For example, the increased demand for transit may allow the frequency to be increased on existing routes. This higher frequency then makes it easier for other users in the community to use this service. This in turn provides benefits to the transit agency, which now offers better service; the surrounding municipality, which has better transit service for its residents; and school districts and businesses, which may have students or employees who now have access to these routes. So, while the pass program may trigger an increase in service, the pass-holders are not the only ones who benefit from this increase. So, the added increment of service cost should not be borne completely by pass-holders. This is a reflection of one of the fundamental operating characteristics of transit, which is quite different than auto travel. When the number of people using transit increases, under a wide variety of conditions the overall performance of the transit system increases; while when more people travel by automobile, the overall performance of the auto system degrades. One approach to this issue is to quantify the use of added service by different user groups. If the university pass-holders make up 25 percent of the users of new service that has to be added, then perhaps 25 percent of the cost of that service should be allocated to the pass program.

Once a pass program is created, it becomes harder and harder over time to calculate what is revenue neutral. As service changes take place, and as the date of baseline information recedes into the past, more and more assumptions need to be made in order to do the calculation. Because of this, a common approach is to agree on a much simpler pricing strategy. This is to tie the contract price to actual ridership by passholders, with a discounted fare paid by the university for each trip. One way of setting this is to agree on a methodology for establishing a revenue-neutral pass price in an early year of the program, then normalize the shadow fares so that the price set by the shadow fares equals the revenue neutral price in that year. This formula can then be used in future years without attempting the calculation of revenue neutrality.

There are a number of other factors to consider in setting the price. One is the impact of passes on the operations of the transit system. In general, it is much faster to board by flashing an ID than it is for a customer to put money in a farebox. This can lead to a significant operational improvement. For example, if there is a 15-second savings per customer, and there are a million rides per year, the total time savings would be more than 4,000 hours. If we value this at a typical transit system cost of $55/hour, these time savings would be valued at $220,000.

There is also a savings from a decrease in cash handling. The administrative burden associated with receiving a handful of payments from a university over the course of a year, compared to the cash handling required for hundreds of thousands or millions of individual fares, is much lower. This savings should be reflected in the pass pricing.

The time value of money also should be considered. In many cases, a pass program pays in advance of much of the annual ridership. This is not always the case, but usually there will be one payment each semester or quarter. This prepayment has value, equal to the interest that would be accumulated during the time period that the fares have been prepaid.

Finally, the overall marketing value of pass programs should not be underestimated. University pass programs build a constituency—of students who are future riders, of employees who are more likely to support funding for public transit, and administrators. Plus, because most universities will build marketing into their pass programs, the transit agency will in effect have targeted marketing provided by the university out of its budget. Once again, there is a real value to these benefits, which should be reflected in the pass pricing.

The issues around pricing are quite different in cities where the transit system is operating at capacity. In this case there is not excess capacity to sell at a discount. In that event, the price that must be charged to achieve revenue neutrality may be considerably higher. The University of British Columbia in Vancouver presents an interesting case study. The UBC and Translink, the local transit provider, began discussing a pass program in 1996, and it took seven years to develop a proposal acceptable to both agencies. In February 2003, in the highest voter turnout in the history of the university, students voted overwhelmingly in favor of a Universal Transit Pass. The pass will cost $20 per month and will be mandatory for all students. In addition, Translink has committed to increasing the number of service hours to UBC by 23,000 per year. Pass holders will be entitled to unlimited use of TransLink buses, SkyTrain, and SeaBus services from September through April. U-PASS holders also will have free access to campus shuttles, bicycle and carpool programs, merchant discounts, and a guaranteed ride home. What is interesting about this example is the magnitude of the fee. At $20/month, it is about four times as high as a more typical $20/semester. However, this is still considerably less expensive than purchasing an individual monthly pass, which would run $63/month for Translink. An economic analysis of the program conducted by the Victoria Transport Policy Institute indicates that it has net benefits for all parties (Litman and Lovegrove 1999).

Fare Increases

An interesting issue is how pass prices should be treated when transit fares increase. Many university pass programs have only been in existence for a few years, so they are only starting to have to address this issue. At first glance, it may appear that this is quite simple—the pass price should increase by the same percentage as fares. However, there are a couple of subtle points to consider. First is the fact that there is elasticity in the individual response to fare increases. That is, when fares go up, some people stop riding, or ride less often. This means that transit agencies must set their fare increase higher than their actual revenue target. But, pass programs are very different. The pass program is either canceled completely because the university decides the price increase is too high, or it is continued completely, with no loss of ridership or revenue. This means that the appropriate increase to the price of the pass program should be less than the fare increase, in order to make the same revenue target.

A corollary to this analysis is that the more users are in pass programs, the more the transit agency is able to simultaneously satisfy two goals: raising ridership and raising revenue. This is an important issue for transit agencies to consider. If their mission is to increase ridership on transit, there are real dangers inherent in fare increases. Litman (2001) points out that transit riders can be broken into two categories when evaluating the ridership impacts of fare increases: transit-dependent and discretionary riders. The transit-dependent individuals may be those people who do not own or cannot afford to own a car and who will have a relatively small elasticity. However, those discretionary riders, who have a variety of transportation choices, may have much higher elasticities. In addition, the long-term elasticity may be larger, as the higher cost of transit leads to some former riders purchasing cars, or making housing or employment location decisions that reduce their access to transit. So, for transit agencies that are attempting to capture new riders—beyond the transit dependent—fare increases have a very significant downside. Having a large number of riders enrolled in a university pass program can buffer this impact.

A related issue is the question of whether fare increases should take place in large increments, separated by a number of years, or whether fares should be increased by smaller increments on a more regular basis. Because fare increases are politically unpopular, transit agencies often put them off, then have a relatively large increase to "get it all over with" at one time. Operationally, this also avoids having to change all of the documents that

BOX 4.1 | **TRANSIT FARE ELASTICITIES**

While actual elasticity will vary depending on many local factors (Multisystems 1997), many agencies use a rule of thumb (based on work from the 1960s) of an elasticity of −0.33; that is, a 1 percent increase in fares would be expected to decrease ridership by 0.335. A more recent study of fare increases in fifty cities (Goodwin 1992) shows an average elasticity of −0.4.

Let's see how this plays out in an example. If a transit agency raises fares by 25 percent, and the elasticity is −0.4, they would expect to lose 0.4 x 25 percent or 10 percent of their riders. Then, the revenue increase will be based on 90 percent as many riders paying 25 percent more; .9 x 1.25= 1.125--the net revenue increase is only 12.5 percent, half of the magnitude of the fare increase. So, if the goal is to raise revenue by the same percentage from pass-holders as from individual users, the appropriate increase in pass pricing is 12.5 percent, half the level of the individual fare increases.

list fares, and get passengers used to paying the correct fare on a regular basis. However, for pass programs the situation may be different. In general, it will be easier for a university to plan for regular small increases to the pass price than infrequent large increases. And pass programs do not have the same operational issues associated with annual fare increases. Once again, the most appropriate approach to increasing prices may be quite different for individual fares and pass contracts.

How Will Users Be Identified?

This is an important logistical detail to work out. Universities generally provide photo ID cards so that currently employed faculty and staff or registered students can be easily identified for purposes such as access to buildings or use of the library. Because of this, the simplest approach is to use this ID as the card for accessing transit. The bus or train operators will need some way of verifying that the ID is current. The simplest approach is through a sticker, which may be issued each semester or each quarter. This approach also works at schools where individuals opt in to the program. For instance, at the University of Washington students who buy a pass place a U-PASS sticker on their "HUSKY" ID card.

An emerging issue is the use of various forms of identification cards that use magnetic stripes or smart card technology. This is increasingly common as schools seek to create cards that have multiple uses (such as cash withdrawal at ATM machines or electronic keys to dormitory doors). These cards also allow universities to limit the number of times they must interact with students to update cards. That is, in the traditional sticker approach stickers must be mailed to all registered students each semester, or students must come in to an office to pick up stickers. By contrast, a magstripe or smart card approach allows registration information to be stored in a database. When a student's registration status changes, the change is reflected in the database. When a student checks out a book at the library, the card reader checks against the database for current registration. Instead of having to provide stickers or some alteration of the electronic information stored on each ID, all information can be transmitted electronically to a discrete number of locations.

This presents a challenge for use of the ID as a transit pass. If the transit vehicles have traditional fare boxes, without the ability to read cards, the transit operators will need some other means to verify current registration or employment. One option is to continue to provide a sticker. There are a couple of downsides, however. First, if the cards are being used for ATM access there may be problems with putting stickers directly on the cards. This can be avoided by placing the sticker on a clear plastic sleeve, although this adds expense. Second, simply the need to add stickers negates the benefit of a card system that does not require physical updating of cards each semester.

As more transit operators move to smart fare boxes, allowing the use of electronic cards, this problem may be lessened. However, there may still be an incompatibility. For most purposes, smart fare boxes will be reading information on a card—such as subtracting fares from a prepaid fare card, or checking the month of validity of a monthly pass. In the college smart card application, however, the fare box will need to check against a database. This requires that updated databases be loaded into each fare box. Close coordination is required between the campus ID office and the transit operator to make the system compatible.

Smart fare boxes also create another option for pricing pass programs, based on charging based on the actual ridership information for a given time period. The *BruinGo* pass program at the University of California–Los Angeles operates in this fashion. The transit agency collects ridership data electronically, then bills the university monthly based on actual ridership. This approach can make it very difficult for the university to budget, however, as compared to a preset annual price.

A final option is to create a separate ID for the transit pass. This eliminates compatibility issues, but it is expensive, poses significant logistical hurdles, and requires users to carry an extra ID. For this reason, few schools choose this option.

Funding Transit Pass Programs

There are a variety of options for funding pass programs. These include:

- Student fee, which usually requires a vote by the student body, just covers students

- General fund sources, although there is often great competition for general fund money
- Parking revenue, which provides incentive, but may be politically difficult, especially at the beginning
- Charges to auxiliary departments
- User fee, which may be easiest to get approved, but may have less impact

For student passes, the most common approach is a dedicated fee for this purpose. Typically, such a fee will require an initial vote by the student body and may require subsequent votes to periodically reauthorize the fee. In some cases, it may be possible for the school administration or a student government to impose such a fee without a vote of the student body. As the following box shows, these fees have done very well at the polls.

The major argument used against student fee funding is one of equity: Everyone pays but not everyone uses the service. Is this unfair to students

BOX 4.2 | **TRANSIT PASS APPROVALS. (MODIFIED WITH PERMISSION FROM BROWN ET AL. 2001)**

In February 2003, students voted by a margin of 69 percent in favor to raise student fees by $20 per month for a U-PASS.
    —University of British Columbia

In February 1997, students voted 4 to 1 in favor of a transit pass program and the program began operating in April of the same year.
    —Ohio State University

The student body reaffirmed their support by voting 15 to 1 in April 1997 to raise student fees to enhance the transit pass program.
    —University of Colorado–Boulder

The transit-pass program originally passed with an approval rate of 58 percent; two reapproval votes in subsequent years passed by 68 percent and 78 percent.
    —San Jose State University

Pitt students voted an overwhelming 93 percent yes to increase student fees to fund their unlimited access program.
    —University of Pittsburgh

4.1
Students often wage
creative campaigns to
win transit pass fee
elections.
Photo by Charlie Johnson

who do not use transit? Opposition to a mandatory student fee transit passes can, in some cases, be quite intense. As an example, when the University of Alberta in Edmonton student government considered the creation of a pass program, the *Edmonton Journal* (August 3, 2002) editorialized against this in strong words: "Any proposal for the U of A student union to charge members for mandatory transit passes does not deserve even to appear on a referendum. Yes, we all know that Edmonton Transit would work more efficiently with higher ridership rates. Sure, it's good for the environment.... But what about students who choose to stay in residence, or to pay high rents for apartments within walking distance of campus? Or those who ride bicycles? Or car-pool? Or need a car, after class, to travel to work? And what about students who simply choose, for reasons that defy understanding, not to stand on cold street corners, waiting for the bus?"

There are a number of responses that can be made to this argument:

- Transit passes are no different than other campus services, such as recreation centers or student union buildings. Everyone helps pay for these services, although some people may use more of one service and others more of another. This is analogous to paying taxes in the broader community. After all, some citizens don't use parks or recreation centers; others ride their bikes everywhere and seldom drive. Should we eliminate public funding for parks and roads as a consequence? While each citizen or each student may not make equal use of every individual service, the aggregate mix of services benefits everybody.
- If the transit pass program reduces driving to campus, then everyone benefits from reduced congestion and air pollution.
- Drivers benefit from lowered demand for parking, making it easier for them to find parking spaces. In addition, as we demonstrated in Chapter 3, this reduced demand can translate into cost savings on parking permits.

It also can be noted that the bulk purchase of transit passes allows individuals to receive passes for a much lower cost than through individual purchase. For a student to buy a monthly transit pass giving access to regional service could easily cost more than $100 per month in many metropolitan areas—a student pass may cost less than this for an entire year.

One other argument against the use of student fees is that, because there is a broad benefit to the campus community that extends beyond students, other campus sources should provide at least part of the funding. The analysis in Chapter 3 indicated that these benefits may be considerable, in the form of lowered capital costs to the campus for parking expansion, and lowered parking fees for individuals who purchase parking permits. Despite this, at most campuses the cost of student pass programs is solely borne by the student fees. A more equitable approach may be to use some combination of parking revenues and student fees.

Parking revenues are less commonly used but can be an important source of funding for both student and employee pass programs. The logic is that there is a rational nexus between parking and transit use. As we explored in Chapter 3, transit pass programs often reduce demand for parking. If this occurs, there is a direct benefit to those who do park on campus in the form of greater availability of spaces. If this reduced demand allows the campus to avoid expensive parking construction, then there is also a financial benefit to both the parking system and individual permit holders. Thus, there is a rational argument that parking users should pay some portion of the cost of the transit pass program in return for these benefits.

The University of Washington U-PASS program, which serves both students and employees, receives about half of its funding from parking revenues. In this example, the university also has increased parking rates in order to adjust the relative price of parking compared to alternatives. An advantage of parking revenues is that in most cases there is substantial room to raise parking rates to increase parking revenue. At the University of Colorado, parking revenues support about half the cost of the faculty/staff bus pass program.

University general funds also can be used. The argument here is that pass programs benefit the entire university, so the entire university ought to provide funding. The difficulty is that there is often intense competition for the use of general fund dollars. Because general funds are used for the university's core purposes of teaching and research, it may be a difficult argument to use the funds for a new nonacademic service. Another variant to this is to use funds from campus auxiliaries to pay some portion of the cost of a program. Here *auxiliaries* refers to service functions on campus that are paid for through self-generated revenues—such as a housing department that generates revenues from student rents or an athletic department supported by ticket sales. For employee passes, it is possible to charge auxiliary departments a "head tax," so that the departmental budget simply covers all or some portion of the cost of travel passes for their employees.

Another possible approach is to build the cost of faculty and staff passes into the benefits package that employees receive. A reasonable estimate is that most institutions contribute approximately 20 percent of an employee's salary to benefits—so that for an employee making $30,000, the institution pays an additional $6,000 for benefits. If a transit pass costs $100/year, this would add about 1.5 percent to the cost of benefits, or about 0.3 percent to the total compensation package.

TABLE 4.2

COMPARISON OF OPT-IN, OPT-OUT, AND UNIVERSAL COVERAGE TRANSIT PASSES.
(COURTESY OF DONALD SHOUP, FROM BROWN ET AL. 2001)

Coverage Options	Partial Coverage: Opt In	Partial Coverage: Opt Out	Universal Coverage
Example campus	University of California–Irvine	University of Washington–Seattle	University of Colorado–Boulder
How program works	The university buys bus passes from the Orange County Transit Authority for $433.50 per month and sells the passes to students for $13 per month.	Students, faculty, and staff are automatically enrolled but can opt out and not pay the fee. Students pay $28 per quarter and faculty and staff pay $37.50 per quarter.	Students are automatically enrolled and cannot opt out. Students pay a mandatory transit fee of $19.52 per semester.
Percent who participate	1% of students	74% of students, faculty, and staff	100% of students
Cost per participant	$246 per year	$130 per year	$41 per year

Opt-in programs present a very different approach to funding. In an opt-in approach, individual students or employees choose to purchase a transit pass. This presents the challenge of "adverse selection." Unlike the universal coverage approach, only individuals who are likely to regularly use the services will pay, so the cost per person is likely to be higher than for universal coverage. In addition, there is less likelihood of picking up new transit users because a student or staff member who does not use transit probably will not opt in. Nevertheless, there are examples of very successful programs built on an opt-in model. Chapter 7 presents a case study of the most successful example we are aware of, the U-PASS at the University of Washington.

The University of Minnesota took an interesting approach to funding. In 2000, the university started a U-PASS program with $6.5 million in seed funding from the federal government. The money was allocated from CMAQ (Congestion Mitigation and Air Quality) funds that come from the federal transportation department to regions that are in violation of federal air quality standards. While this probably cannot serve as a source of long-term program funding, it may be a model that other campuses can use for initial seed funding.

Guaranteed Ride Home Benefits

One of the common elements of transit pass programs for employees is a guaranteed ride home. The idea is that there are occasional "emergency" reasons that may come up where an employee needs to get somewhere quickly, and the transit system can't serve this need. For example, someone's child might get sick, and the employee needs to get to the school and take the child home. The fear of being stuck, unable to respond to this type of situation, is a major barrier for many people, reducing their willingness to give up a parking permit and leave their car at home. In response, it is common for transit pass programs to offer a reimbursed ride home program.

Typically, an employee's supervisor will have to authorize the trip; the employee can then use a taxi and get reimbursed. In practice, these services are seldom used, and the cost of providing the guaranteed rides is low. For students, the situation is a bit different. Because student schedules are so variable and there is not the same type of ability for a supervisor to certify that a trip is legitimate, student transit pass programs generally do not include this benefit.

Infrastructure for Transit

There are also a number of infrastructure investments that campuses can make to support transit use. These include bus shelters, transit stations, real-time transit displays, and dedicated bus lanes. The goal of these improvements is to make transit service more convenient, pleasant, or faster.

Bus shelters may seem like an obvious investment, but in many areas they are few and far between, forcing transit riders to wait outside in inclement weather. Investing in bus shelters is a relatively inexpensive way to make the waiting time of transit users more comfortable. A variety of off-the-shelf bus shelters are available or the campus can design its own. Some communities have tried to crate a unique identity for their shelters; a notable example is the city of Tempe, Arizona, where bus shelters were designed by local artists. Stops and shelters should be placed so that they are easily accessible by both cyclists and pedestrians. In addition, providing bicycle parking at stops can make it easier for users to combine bicycling and transit use.

A relatively recent innovation is the provision of real-time transit location information to transit users. The concept is relatively simple. Global positioning system transmitters located on the transit vehicles transmit their actual positions to a computer server. The server then uses a software package to calculate the likely arrival time at a designated stop. This data can then be accessed in a number of ways. It can be placed on the Web, so that a student or staff member can check bus arrival time on the computer before leaving their office or home; it can be accessed by portable digital devices or cell phones; and it can be transmitted to displays at bus stops or shelters. This can provide a level of comfort to transit users by allowing them to know how long they need to wait and whether or not they have missed a bus.

A number of campuses have invested in full transit stations. For example, the Colorado State University in Fort Collins has planned a transit station linked to their student union building. Because the density of travel is so high in this core area of campus, it makes sense as a location for a transit center serving as a hub for multiple routes. Campus planners were persuaded that the new transportation hub should be situated next to the center of student life, the place where most students go every day. University leaders were likewise tempted by the federal dollars that would flow into the project should it be approved. The plans include a transit center, climate-controlled waiting areas, and retail space, including a midsized grocery store. City and university officials are seeking federal discretionary grants for the center.

Many campuses have pedestrian-oriented core areas with limited vehicle access. Dedicated transit lanes may allow vehicle access to core campus areas that are otherwise only accessible to pedestrians, cyclists, and service vehicles. Some of the campuses that allow transit access into these types of core areas include Oregon State University, Stanford University, the University of Alberta–Edmonton, the University of Arizona–Tucson, the University of California–Berkeley and University of California–Davis, and the University of Minnesota–St. Paul. A number of campuses also have worked with the surrounding communities to develop dedicated transit malls on nearby city streets, including the University of Minnesota, the University of Oregon, and the University of Wisconsin–Madison (Nelson/Nygaard 2000).

Innovative Transit Services: The Boulder Example

In addition to pass programs, improvements to transit service also can significantly increase ridership by the campus population. In many areas, bus service is treated as a social service, rather than as an integrated part of the transportation network. That is, it is designed to serve the needs of transit-dependent populations, rather than to serve discretionary trips by people who have other options. This means that routes are often designed to maximize coverage so that many people have the option to use the route if they need to, but at very low frequencies. The result is that most people who have any other option use it.

It is possible to redesign services to increase ridership. There are a number of changes that can cause many new people to ride the bus. In order to attract these choice riders, a number of issues must be addressed. In general, people want bus routes with a number of characteristics:

- Easy to understand where the buses are going
- Fast and direct routes
- A friendly, pleasant experience
- Routes that go where people want to go
- High enough frequencies that service is "schedule free"

This is a very different paradigm than typical bus service offered by transit agencies in the United States. The typical model is one of complicated bus routes, often on a hub and spoke system requiring at least one transfer for most trips, at low frequencies, with waits anywhere from 15 minutes to an hour between buses. And riding the bus can be an unpleasant experience, where drivers are not expected to have an ethic of customer service.

In some ways there is a classic "chicken or the egg" problem here. In order to attract discretionary riders, it is necessary to invest more funding in service. But it doesn't make financial sense to invest heavily in service that does not have high ridership. It takes leadership—by the campus, the surrounding community, the transit agency, or all three—to get past this dilemma. And the creation of unlimited access pass programs can create the demand that allows rational investment in high levels of service.

The partnership between the University of Colorado, the City of Boulder, and the Regional Transportation District (RTD) provides an instructive case study in the opportunities—and the pitfalls—of such an effort. Prior to the early 1990s, transit was the exclusive arena of RTD. There were no unlimited access programs, and other than a few regional express routes serving commuters, the bus system was focused on providing service for the transit dependent. In a city of 100,000, local bus routes carried a total of 5,000 one-way trips per day. Transit was not viewed by the community or the university as a major player in addressing access, mobility, or congestion.

In 1990, the city adopted a new transportation master plan, which emphasized transit and transportation demand management. The city created a new department known as GO Boulder as a think tank to create new innovations in alternative transportation. One of the first things GO Boulder did was to propose the creation of a student bus pass program. The city and the university teamed up and together approached RTD. The initial negotiations were quite difficult, but ultimately all of the players agreed to a pass that would give free access to the local bus system and a discounted fare on regional buses. Each student would pay a $10 per semester fee, generating about $550,000 annually for RTD. In addition, the city agreed to invest in the program, paying 25 percent of the program cost during the first year, gradually phasing out their contribution over a five-year period. Students voted by a 4 to 1 margin to support the fee increase and to allow it to be increased by up to 10 percent a year without another vote of the student body.

The impact on ridership was immediate. Before the passes were issued, a survey by RTD indicated that 300,000 student bus trips took place in the 1991–1992 school year. Within three years this number grew to 900,000. By the year 2001, student ridership grew to more than 1.85 million. A 1995 survey indicated that 42 percent of these trips would otherwise have occurred in automobiles. A follow-up survey in 2000 showed that 64 percent of bus trips would otherwise have taken place in private automobiles.

The success of the student pass program quickly led to the creation of employee pass programs, first in downtown Boulder, then in Denver, and then in other areas across the RTD district. The increased number of transit riders spurred the City of Boulder to propose a new approach to local

Why don't you ride your bike or take the bus?

You don't like anything that's free?

You love traffic jams?

You think smog looks nice?

You're already in shape?

You don't know a good thing when you see it?

Cool people ride their bikes and take the bus.

FIG. 4.2
Students at the University of Colorado can get very creative with their marketing efforts, as shown by this poster promoting transit use. (Courtesy of Ben Everson and Ryan Patterson)

transit, based on a series of surveys and focus groups that asked potential transit customers what they wanted. The city proposed a network of simple, high frequency routes served by small, friendly-feeling buses. Initially, RTD was not interested. The city obtained earmarked federal funding to create the first new bus, the HOP, which began operations in 1994, using a local nonprofit paratransit agency as the service provider. The HOP was a circulator shuttle, linking the university campus, the downtown, and the local shopping mall. Ridership quickly exceeded expectation, and more than 50 percent of the riders were students. The service was so successful that the city felt an obligation to maintain it after the federal grant ran out, even though Boulder had never been in the business of funding transit operations.

In 1997, RTD agreed to create the next link in the network. The SKIP was another small-bus, high-frequency service, running in a straight line on Broadway, the main north–south route, which runs through the downtown and next to the campus. The frequency was set at every 5 to 7 minutes during peak periods, and 7 to 10 minutes off-peak. The SKIP replaced a previous route, which ran every 15 minutes during peak and 30 minutes off-peak, and which used to leave Broadway to connect to the downtown transit center— adding several minutes to crosstown trips. The impact of the SKIP was extraordinary, with ridership almost three times the route it replaced. In 2002, the SKIP alone carried more riders each day than the entire Boulder local system did in 1990.

This success also created financial strains. In response, students went back to the polls to increase their bus pass fee. Students voted by a margin of 16 to 1 in favor of a $5 fee increase to support the HOP and SKIP services. In 1998, the university decided to extend pass benefits to the 6,700 permanent full-time faculty and staff.

The city continued to pursue new "community transit" routes. In each case, the city applied for federal funding under the CMAQ program to pay for the first two years of the cost of a new route. RTD agreed to take the funds that were going into existing routes that were replaced and use this as the local match for the federal funds. Using this model, funding was approved for the BOUND, JUMP, LEAP, DASH, DART, and STAMPEDE. RTD agreed that if the routes were successful, meeting ridership projections at the end of two

4.2
The HOP high-
frequency shuttle
connects the campus,
the downtown, and
several student housing
locations in Boulder,
Colorado.
Photo by Spenser Havlick

years, they would be absorbed into the system, and funding would be continued. The STAMPEDE is a service that links the main campus and east campus of the university. The university developed the proposal for the STAMPEDE, and the city then applied for the federal funding. The routes are all brightly painted so that they are easily recognizable from a distance. Community design groups help to design the route, the schedule, and the appearance of the buses. And the nontraditional route names help create "branding" for the routes. Pass programs continued to spread, with the addition of a faculty/staff pass, neighborhood passes, and many businesses offering transit passes. By 2002 nearly 60,000 residents and employees in Boulder were eligible for a transit pass through their school, employer, or neighborhood.

The result of all this has been a very large increase in transit use. As of 2002, daily ridership on local routes approached 22,000—four-and-a-half times larger than in 1990. The city's population only grew by 13 percent during that time, so the increase is not due to population growth—it is pretty clearly related to the creation of pass programs and the community transit network.

Another innovation initiated in 1996 was a ski bus to provide students and staff with the option of taking the bus to downhill ski area destinations during winter weekends. The student bus pass provided full coverage of RTD regional service, including the nearby Eldora ski area. The missing link was service to other mountain resort destinations. The idea was to provide an inexpensive, safe alternative to mountain driving. The ski bus program further facilitates a student's ability to attend the University of Colorado without owning a personal vehicle.

However, difficulties also began to emerge. As the network expanded, the cost of the program increased. While the cost per rider is still relatively low compared to many routes within the RTD system (due to the high ridership), nonetheless the total number of dollars spent on transit service within Boulder began to raise eyebrows in other parts of the RTD region. When a national economic downturn hit in 2002, RTD responded by backing away from funding some services past the grant period. In a more far-reaching proposal, RTD staff floated the idea of eliminating all employee transit pass programs across the district, with the hope that this would increase farebox revenue. Upon analysis, it is unlikely that this would actually generate net new revenue for RTD. In the summer of 2003, RTD decided to retain the pass programs. However, there is a clear warning here that a transit pass program can be "too successful." It is important to work with all of the partners in a pass program to assure that enough funding is generated to allow the program to thrive.

Another approach to student transit involves the college or university actually operating the transit system. This may be the only option if there is not transit service in the area, or it may be a way of offering targeted service that the city or transit agency will not provide. In the latter case there are two transit providers, with the challenge of coordinating service, fares, and pass programs. There are many examples of university-operated bus systems (Miller 2001). There are also examples of systems that are jointly operated by the university and local government. Cornell University in Ithaca, New York, and Clemson University in Clemson, South Carolina, are examples of the joint approach. Another interesting example is the University of Massachusetts Transit that connects and serves five campuses in the Amherst area. Mount Holyoke, Smith, Hampshire, Amherst colleges and the University of Massachusetts–Amherst are in the transit network. Without the university programs, these areas would not be served by public transit.

On the positive side, operating the transit system gives the educational institution considerably more control over the transit services provided. On the negative side, there may be a significant financial and administrative burden. It is important to understand the financial issue. In the United States, public transit is primarily tax supported. Typically, fares paid by riders cover only 20 to 30 percent of the operating costs of a transit system, with the remaining 70 to 80 percent covered by local sales or property taxes. If the university is in the role of purchasing access to the system for students and employees, it is paying that 20 to 30 percent of costs. But, if the university is operating the system, it also has to cover the other 70 to 80 percent. Now, the university may be able to operate a transit system at lower cost than a large transit agency, so this can partially offset having to pay the full costs. At some schools, student employees serve as the drivers, creating very substantial costs savings. A student with a work-study award may cost the university as little as $2 to $3 per hour, compared to a unionized employee with full benefits, who may cost $15 per hour or more. Nonetheless, there are significant financial challenges associated with operating a university transit system.

Conclusions

Transit plays an important role in nearly every successful university TDM program. Perhaps the most important and fastest-growing approach is the provision of universal transit passes to students and to employees. The demand for transit use that this generates also can be leveraged to provide significantly expanded levels of transit service.

References

Brown, J., D. Hess, and D. Shoup. 2001. Unlimited Access. *Transportation* 28(3):233–267. See also www.sppsr.ucla.edu/its/ua for profiles and contact information on university transit pass programs.

Goodwin, P.B. 1992. A Review of New Demand Elasticities with Special Reference to Short- and Long-Run Effects of Price Changes. *Journal of Transport Economics and Policy* 26(2):155–163.

Litman, T. 2002. *Transit Price Elasticities and Cross-Elasticities,* found at www.vtpi.org/tranelas.pdf. Victoria Transport Policy Institute, Victoria, B.C., Canada.

Litman, T., and G. Lovegrove. 1999. *UBC TREK Program Evaluation: Costs, Benefits, and Equity Impacts of a University* TDM *Program,* found at www.vtpi.org/utrek.pdf. Victoria Transport Policy Institute, Victoria, BC, Canada.

Meyer, J., and E. Beimborn. 1996. *An Evaluation of an Innovative Transit Pass Program: The UPASS.* U.S. Department of Transportation, Washington, DC.

Miller, J. 2001. TCRP *Synthesis 39: Transportation on College and University Campuses, A Synthesis of Transit Practice.* National Academy Press, Washington, DC.

Multisystems. 1997. Coordinated Intermodal Transportation Pricing and Funding Strategies. *Transportation Cooperative Research Program Research Results Digest* (14):12. Also found at http://216.239.33.100/search?q=cache:8hitkRnTvKEC:gulliver.trb.org/publications/tcrp/tcrp_rrd_14.pdf+elasticity+percent2B+fares&hl=en&ie=UTF-8.

Nelson/Nygaard Associates. 2000. *City of Fort Collins University Area Strategic Transportation Study: Existing Conditions and Opportunities.* Colorado State University, Fort Collins, CO.

University of Washington Transportation Office. 2001. *2000–2001* U-PASS *Annual Report,* Seattle, WA, found at www.washington.edu/upass/news_and_reports/upass_reports/annualreport2001.pdf.

Chapter 5

Promoting Nonmotorized Transportation

This chapter examines the importance of nonmotorized transportation on college and university campuses in greater depth and provides some ideas for encouraging alternate modes of transportation. The primary reasons to encourage walking and bicycle use include cost savings to institutions and students, health and safety benefits, and environmental benefits. We will present a detailed list of pedestrian and bicycle facility ideas and policies that have been implemented at colleges and universities.

There are several dozen institutions that have pioneered innovations in facilities that support nonmotorized transportation. We will reference some, but certainly not all, of the institutions where biking and walking have become the mode of choice by faculty, staff, and students. Most campus communities are well-suited for high levels of walking and bicycle use due to the short distance of many trips and the age and ability of traditional student populations.

A number of United States campuses have achieved very significant levels of student bicycle use. For example, as of 2000, 31 percent of all trips taken by University of Colorado students were on bicycles, and 19 percent were on foot. For trips from home to campus, 23 percent were by bike and 55 percent on foot (National Research Center 2001). Several of the University of California campuses also quote nonmotorized mode shares of more than 50 percent (Balsas 2003).

It is worth pondering the economic importance of these numbers to university administrators. It is relatively inexpensive to provide the basic infrastructure needed by pedestrians and cyclists. Bicycle parking can cost as little as $30 per space, compared to $15,000 to $30,000 per space for new automobile parking spaces. Sidewalks and bike paths are much cheaper to

5.1

One car parking space
can provide parking for
at least 12 to 15 bicycles.

Photo by Spenser Havlick

build and maintain than street networks. And the cost of this infrastructure is much less than the cost of operating a transit system.

Given this context, policies that shift student or staff trips from motorized to nonmotorized modes offer real fiscal benefits to the campus. At the University of Washington biking and walking account for 30 percent of trips to campus, but at $100,000 per year they take less than 1 percent of the transportation budget (U-PASS Report 2000–2001). It is clear that there would be enormous costs to the campus if many of these trips were shifted to driving. Unfortunately, there are not good data available to calculate the cost to shift one commuter from automobile to nonmotorized modes. One analysis of transportation programs at Stanford estimated that an expenditure of $2.75 million on bicycle infrastructure would yield 1,475 new riders for a capital cost per new rider of $1,864—much lower than the marginal cost of a new structured parking space.

Nonmotorized transportation also has significant health benefits. In the last few years health researchers have begun to look closely at the link between land use, transportation choices, and health. Despite all of the efforts made to promote exercise, children and adults in the United States are increasingly inactive. Obesity among young people and adults has become a serious health problem. As of 2000, 27 percent of adults are sedentary, with 70 percent achieving less than recommended levels of exercise. This contributes directly to the fact that 64 percent of adults are overweight and one in three are clinically obese. These conditions increase the risk of cardiovascular disease, cancer, and diabetes. Physical inactivity is a primary factor in 200,000 deaths each year. And young people are a part of this problem. One third of high school students engage in no strenuous physical activity, and one in seven young people ages 6 to 19 are overweight. The evidence indicates that organized sports and athletic activities affect only a small percentage of the population, while most of the population gets less and less exercise, primarily because of a decline in nonmotorized trips. There is also significant evidence that smart community design can affect these trends. Surveys have indicated that people who have easy access to sidewalks and trails are much more likely to be physically active, and that 46 percent of Americans claim that they would walk or bike to work if they had safe and convenient facilities. While this may overstate the case, we have seen that some towns and cities, especially university communities, have been able to buck the trends and maintain nonmotorized mode shares an order of magnitude higher than the national average.

In the last fifty years the use of bicycles for transportation has declined in the United States. In the last twenty years, trips to school by walking and biking decreased by 40 percent. Among children aged 5 to 15 nearly half are driven to school in cars, another third take a bus, about 13 percent bike to school, and only 10 percent walk to school. For people aged 16 to 24—which covers many of those who are about to enter or who are in college—bicycling accounts for only about 1 percent of all trips, and walking for about 6 percent (Killingsworth 2003). This poses a formidable challenge to campus leaders who seek to increase nonmotorized mobility for students. The use of nonmotorized travel for trips to work also has declined substantially. Table 5.1 shows the trends since 1960.

Local land-use planning, cultural trends, and government policy affect these trends. Pucher and Renne point out that, "while over $75 billion a year is spent on federally-assisted roadway projects, less than $1 billion a year is

TABLE 5.1

CHANGES IN MODE SHARE FOR THE COMMUTE TO WORK IN THE UNITED STATES SINCE 1960.
USE OF NONMOTORIZED MODES OF TRANSPORTATION TO COMMUTE TO WORK
HAS DECLINED DRAMATICALLY. (COURTESY JOHN PUCHER AND JOHN RENNE 2001)

Mode	1960 Census	1970 Census	1980 Census	1990 Census	2000 Census
Total auto	66.9	77.7	84.1	86.5	87.9
Public transit	12.6	8.9	6.4	5.3	4.7
Walk	10.3	7.4	5.6	3.9	2.9
Bicycle	n/a	n/a	0.5	0.4	0.4
Work at home	7.5	3.5	2.3	3.0	3.3
Other	2.6	2.5	1.1	0.9	0.8

Source: U.S. Decennial Census, Supplemental Survey: Journey to Work, various census years, 1960 to 2000, as tabulated by Alan Pisarski and reported in A. Pisarski, Commuting in America III. Washington, DC: Eno Transportation Foundation, 2003.

spent on pedestrian and bicycling projects. Only 0.7% of federal transportation funds are spent on improving the pedestrian environment and making it safer to walk" (Pucher and Renne 2003).

Let us compare the efficiency of the bicycle with the efficiency of a pedestrian. Pound for pound, a student or faculty member on a bicycle expends less energy than any other creature or machine covering the some distance. In fact a human walking spends *three times* as much energy per pound as the same person traveling on a bicycle. John Ryan's book *Seven Wonders* states, "The bicycle is the most energy efficient form of travel ever devised" (Ryan 1999). Ryan goes on to say that about 50 million American adults and 40 million children ride bikes at least once a year, but of this 90 million ridership only about 2 million are regular bike commuters. Many compact European and Asian cities have much higher percentages of daily bicycle commuters compared to automobile commuters. Copenhagen and other Danish cities experience 20 to 25 percent bicycle ridership in total trips, and most cities in China and the Netherlands have bicycle use well over 35 percent. But the increasing safety threats from increasing automobile use are beginning to reduce bicycle commuting. Where there are bicycle-friendly bike facilities, such as in college towns in the Netherlands; in Davis and Palo Alto, California; Vancouver, British Columbia; and Boulder, Colorado, bicycle use for commuting and recreation is holding its own or slightly increasing up to 10 to 12 percent of daily trips.

It is also important to realize that nonmotorized modes are important at community colleges and other commuter campuses, not just at universities that have a significant number of students living on campus. Fresno State University in California provides an interesting example. With 20,000 students and only 1,100 students living on campus, 95 percent of students commute. Fresno nonetheless has developed a very successful bicycle program. The program works like this: Old bicycles are brought into a nearby prison where the prisoners rehabilitate the bikes and get them into working condition. The bikes are then painted red and brought over to the university. These bikes are then rented to the students for a semester. Students must pay a $25 deposit and $5 for a lock. The funding for the program comes from parking citation revenue. As of 2002, there were 200 bikes, with a long waitlist for more students interested in renting a red bike for the semester.

The redesign of the physical "transportation environment" of a campus and the campus neighborhood to slow speeds and isolate users is the most effective approach to increasing safety (Havlick and Newman 1998). This redesign includes separation of vehicles from cyclists and pedestrians and separation of bicyclists from pedestrians in high-volume situations. It is especially important near college campuses.

We will describe a number of approaches that colleges and universities have taken to provide infrastructure, education, and encouragement to people who walk and therefore make campuses safer and more pleasant. In order for pedestrians and bicycles to regain a larger modal split of the transportation pie several steps are needed. It is advantageous to have national, private, provincial, regional, or state funding that moves an institution of higher education away from auto-dependency. But local jurisdictions have

BOX 5.1 | **UNIVERSITY OF OREGON TANDEM TAXI. (POINSATTE AND TOOR 1999)**

Tandem Taxi Service: This innovative service is a free, evening transportation option for students, staff, and faculty at the University of Oregon. Those needing a ride can flag down the tandem (two-person) or triplet (three-person) bikes and receive rides to wherever they need to go. The taxi service offers Sunday night Amtrak and Greyhound pickups, bike-rack security patrol, emergency repairs for other cyclists, and direct communication with public safety.

5.2

(ABOVE LEFT)

Separate bike paths
enhance safety for
cyclists.

Photo by Francoise Poinsatte

5.3

(ABOVE RIGHT)

Bike traffic on some
campuses requires
double-flow lanes.

Courtesy of Colorado State
University

excellent opportunities to implement pedestrian/bicycle facilities and programs as well. At least three strategies have been successful in most pedestrian- and bicycle-friendly campuses in the United States and around the world. Improved safety, citizen involvement, and pro-pedestrian/biking marketing are essential.

Improved Safety

Traffic accidents are the leading killer of North American children. Vehicle speed is the decisive factor in determining neighborhood safety for kids aged 5 to 12. As Ryan (1999) recites the literature from pedestrian injury research, it is shown that a pedestrian hit by a car traveling at 40 mph (65km/h) has a 15 percent chance of surviving; the same individual has a 55 percent chance of survival at 30 mph (50km/h) and a 95 percent chance at 20 mph (30km/h). College-age cyclists and pedestrians also are prone to unsafe behavior and have high accident rates.

Traffic-calming schemes have been shown to dramatically reduce pedestrian and bicyclist deaths and injuries in many European cities. Seattle shows a 94 percent reduction in accidents where traffic circles and other engineered traffic-calming projects have been evaluated for twenty years. According to Newman and Kenworthy (1999) in Portland, Oregon, seventy traffic circles and 300 speed bumps have decreased reported accidents by 50 percent. When pedestrians and bicycles are separated from roadways by buffers, grade separations, and well-designed engineering devices, not only is safety improved but also use by pedestrians and bicycles dramatically increases. These transformations do not happen by chance.

Pedestrian and bicycle safety is increased by campus bicycle-mounted police. The presence of bicycle-riding law enforcement officers, especially in larger campuses, has been shown to be a strong incentive for abiding by pedestrian laws (i.e., against jaywalking), and bicycle laws (operation without lights or bell). The mobility of well-trained bicycle police serves as an additional disincentive for crime on campus as well as increased enforcement of other violations. About twelve years ago San Antonio, Texas, trained 135 officers to become bicycle-mounted police. They are fully equipped with high-quality mountain bikes and a radio network compatible with, but different from, the emergency communication system in police patrol cars. Today 1,200 police departments in Canada and the United States have police bicycle squads to provide enhanced safety in urban areas with high pedestrian density, such as shopping malls and public markets. Almost every college campus has bike police today. Emergency response time for police officers on bikes is quicker and more efficient than the response time from patrol car officers. Many cities, including Boulder, Colorado; Vancouver, British Columbia; Seattle, Washington; and Portland, Oregon, also use bicycle-mounted police to provide assistance on bicycle paths and to issue

BOX 5.2 | **SAFETY COUNTS AT THE UNIVERSITY OF CALIFORNIA–BERKELEY.**
(POINSATTE AND TOOR 1999)

The University of California–Berkeley sits in one of the most densely populated areas of the United States. UC–Berkeley is largely a pedestrian campus, with 50 percent of students citing walking as their primary mode. A strong plan and realistic regulations had to be set to ensure safe bicycle riding and pedestrian transportation. University administrators have tried to alleviate potential dangers for pedestrians by implementing safety measures through the "Safety Counts" campaign.

- *Campus Patrols.* Uniformed and nonuniformed officers patrol the campus on bicycles and on foot (as well as in cars and on motorcycles) 24 hours a day, enforcing regulations and ensuring pedestrian and cyclist safety.
- *Night Escort Service.* Community service officers, who are trained student employees of the University of California Police Department, provide a walking escort for students,

summons to bicyclists who are breaking bike path speeding laws on congested multiuse paths. A typical paved urban bikeway speed limit is usually 10 to 15 mph (16 to 20 km/h).

Citizen Involvement

Victories in the campus ped/cyclist arena have been most effective when a student group works with the campus or municipal department of transportation. This group serves as a watchdog, as an advocate for non-auto transportation improvements in safety and facility maintenance. Student activists are more often drawn to bicycles than to other alternate modes, so this is a good area for student creativity and commitment to make a difference.

There are many colleges that do not have a pedestrian/bicycle coordinator as part of the transportation staff. In those cases, if ped/bike safety and facilities needs do not have an advocate or champion within the college or university, it is imperative that interested students form their own organization for lobbying purposes. Almost every ped/bike mobilization began with one or two individuals who had ideas for improvement and then they organized friends, fellow students, or colleagues into an action group. Often the focus begins with a dangerous intersection where accidents have

staff, and faculty during the evening hours. Individuals can be escorted to nearby residences, parking structures, or public transportation facilities.

- *Night Safety Shuttle.* The university offers a shuttle service that takes students to and from the campus during the evening hours, providing door-to-door service on the north side of campus. This service is offered by Parking and Transportation and is an extension of their regular daytime shuttle services. It is aimed at safe transit to and from the campus for students in evening classes or those studying late at night. Students who walk or bike to campus during the day and feel unsafe doing so at night can take the shuttle.
- *Lighting/Emergency Telephones.* The university installed emergency phones, clearly indicated by blue lights, throughout the campus for those in need of police or medical assistance. As an added safety measure for walking, biking, and bus riding students, the university installed new "Code Blue" phones in the Night Safety Shuttle stops and the nearby parking areas.

been common. Another motivation for student intervention could be frequent car speeding on or near a campus street where many students are present.

Pedestrian/Bicycle Marketing

Once the pedestrian/bicycle safety and mobility facilities have been installed, the need for continuous marketing and public information is paramount. With each new ped/bike underpass there should be a ribbon-cutting ceremony and press conference. For every new pedestrian connection or special footpath the developer who may have dedicated the right of way should be showcased and honored at the opening ceremony. Adopt-a-path or adopt-a-trail programs can involve volunteer maintenance by student dorms or environmental clubs. As the popularity of a ped/bike artery increases and as a path is more heavily used, a good marketing plan can and should solicit alumni investment for special features such as drinking fountains, historic signage, ecological interpretation, and resting areas. In Boulder, Colorado, individuals and families have made significant financial contributions for the construction and maintenance of dozens of benches, waterfalls, drinking fountains, and contemplative areas in memory of a family member. Pavement-embedded, flashing crosswalk lights had to be marketed and publicized for widespread use in Kirtland, Washington. Walk to work, bus to work, or bike to work days that are held monthly in some cities must be marketed well in advance. On the special "no car" days many restaurants are encouraged to give free breakfast to non-car commuters from the campus community. There should be awards established by deans, chancellors, presidents, and other key university administrators.

Pedestrian Improvements

Walking to campus is one of the most common forms of transportation, especially among students whose housing is clustered within a mile. Distance, and the time involved traversing it, is certainly a major reason why more people do not choose this simple and healthy form of transportation. Another factor many people cite is the lack of safe, convenient access to their destination. Often lack of aesthetic interest contributes to a hostile pedestrian environment. Universities can work with the surrounding communities to mitigate these deterrents through land-use and pedestrian facilities planning.

Let's consider the distance factor. Universities and colleges that provide for housing on or near campus will have a far greater percentage of students walking to campus. This is especially true if the short distance has reasonably good pedestrian amenities. The University of California–Berkeley, for example, has 51 percent of its students citing walking as their primary mode of transportation to campus. The compact design of the neighborhoods around the campus with ample student housing clustered nearby accounts for this high number. In fact, 59 percent of University of California–Berkeley students live within one mile of campus.

University leaders should keep the proximity to student housing in mind as they consider campus expansions. When satellite campuses are created far from the core area of the central campus, local businesses, and housing, they can create transportation problems. University planners need to also consider how the construction of parking facilities affects the pedestrian environment. Often parking lots are placed on the fringe of campus because this is where land is available. If this location is between the campus and a residential district it can greatly diminish the desirability for walking. Most people simply don't like walking through a sea of asphalt to reach their destination. Furthermore, a parking lot's large driveway can produce hazardous conditions for pedestrians. Even adding the basic amenity of a sidewalk will not make this an aesthetically pleasing experience, even if it is a safer one. If a university wants to promote pedestrian travel, the campus master plan should prioritize convenient, safe, and interesting access. Mixed land use, such as stores and restaurants interspersed with residences, creates a more appealing pedestrian environment.

The primary pedestrian facilities are the sidewalks that link the buildings within campus and link the campus to adjacent neighborhoods. Sidewalks should be wide enough to accommodate foot-traffic flows in both directions. Ideally, they should be set back from the street to minimize the negative effects of vehicle traffic such as noise, pollution, hazards, and splattered mud puddles. Barring the possibility of a landscaped strip, at least a row of parked cars can serve as a barrier. Sidewalks should be in good repair and free of encumbrances such as cracks and heaved, uneven concrete. Curb cuts at intersections are useful for everyone but essential for wheelchair users and people pushing strollers. Joint planning with the surrounding community is needed to create good pedestrian facilities.

Conflicts with motorists, and to a lesser extent with bicyclists, discourage many pedestrians. Clearly marked routes and crosswalks are critical for promoting a safe walking environment. Signage also plays a big role. Motorists need to clearly understand that pedestrians have priority in the crosswalk at stop signs and stop lights. In certain cities, pedestrians are supposed to have priority at any signed crosswalk whether or not there is a stop sign or light. Unfortunately, however, motorists do not always yield the right-of-way, creating a dangerous situation for pedestrians. Enforcement of traffic regulations and severe citations for moving vehicle violations may help remedy the safety issues. This is where close collaboration between the university and the municipality can really help. Campus police can enforce traffic regulations on campus, but it is up to the municipal police to enforce them in adjacent areas outside campus. The better the working relationship between the university and the community, the more cooperation will exist in enforcing safety laws. In addition, there are many physical improvements that can make pedestrian crossings much safer.

Providing clearly marked bike routes that are well-separated from pedestrian routes can mitigate pedestrian conflicts with bicycles. Creating safe and convenient access for cyclists will go a long way in reducing conflicts. Often cyclists don't want to get mixed up with pedestrians, because it slows them down and can cause accidents, but they end up jumping on sidewalks to avert a dangerous situation with motorists. The other reason cyclists ride on pedestrian paths is to take a shorter route. Providing express cyclist routes on campus will give them a quick and convenient alternative.

All forms of transportation ultimately end up with walking, whether it is walking from a transit stop, parking lot, or bike rack. It is critical that this cornerstone form of transportation be given high priority in planning if university leaders want a pleasant, safe, and accessible campus. Besides the basic safety measures already discussed, innumerable other factors will contribute to a desirable pedestrian environment. They can range from the

expensive and large scale, such as a pedestrian passage tunneled under a busy street, to the small and inexpensive such as chairs and tables set out in front of a cafe. Interesting architectural facades, inviting porches and storefronts, pedestrian plazas, and arcades are all components of a pedestrian-friendly atmosphere that the university can help promote on and off campus. Higher density and mixed-use developments around campus also will encourage walking as a primary mode to campus. The following is a list of pedestrian enhancements:

1. *Pedestrian-activated crossing lights embedded in crosswalk pavement.* A relatively recent technology has been developed whereby flashing yellow strobe lights are partially embedded in the roadway surface. A pedestrian, before crossing the street, activates the flashing lights either by pushing a button near the curb or by crossing a photoelectric beam. Motorists in Kirkland, Washington, had a compliance rate of 47 percent (those who stopped for pedestrians in the crosswalk) before the flashing lights were installed, compared with a 97 percent compliance rate after installation. Head-level flashing yellow lights at pedestrian crossings are effective also but not as unusual to the motorist as embedded lights.

2. *A Pedestrian Bill of Rights for college and university students, staff, and faculty.* Educational institutions have honor codes, nondiscrimination mandates, and other rights and obligations about campus life. We propose that a pedestrian (and cyclist) bill of rights be drafted to provide safety, courtesy, and convenience guidelines. (See Box 5.3.)

3. *Raised pedestrian crossings with differential paving material.* Whenever there is heavy vehicle traffic and heavy pedestrian traffic crossing the roadway on a campus it has been shown that motorists are alerted effectively to a student crosswalk when that crossing zone is slightly elevated and well-marked. A different-color pavement or a different texture paving material helps the motorist to see the pedestrian crosswalk more clearly.

4. *Pedestrian crossing light with digital display of seconds remaining to cross.* In addition to the pedestrian "table crossing" or raised crosswalk mentioned above, the student crossing can be equipped with flashing yellow for the pedestrian to cross. When the pedestrian headlight is located midblock or at an intersection it is a very helpful safety convenience to know how many seconds remain before the automobile traffic signal turns to green. In many campus applica-

---

Good pedestrian facilities are often a neglected consideration or an afterthought on campuses. At construction and road building sites the pedestrian is too frequently treated as a second-class citizen when compared to the motorist. We suggest the establishment of special considerations or "rights" to be afforded to those who choose to walk or bicycle as their major mode of transportation. Some schools may find a type of bill of rights to be a useful policy document.

1. The right of campus pedestrians (and bicyclists) to use university or college pathways or pedestrian ways at night thanks to adequate lighting, police presence, and easily visible emergency phones.

2. The right of campus pedestrians to be able to cross streets at walk signals in an appropriate span of time.

3. The right of campus pedestrians to be safe from ice, snow, deep water, and broken surfaces as they use school walkways.

4. The right of campus pedestrians to have pedestrian overpasses or underpasses when the vehicular roadway reaches a specified capacity or poses a serious threat to people who must cross the street or highway.

5. The right of the campus pedestrian to have the right-of-way at all pedestrian crossings and designated school and neighborhood crosswalks and that this be strictly enforced.

tions 20 to 25 seconds are time spans that enable a pedestrian to cross four lanes. If the digital display is counting down 7, 6, 5, and so on, it alerts the pedestrian that it is no longer safe to begin crossing the intersection.

5. *Doubled fines for speeding in pedestrian areas, such as school zones and other areas of high pedestrian activity.* Throughout the United States on interstate highways and other major roadway construction areas fines are doubled for speeding in the work zones; fines are also often increased near elementary, middle, and high schools. We suggest that speeding fines be doubled or tripled as a strong message not to speed on or near a campus where pedestrians and cyclists are present. Student, staff, and faculty populations who have chosen to use walking, biking, and busing as an alternative to the car should be given as much protection as highway crews who are working in a

6. The right of the campus pedestrian not to be impeded by vegetation or structural barriers on city sidewalks and to be protected from harmful traffic noise.

7. The right of the campus pedestrian to a pleasant walking experience due to increased number of benches, use of public art, fountains, and other aesthetics including creative, protective landscaping.

8. The right of campus pedestrians to move conveniently and well protected from rain, snow, or excessive summer sun in the high-density campus areas with the assistance of canopies, archways, or covered walkways.

9. The right of the campus pedestrian to be safe and well separated from roadways by protective splash rails, adequate safety fencing, or vegetative barriers.

10. The right of the campus pedestrian to know where the retail outlets exists, where transit stops are available, and where recreational facilities and other basic needs are available with the help of useful maps and signage.

11. The right of the campus pedestrian to a reasonable "peace of mind" through increased enforcement where red and yellow lights will not be run by autos, where campus and town speed zones will be enforced.

12. The right of the campus pedestrian to be able to activate midblock crosswalk signals, especially along city streets of high density and high traffic volume.

A digital display of the
seconds remaining to
cross the street safely is
a pedestrian-friendly
campus idea.

Photo by Spenser Havlick

car-dominated environment. We believe that as safety increases for
people coming to campus more students and staff will be encouraged to bus, bike, and walk to campus.

6. *Enforcement of pedestrian priority at crosswalks and intersection
    crossings.* California is not the only place in North America where the
    pedestrian who is in the crosswalk has the right of way. The enforce-
    ment by the California State Highway Patrol and all municipal police
    agencies made this law well known and carefully observed. Most
    Canadian law enforcement agencies strictly enforce the pedestrian-
    in-the-crosswalk priority. Fines in British Columbia are $150 for the
    first infraction, $300 for the second, and up to $450 for the third
    with potential jail time, community service, and loss of license as
    additional penalties. But no campus or town can afford to have a
    police officer at every pedestrian crossing. Laws to protect pedestri-
    ans at crosswalks are most effective when motorists know the rules

and are alerted to crosswalks by zebra stripes, appropriate lighting, and signage.

7. *Citywide pedestrian maps/bicycle maps and bus routes to show most direct routes to key destinations beyond the university, junior college, or other school campus.* Students we have interviewed often cite the need for a car in college as a means to get to key destinations easily. If this were true it would be useful for new students to be given a map not only of their campus but also of the direct bicycle, pedestrian, and transit routes to destinations important to students in their college town. The theory here is that if easily read maps show how to walk, bike, or take the bus to a local attraction, a larger number of students and staff will use alternate modes in good weather.

Bicycle Improvements

The bicycle is an integral form of transportation on many university and college campuses across the country. Bikes are used for commuting to campus, for getting around on campus and for general recreation and exercise purposes. Some of the reasons they are so widely used is because they are quick, energy efficient, relatively inexpensive, and pollution free, and their use contributes to a reduction in automobile traffic.

The level of bicycle use, though, is dependent upon the availability of various facilities and services such as bike paths and lanes, proper signage, bike parking, measures taken to deal with safety issues, and the level of cooperation between the school and the town or city in which it is located (Balsas 2003).

The following are a set of techniques that can be used to improve bicycling in campus communities:

1. *Bike paths/bike lanes.* Bike paths and lanes are essential to any successful bike plan. Cyclists should have designated routes on which they can travel—routes that connect between key areas of campus and the surrounding community. The choice between lanes and paths depends on several factors.

    Bike lanes are areas of the street that are designated for

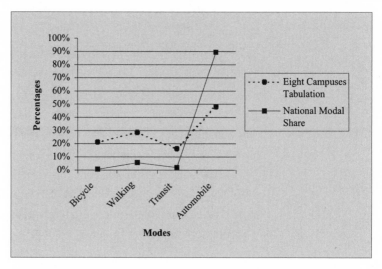

FIG. 5.1
Campuses often have a far higher percentage of trips by nonmotorized modes than the national average. Comparison of 1995 national average mode share to the mode share average for eight campuses (Cornell University, Stanford University, University of Colorado–Boulder, University of California–Santa Barbara, University of California–Davis, University of Oregon–Eugene, University of Washington–Seattle, and the University of Wisconsin–Madison). (Courtesy of Carlos Balsas)

bicycles. Cyclists are generally expected to follow the same rules of the road as motorists and to stay inside the designated lanes. The required width of such lanes may vary for different areas of the country, but the City of Davis, California, has an 8-foot width guideline when a lane is adjacent to the curb and a 7-foot guideline for streets where parking is allowed. Lanes provide safe and efficient bicycle circulation and have been shown to significantly reduce conflict between bikes and cars.

Bike paths are off-street routes that are designated for bike-only travel or for combined bike–pedestrian travel (sometimes with a median or divider to separate the two modes). Paths are independent of roads but are often found following the route of major city streets. Bike paths are useful in areas where motor vehicle speed is unsafe or uncomfortable for cyclists. Generally, any street with speeds more than 35 mph should have a separate path rather than a lane for cyclists. Paths are also good in open space or greenbelt areas. One problem with paths is the presence of driveways and side roads. They act as unsignaled intersections for cyclists and can prove to be dangerous. With proper planning and placement of signs, these problem areas can be mitigated.

2. *Dismount zones.* It is common to have significant conflict between pedestrians and cyclists in the campus environment. While these seldom lead to fatal injuries (as in pedestrian–car and cyclist–car interactions) they can lead to accidents. When cyclists weave their way through dense crowds of pedestrians during class-change hours, the results can be unpleasant.

   One solution many campuses have implemented is dismount zones, where cyclists are required to walk. Dismount zones come with a cost, however. Enforcement can be quite expensive, requiring the use of police or specially hired enforcement personnel. If dismount zones are too pervasive they also can discourage the use of bicycles. One of the advantages of cycling is that at many campuses it allows travelers to park right at their destinations, rather than at outlying lots. This can give bikes a time advantage compared to driving. If dismount zones do not allow direct access to academic buildings, this incentive can be lost.

3. *Signage.* The use of signs on bike paths and lanes is essential for a successful bikeway plan. Proper signs include:
   - Route identification signs (bike path, pedestrians only, etc.)
   - Orientation signs (maps)
   - Directional signs (to downtown, to stadium, etc.)
   - Traffic control signs (stop, yield, dismount)
   - Advisory signs (bumpy pavement ahead)

   Signs such as these help cyclists have safer and more efficient trips. Riders not only know where a particular path will take them, they know which areas to avoid (pedestrians only). This type of planning increases ridership because it makes the experience easier and more efficient for the rider. Students will be more likely to take up bicycling as a means of transportation if they know how the routes work and that they will receive guidance (signs) if they need it.

4. *A bicycle service station.* Stanford University, Colorado State University,

the University of California–Davis (the Bike Barn), and the University of California–Berkeley are schools that provide bicycle service stations on or near campuses. Students can rent bikes, purchase bike equipment, store bikes, and obtain minor repair services. Flat tire repair or replacement is a well-used service. Bicycle rentals or "checkouts" are available at the University of Montana, the University of New Hampshire, and the University of British Columbia in Vancouver.

5. *Bicycle racks on the bus fleet.* Many college towns provide bike racks on local buses. In Portland, Seattle, and Denver the regional transit district buses have front bike racks and also storage bins underneath for bicycles. A student who lives several miles from a transit stop can ride a bicycle to the bus stop, place the bike on the bus bike rack, and use the bicycle to access classes and do errands during the day. The student cyclist can ride the bike home or place the bike on the bike rack to help expedite the journey home. This is another incentive to use mixed modes of transportation that do not involve the personal auto.

6. *Bicycle path separation from campus roadways.* There is often a debate on college campuses whether or not bike paths should be separated from roadways. Our recommendation favors bike paths separated from streets and bike path separation from the pedestrian sidewalk whenever possible. Costs may prohibit the optimum configuration. However the long-term safety and reduced accidents should be considered. Advanced and Olympic-class cyclists prefer on-road bicycle lanes. But for the average and novice campus cyclists the on-road or on-shoulder bicycle lanes have a higher percentage of serious accidents due to close proximity to moving vehicles, roadside debris,

and dangerous surface conditions, such as curbs and storm-sewer grates.

7. *Roadways striped for bicycle lanes to give motorists the optical illusion of a narrower street, thus slower speed.* The visual impression of a narrowed roadway prompts motorists to drive at lower speeds than would be the case on a street with no painted bike lanes. Planted medians also give an optical illusion that a street is more narrow. As a result, motorists tend to reduce their speed. If cyclists going to a campus wish to ride streets and desire increased safety from fast-moving traffic, bold striping on the bike route may provide some relief.

8. *Striped or painted bicycle climbing lanes as a safe zone for bicyclists (not all college students are Olympic racers).* Whenever there is a campus street or city street near a campus with a considerable hill it has been shown that a striped "climbing lane" slows motorists and encourages bicyclists to use that street. In an optimum arrangement there may be two lanes of traffic using the uphill lanes. If one of the 16-foot lanes has a 6-foot wide (striped) climbing lane for cyclists, the other 10 feet of the right lane can be striped or painted as a no-car buffer zone to give extra protection to the cyclist peddling up the hill.

   As with the addition of any successful change in roadway design on a campus or in the community, generous time should be spent at public meetings to explain to the general driving public and to neighbors and businesses the advantages of reducing auto speeds and increasing cyclist safety on striped "climbing zones." Videos of successful application and testimony from other campus and city planners are invaluable tools.

9. *Free bicycles, distinguished by color, for on campus short-term use.* Some campuses and several cities around the world have tried to reduce auto dependency on a campus or in the city by free public bicycles. The theory is that if a campus or a downtown is flooded by a large number of bicycles for short errands, fewer cars and fewer parking spaces would be required on a campus in a central business district. Bicycles that are abandoned and donated from bike shops can make up the basic inventory, or uniform bikes can be purchased.

In some cases the bikes are available after the potential user deposits a coin to free the lock, in others, a university ID must be shown. The bike is used and then locked at the end of the use period and the coin is returned. The fleet of several thousand white bikes in Copenhagen, Denmark, operates by coins; the checkout systems at the University of Colorado and University of Montana require student IDs and signed liability waivers.

At the National Taiwan University in Taipei, Taiwan, 300 bright yellow bikes were placed on the campus. However, over several years few were still usable because no maintenance or repair program was part of the effort. Therefore, without a replacement of lost or displaced bicycles and a diligent upkeep and repair program the campus or community "share-a-bike" program has mixed success. Careful check-out procedures that require the user to take responsibility for the condition of the bike are critical, as are ongoing maintenance funds.

10. *Zero-interest loan programs.* A handful of schools have teamed up with local banks or credit unions to offer low-interest or no-interest loans to students to buy bicycles. This serves as a marketing tool for the bank and for the school's bicycle program, and it opens up bicycle ownership to some students who otherwise might not be able to afford one. At the University of Colorado, the maximum loan amount is set at $500, in order to assure that it is targeted at students buying bicycles for commuting, rather than expensive high-performance mountain or touring bikes.

11. *Pedestrian/bicycle grade separation underpasses or overpasses at busy roadways.* As traffic congestion increases on or near a campus, it is important to incorporate grade separation at busy pedestrian–automobile intersections. Whenever a roadway is scheduled for enlargement or repaving at congested intersections, it is prudent to consider an underpass or overpass to increase pedestrian safety that also encourages greater use of bicycles and walking on a campus. Although this physical improvement is the most costly (up to $1.4 million for one pedestrian bike underpass) it does have significant benefits in terms of student lives saved or injuries avoided over the life of the underpass.

12. *Showers and bike storage space for bike/pedestrian commuters.*
A campus that provides secure bike locker storage and showers for
bike commuters increases the probability that more faculty, staff,
and students will consider the healthier walking and biking modes
of travel. By increasing amenities for those who use "muscle power"
to come to campus, one can be certain that more of the university
population will be attracted to non-auto modes.

13. *Awards to colleges or departments within a large university (like
an intramural program) with the highest percentage per capita of
ped/bike commuters.* University populations tend to enjoy competitive events in scholarship, athletics, music, and other endeavors. This
is a suggestion to enable departments, dormitories, or other logical
campus units to compete for prizes or awards for the unit with the
highest per capita of alternate-mode users. This monthly or semester
program for nondrivers could be patterned after a sports intramural
program with a minimum of administrative care. Awards to the

5.10
Bicycle traffic at
the University of
California–Davis is so
high that they have
installed traffic circles
for bicycles.
Courtesy David Takemoto-
Weerts and University
of California–Davis
Transportation and
Parking Services

highest nondriving department would tend to make many people on a campus aware of the alternative modes of transportation that are available.

14. *Well-designed traffic circles or roundabouts with ped/bike crossings clearly marked to calm traffic near a campus but these must favor cyclists and walkers.* When compared with other campuses and cities in Australia, Canada, most of Europe, China, and India, the United States has relatively few roundabouts or traffic circles that, when well designed, calm traffic. Congestion of motorized traffic tends to be severe near many large campuses. Town and campus transportation planners should be advised that the turning radius of a traffic circle must be large enough to accommodate the more gentle flow of traffic, and it also must be designed for adequate protection to the pedestrian and bicyclist as they navigate the traffic circle.

15. *Full-time campus pedestrian and bicycle facilities coordinator on campus.* A full-time pedestrian/bicycle/alternate mode coordinator is needed on large campuses to organize and market programs to promote non–single-occupancy vehicle use. The Federal Intermodal

Surface Transportation Act funding has helped establish alternate mode coordinators, state Rideshare programs, and other incentives to discourage auto dependency. A campus ped/bicycle coordinator is essential in promoting a multitude of transit, carpooling, biking, and pedestrian programs. This individual is seen as an advocate for improved campus safety for cyclists and pedestrians. The coordinator would promote non-auto competition, bike/bus/walk to campus days, and would work with facilities managers for more and better physical facilities, which, over time, would increase the percentage of non-auto trips to and from a campus.

If the campus is small there may be an opportunity for the ped/bicycle coordinator to be a shared and jointly funded position between the college and the town. Even in a large campus in a large city the coordinator's functions are important to ensure complementary coordination in similar programs being carried out in the city and on the campus. In most communities where a coordinator is effective, town-gown traffic congestion reduction is a shared objective with funding coming from parking fees and permits.

16. *An effective bicycle path and sidewalk maintenance program with cost sharing between town and college.* Once a campus bicycle network and pedestrian-safe sidewalk plan are built, the college or university must make a financial and staff commitment to maintain the system. As user numbers increase the network may need expansion. But if maintenance is not provided on a regular year-round basis the system will fall into disrepair and lower usage. Debris must be cleaned, potholes repaired, branches and other obstructions eliminated, and signage kept clean and graffiti-free in order to sustain maximum use. The maintenance of pedestrian and bike facilities and the advocacy and marketing for this infrastructure are key roles of the campus alternate mode coordinator.

17. *Bike to work/walk to work day for the campus and community.* Special days each month or on an annual basis can be publicized as bike to class, bus to campus, or walk to work in a community- and campuswide effort to promote alternate modes of transportation.

If the bike/pedestrian coordinator made contact with campus and town restaurants, bakeries, and so on, free breakfasts could be used as a special incentive to get motorists to try other modes on these special no-drive days. Excellent publicity in local media outlets, prizes for the longest bike commute to campus, and other incentives create a festival atmosphere and increase participation by townspeople and university commuters.

Conclusions

The implementation of a campus environment friendly to pedestrians depends on the mandates of a campus transportation master plan. The policies and financial resources need to be mobilized in order to promote a safe and pleasant pedestrian experience on a college campus. Administrators at most academic institutions need encouragement to provide nonmotorized transportation facilities. Organized students and faculty and staff who present very specific objectives and mechanisms to fund the improvements can enhance lobbying for bike and pedestrian improvements.

The benefits of promoting nonmotorized transportation on college campuses and in college communities extend beyond the recognized cost savings to an institution for extensive automobile parking. There are significant benefits, including health, safety, efficiency, campus aesthetic appeal, and convenience to students and faculty who are able to walk or bike on the campus easily as well as accessing the campus without a dependency on a car. The administration and student leadership that plans for and implements nonmotorized transportation facilities and programs will create a learning and living environment of appealing and sustainable dimensions.

References

Balsas, C. 2003. Sustainable Transportation Planning on College Campuses. *Transport Policy* 10:35–49.

Havlick, S., and P. Newman. 1998. Can Demand Management Tame the Auto in a Metropolitan Region? *World Transport Policy and Practice* 4(1):30–35.

Killingsworth, R. 2003. *Active Living: A New Public Health Paradigm*. Active Living Network, found at www.activeliving.org/tools_toolkit_powerpoint.htm.

Newman, P., and J. Kenworthy. 1999. *Sustainability and Cities*. Island Press, Washington, DC.

Pucher, J., and Renne, R. 2001. Socioeconomics of Urban Travel: Evidence from the 2001 NHTS. *Transportation Quarterly* (Summer).

Ryan, J. 1999. *Seven Wonders: Everyday Things for a Healthier Planet*. Sierra Club Books, San Francisco, CA.

University of Washington. 2002. *U-PASS Annual Report*, found at www.washington.edu/upass/news_and_reports/upass_reports/annualreport2002.pdf.

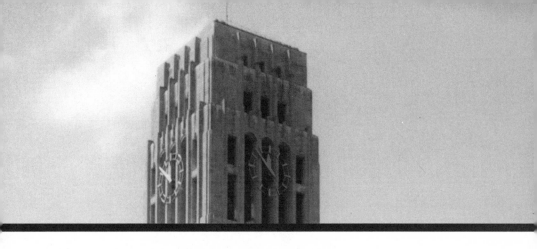

Chapter 6

Developing a Campus
Transportation Plan

In many ways, the central question of campus transportation planning is one of determining the right balance between building more parking and providing transportation alternatives. One common planning assumption is to assume that the modal split is fixed. As an example, suppose that 30 percent of trips to campus are currently by automobiles that park on campus. Then the assumption is that as the campus grows, 30 percent of the trips will continue to terminate at a campus parking space. So, if the university population is projected to increase by 10,000 in the next decade, it should plan on adding 3,000 spaces.

This plan also must recognize the fact that some existing parking spaces will be lost as new buildings are constructed on current surface lots. Thus, the total number of spaces that must be built includes replacement of lost spaces. In our example, let's say that the master plan calls for new buildings to displace 750 parking spaces. Then the campus will need to construct 3,750 new spaces in order to provide 3,000 net new spaces.

So far, this is pretty straightforward. However, there is a substantial conceptual problem—the assumption that the mode share and parking demand per person is fixed is only reasonable if the price also is fixed. In many circumstances, as we have seen above, the permit fees required to build the "needed" additional parking will be substantially higher than initial fees. In fact, if some of the increase to the university population is coming from new buildings on existing parking lots, it may require substantial fee increases just to maintain the initial parking supply. The increasing cost of parking will lead to a reduction in demand. That is, if the projected number of parking spaces required is actually built, there will be many empty spaces. Figure 6.1 illustrates this point.

To calculate the expected demand, we must then make assumptions

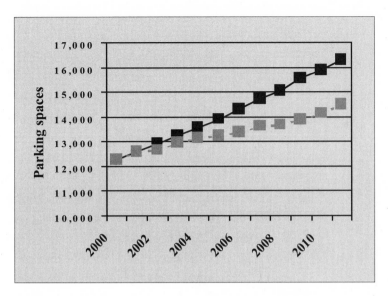

FIG. 6.1
The schematic diagram shows parking demand over time as a campus grows. The upper line is the demand at constant price; the lower line is the price elastic demand. (Courtesy of Nelson/Nygaard Consulting Associates)

about the price elasticity of demand. If the institution is on the cusp, where maintaining or expanding parking supply will require a shift from surface parking to a high percentage of structured parking, the price increases required will be so large that existing local data on the elasticity of demand as a function of much smaller price increases will not give good information on the demand impacts. Because we are looking at such a large range of parking permit fees, we would expect a nonlinear demand response over this large range of prices. Most campuses will have no experience with prices anywhere near the high end of the range and may have little confidence in the demand estimates at these prices. In this case, a prudent policy may be to raise the parking fees to the level required for construction *prior* to committing to the construction, and determine the impact on demand prior to locking in decades of debt.

Colorado State University provides a very instructive example. When planners first looked at the CSU master plan based upon the expected increases in the university population, they projected that the parking supply would need to be expanded from 12,259 spaces to 19,803 spaces over a twenty-year period (Nelson/Nygaard 2000). However, when they looked at the permit fees that would need to be charged in order to build enough parking structures to provide this supply, they projected that permit fees would need to increase from $5/month to $40/month—and that such a large price increase would cut the demand to 10,000 spaces—even with the projected twenty-year increase of campus population.

It is possible for an institution to get in serious trouble by building more than the cost elastic demand for parking. The University of California–Santa Barbara has decided to expand its parking supply by building a parking structure on an existing surface lot. In 2000–2001, parking permits cost $35/month. However, the UCSB Parking and Transportation Committee projects that permit fees will have to be raised by approximately $100/month over the next five years in order to cover the costs of the new garage. They are proposing that this be accomplished by increasing the permit fees by $20/month for each of the next five years. They do not have good data on the elasticity of demand. In the words of the committee in their recommendation for the 2001–2002 rate structure: "There's some possibility that extremely high parking fees will lead to a substantial exodus to alternative transportation, a plus from an environmental standpoint, but a serious problem for supporting loan payments for the expensive new garages; e.g., we could even face a 'death spiral,' in which high rates reduce permit demand leading to even higher rates, etc. The new rates will produce some information on elasticity of demand; should demand prove more elastic than we expect, we may have to rethink the strategy for the future" (University of California–Santa Barbara 2001).

In order to determine the most cost-effective scenario, it will be necessary to model a series of scenarios that provide different levels of parking supply and of alternative modes. Each scenario will have a cost made up of the cost of providing the parking added to the cost of providing the additional access by alternative modes, and any cost incurred in providing financial incentives. Each scenario also will have a parking demand determined by the campus population, the price of parking, and the availability of alternatives. The most cost-effective scenario is that which minimizes the total cost subject to the constraint that the parking demand at this price is met. This is clearly a much more complicated analysis than the simple fixed-mode share projection of parking demand. Under a wide range of circum-stances, this type of analysis will show that the cost-effective level of park-ing supply will be substantially lower than the simple fixed-mode share projection would suggest. The most cost-effective scenario involves some combination of investment in new parking and some level of investment in transportation alternatives. This may require that parking rates be raised not only to pay the cost of providing any new parking that is constructed but also to pay for a range of transportation alternatives. This is illustrated in Figure 6.2.

At Stanford University, this approach has allowed the university to add 5 million square feet of new building space with no net increase in vehicle traffic, and at a cost savings compared to a conventional parking supply approach. The University of California–San Diego planned to build thirteen new parking structures over a ten-year period to accommodate expected growth. In response to an economic analysis, this has been modified to six

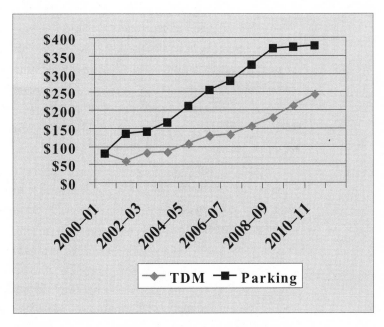

FIG. 6.2
This schematic diagram shows the parking fees that must be charged in order to support parking expansion, compared to the fees that must be charged to support a demand management scenario. (Courtesy of Nelson/Nygaard Consulting Associates)

structures plus TDM measures, eliminating 4,000 planned parking spaces at a net cost savings. The University of Colorado–Boulder is using parking revenues to support the faculty/staff ecopass program at substantial cost savings compared to building new parking. Cornell University made the decision to invest in a transportation demand management program, rather than building the 3,100 new parking spaces they were originally contemplating. In the ensuing six years, they only built 350 spaces. The Cornell Transportation Department estimates that the campus saved nearly $12 million in the first six years of the program, compared to what would have been spent on an expanded parking supply (Eagan and Keniry 1998).

6.1

Car parking structure costs of construction and operation are often heavily subsidized and seldom known by those who use them.

Photo by Spenser Havlick

How Much Parking Should Be Supplied When Building Student Housing?

There are some special considerations when it comes to providing parking for student housing. While many educational institutions have a requirement that parking pay for itself (albeit with land considered free), this is often not the case for parking that is provided by the housing department. It is up to the housing department to decide whether parking will be charged separately or simply included as part of the rental rates. If parking is paid through rent, this will tend to increase the demand for parking compared to charging a separate parking permit fee. A survey of twenty-three colleges and universities performed in 2001 showed a range of parking permit fees charged to students living in residence halls, from a minimum of $23/semester to a maximum of $318/semester, with a mean of $91/semester (Daggett 2001).

One university transportation consultant had the following advice on this issue, "While there may be sound employee retention reasons for continuing to subsidize parking for staff, there is no reason to subsidize parking for students. In fact, charging students less than the full cost of parking is regressive and unfair to students who do not drive. Housing rents are raised for all students to subsidize a minority of the wealthiest students who bring cars to campus. While there may be some low-income students with off-campus jobs who have a genuine need to store a car on campus, this need should be handled through financial aid" (Tumlin 1999).

The decisions made about parking supply will have broad implications for the entire housing system. One major determinant of the land available for housing at a given site is how much land is allocated toward parking. If "free" surface parking is provided, a significant portion of the land set aside for housing may be used to house cars rather than students. The land required will be reduced if the parking is placed in structures and will be reduced still more if demand is lowered by separating parking permit fees from the general rent.

There is a wide variation in the amount of parking provided for student housing. The University of California–Berkeley provides essentially no parking spaces—you simply cannot bring a car if you live in a residence hall. Cornell University requires 0.15 to 0.25 spaces per student bed. Existing student housing at the University of Colorado–Boulder provides 0.37 spaces/bed, the university is considering providing 0.75 spaces/bed for new housing. At the high extreme, there are some schools that provide more than one space/bed. One study performed by Walker Parking Consultants of multiple universities from 1986–1995 showed an average of 0.48 spaces/bed.

Since surface parking requires about 300 square feet of land per space, about 124 spaces per acre, we can calculate the land demand of these parking requirements. It can be a very significant percentage of the total land available. As an example, for two- story buildings, assuming 250 square feet of living space per student, a school could fit 280 students/acre with no parking, 176 students/acre at 0.5 parking spaces/bed, and 128 students/acre at 1 parking space/bed (Litman 1999).

An alternative approach, of course, will be to provide structured parking. While this will decrease the impact of parking requirements on the number of units that can be provided, it will increase the impact on the price of the housing. We have seen that a parking structure will typically cost $10,000–$20,000/space. If the cost of new residence hall construction is $50,000/bed, then a requirement of one parking space per bed can add 20 to 40 percent to the cost of the housing. If this is folded into the base rents, it will represent a significant increase in housing costs for all students—regardless of whether or not they own a car. If it is not included in the rent, and instead residents must rent a parking space, then the parking requirements should reflect the expected reduction in demand at this price.

A residence hall parking and transportation analysis should look at a number of issues. Given the land-constrained environment that many educational institutions face, it may make sense to maximize the amount of housing that can fit on the site, subject to the constraint that lack of parking not jeopardize the ability to attract tenants. This is a very different approach than just saying that if the average off-campus student has, for example, 0.65 cars, then student housing should provide 0.65 spaces/person. Instead, one could take a demand management approach, using pricing strategies and alternative approaches to provide student mobility.

One key factor influencing the approach may be the ability to constrain overflow parking in the surrounding neighborhood. If student housing is located in an area surrounded by a residential neighborhood, any approach other than providing abundant cheap parking may simply displace student parking into the neighborhood. In this case, any alternative strategy may require some sort of parking management in the surrounding neighborhood, such as metering the on-street parking, or instituting parking permit zones. This issue is discussed in more detail in the next section.

Another factor will be market conditions. In general, an educational institution will need to borrow funds to build student housing, and will then pay off this debt and the operating costs of the housing through the rents that are charged. While there are some areas where the market will support housing with no parking, in many areas it will not be possible to fill the beds without some parking availability. This will vary dramatically and needs to be carefully studied for the particular area before making a decision about the appropriate level of parking supply. There also will be a relationship between the type of student housing provided and the associated parking demand. In general, dormitory-style housing is likely to generate less parking demand than apartment-style housing.

The supply and price of housing also will influence the type of students who choose to live in a housing development. If the residence hall provides little or no parking, or "unbundles" the cost of parking from the rent, it may selectively attract students without cars. At the University of California–Davis, there are two apartment complexes for upperclass students that provide parking at a ration of 0.75 spaces per bed, with no charge for the parking. This is a higher ratio than the percentage of Davis students who own cars—but the demand for parking at this complex is greater than

the supply. This "free" parking selectively attracts students who do own cars and leads to a parking demand problem despite the large amount of parking provided.

An interesting approach that has been examined at a few institutions is based on the fact that very few students who live in student housing use their cars daily, but many students store their cars for occasional use and weekend trips. It may be possible to provide this type of mobility through an on-campus car rental program that will rent to students, or by a car-share program. Easy access to rentals could be cheaper for many of these students than paying the real cost of a space in a parking structure. Later in the book we will provide case studies of both on campus car rental and car-share programs. The common theme is that it may be cheaper for students and the educational institution to provide mobility without individual car ownership than to provide abundant cheap parking.

Noneconomic Factors Affecting Parking Decisions

As the preceding material has demonstrated, the most cost-effective approach to campus transportation will generally involve some mixture of expanded parking supply, financial incentives to drive less, and expanded alternatives to the automobile. In real world decision making, of course, there are other factors that come into play beyond strict economic efficiency. These will tend to shift the appropriate mix.

Campus green space is very important at some institutions. While most of our analysis has focused on the conversion of surface parking lots to parking structures, another alternative that may be possible is the conversion of playing fields, or lawns used for passive recreation and picnicking, to parking lots or parking structures. Every 124 surface parking spaces will require about an acre of land. That means that a campus with 10,000 spaces of surface parking is devoting 80 acres to parking. If some of the parking is in structures, the land need is reduced—but not as much as you might think. Because of the space that must be devoted to ramps and to structural needs, about one-third less space will be available on each level of a parking structure. Thus, a three-story parking structure on an acre of land will provide about 3 x 124 x 2/3 = 248 spaces—double the capacity of a surface lot, rather than triple. At some campuses, existing fields may seem like a cheap source for some of this land. This can arouse strong emotions among campus constituents. Building parking lots on green space tends to raise more opposition than converting open land to academic or other building uses. A number of institutions have faced major controversies over this issue. The desire to preserve campus green beauty was a major factor in both the University of North Carolina and Cornell University's decisions to manage demand rather than significantly expand their parking supplies.

Another factor is the traffic generated by the campus. Trips back and forth to the campus will be taking place over public roads. The amount and price of parking that the campus provides will be one major determinant of the number of vehicle trips (U.S. EPA 1998). As we have seen, the price of parking affects the modal choices made by individuals commuting to campus. In the example of Los Angeles businesses shown in Table 3.6 on parking cash-out, converting from employer-paid to employee-paid parking reduced the percentage of people who drive alone by 30 percent and reduced total vehicle miles traveled by 25 percent. More generally, assuming that there is not easy availability of free or cheaper parking off-site, the reduction in parking demand as price is increased will directly translate into a reduction in vehicle trips to campus. On the other hand, expanding the supply of parking will generally lead to an increase in the number of automobile trips to campus, increasing off-site traffic impacts. While the importance of traffic problems will vary by location, in many areas off-site traffic generated by the educational institution is a major source of controversy. If this is the case, it will be another factor that will tend to shift the appropriate mix toward less parking and more alternative modes. This has played a very important role in decision making for many institutions and was a dominant factor in the adoption of two of the most successful campus demand management examples—Stanford University and the University of Washington.

It is also important to remember one of the fundamental distinctions between the operating characteristics of auto travel and of transit. With auto travel, increasing the number of travelers reduces the overall performance of the system because it uses up roadway capacity and degrades travel times. By contrast, as more people use transit it becomes economical to decrease the time between buses, thus improving overall performance and reducing travel times. So policies that increase transit use by students and employees will have a positive effect on the broader community, unlike those that tend to increase automobile use.

Air quality and greenhouse gas emissions also may be an important factor. Nearly half of the population in the United States is exposed to dangerous levels of air pollution. Thus, in many localities there will be public health considerations that will tend to drive parking policies in directions that favor lower automobile use. In addition, a number of institutions have adopted policies to limit their emissions of greenhouse gases. Overall, transportation is responsible for about one third of total greenhouse gas emissions. While this will not necessarily be the case for individual institutions, in almost all cases transportation will be a significant contributor. In order to reduce the transportation contributions, the basic choices are reducing the carbon intensity of travel by changing vehicle technologies, or by shifting trips to lower carbon intensity modes such as walking, bicycling, and transit, or reducing total travel required by shortening trip lengths. Because parking policies will affect modal choice, they are one tool that can be used.

Developing a Campus Transportation Plan

The previous discussion presumes that the planning process is taking a comprehensive look at transportation issues. The vast majority of educational institutions do engage in long-term master planning for facilities. However, this does not mean that there is a comprehensive transportation element in the master plan. One study (Daggett and Gutkowski 2002) found that while a large majority of campus master plans include parking, pedestrian circulation, and traffic circulation, a considerably lower percentage include a transit or a bicycle element. Even those plans that do include all of these elements may not incorporate them in a framework grounded in a good understanding of transportation demand and transportation finances. Very few planning processes include an effort to truly identify the least cost approach to transportation.

A student who just had a good idea created many of the innovations that are profiled in this book as stand-alone programs, often outside of the context of a comprehensive plan. However, the most successful comprehensive programs have emerged from master planning processes. A good campus plan can help the institution set transportation goals, and then identify the appropriate physical infrastructure, program development, incentive structure, and departmental structure and staffing to support these goals.

So how do you get started on creating a smart transportation plan for your campus? The first and most important step is to ask the right questions. If the scope of work asks the planners to project future parking demand and identify where to build new lots and structures, and what intersections may need to be expanded to accommodate this new automobile demand, you will get back a plan that is focused only on automobile infrastructure. A smart plan starts with a much broader scope of work.

The focus of the planning effort should be the identification of a comprehensive transportation strategy that will provide mobility for the university population and support the campus's needs as projected by the master plan. The plan should provide access to campus while maintaining the quality of the campus environment and minimizing financial risk to the university. A comprehensive planning effort will identify and recommend prioritized parking facility, transit, bicycle, pedestrian, and transportation demand management program options that can be implemented to support campus access by students, faculty and staff, and visitors. The plan should identify recommended timetables for the implementation of proposed facility or program development, identify the estimated costs of recommended facility or program development, and make recommendations for preferred mechanisms for funding the proposed options. The plan should be designed to integrate with the transportation master plan for the surrounding city or county.

The following illustrative list may not be appropriate for every campus, but it provides an overview of planning elements that should be considered when developing a scope of work for a transportation plan. It is loosely based on the work of Jim Baily and David Cook at the University of Colorado.

- Develop a geographic locator map identifying the locations of students and staff residences.
- Develop existing baseline of mode shares for trips to campus by each element of the campus population.
- Quantify the existing parking supply and the amount that is expected to be lost as a result of campus construction during the planning period.
- Develop parking supply and demand analyses for the planning periods, assuming no new alternatives or financial incentives. The analyses should provide parking supply/demand data and analysis for faculty, staff and students, visitors, and service vehicles. This should look at demand based on the parking fees that would be required to provide that level of parking.
- Identify potential parking demand reduction strategies. These may include pricing strategies, student parking limitations, parking cash-out, and other strategies. Assess the viability and effectiveness of these parking demand reduction strategies. Assess the impact of these strategies on the surrounding community and on the "marketability" of the campus to potential students. Compare this to the impact on marketability from raising campus parking rates to the level necessary to increase the parking supply to meet demand.
- Identify existing and planned transit services to and from the areas identified on the geographic locator map. Identify the current volume of university affiliate use on existing transit routes. Develop projected transit use volumes by university affiliates for the planning period. Analyze transit program options that could be employed to reduce parking demand on campus. Identify the projected costs and debt capacity that will be required to finance these options. Quantify the projected reduction in parking demand.
- Analyze nonmotorized transportation program options that could be

employed to reduce parking demand on campus. Using geographic information, identify the population base within walking and cycling distance, and the existing availability of safe and convenient routes. Identify the projected costs and debt capacity needed. Quantify the projected reduction in parking demand.

- Analyze ridesharing programs and incentives that could be employed to reduce parking demand on campus. Identify the projected costs and debt capacity needed. Quantify the projected reduction in parking demand.

- Using the results of the previous elements, prepare a series of options incorporating different mixes of parking, transit, financial incentives, ridesharing, and nonmotorized transportation to evaluate the cost, use of debt capacity, and ability to meet demand for access to campus. For each alternative, evaluate the parking permit fees that will be required and factor this in when calculating demand.

- Compare the marginal cost of accommodating one additional person through providing a parking space, versus shifting one person's travel to transit, walking, bicycling, or ridesharing.

- Identify the total amount of university land that is dedicated to parking or other transportation needs, rather than to other academic or support uses, for each option.

BOX 6.1 **UNIVERSITY OF IOWA: DESIGNING A WALKABLE CAMPUS.**
(POINSATTE AND TOOR 1999)

The University of Iowa in Iowa City provides an example of a school that has examined its transportation and planning needs and developed a plan for instituting solutions. The plan includes a strong emphasis on making the campus pedestrian oriented. *Achieving Distinction 2000, A Strategic Plan for the University of Iowa,* identified problems including:

- Conflicts among vehicles, bicycles, and pedestrians
- Too many vehicles on campus
- Access difficulties for people with mobility problems

The goal of the University of Iowa's Pedestrian-Oriented Campus Plan is to maintain, expand, and emphasize safe, efficient, and effective pedestrian movement through campus. The university's Campus Planning Framework states that giving priority to alternative modes of transportation such as bicycles and buses over automobiles will promote a

- For each option, analyze the impact upon other goals laid out in the campus master plan. These may include preserving or creating a pedestrian campus core, preserving or creating green spaces, addressing air quality concerns, and maintaining acceptable levels of water quality in campus discharges to stormsewers.
- Perform a series of iterations to identify the least cost approach to meeting transportation demand. Identify the amount of university debt capacity that will be required to finance these options. Analyze the impact on peak-period traffic volumes and level of service at intersections adjacent to campus.
- Identify potential partnerships for funding or implementing program options. Identify which projects may be eligible for state or federal funding, and the procedures and timelines for applying for these funds.
- Gauge the preferences of various campus constituency groups and of important off-campus constituencies.

The criteria to be used for selecting the preferred options will need to be set based upon the particular goals of each institution. The set of planning tasks laid out above would provide the information necessary to make intelligent decisions on a range of criteria.

pedestrian-oriented campus. Planners realize that to achieve this, extensive paths and walkways and an efficient transit system are necessary. Standards that the University of Iowa has chosen are as follows:
- Pedestrian movement takes priority over vehicular movement.
- Vehicles and bicycles must always yield to pedestrians.
- A continuous pedestrian system must connect buildings, parking areas, and exterior spaces and minimize potential conflicts with motorized vehicles.

Their plan will be implemented by minimizing the intrusion of vehicles into campus and keeping general vehicular circulation to the campus periphery, recognizing that bus service, emergency, and service vehicle access must be provided. Numerous pedestrian-oriented routes, pedestrian bridges, gathering sites, open space areas, corridors, and pedestrian connections are a part of the university's Campus Planning Framework.

6.4

The University of
Georgia–Athens
has undergone an
ambitious effort to
reclaim campus green
space. The first picture
shows Herty field as a
parking lot. Today,
Herty field is a quiet
student gathering
space.

Courtesy of University of
Georgia Public Affairs

Land-Use Planning

The planning discussed above is very much focused on parking and transportation programs. Another equally important process is the development of the land-use vision for the campus. There is a strong connection between transportation and land use. For example, a decision to create a satellite campus may generate thousands of new daily car trips between campuses, whereas a decision to add student housing on campus may shift thousands of trips to nonmotorized modes.

First is the density of the campus. In general, people are most willing to walk for trips that are under a half mile. If the campus is very spread out, with many destinations requiring trips longer than this, much of the campus population will use other modes for daily intracampus trips. By clustering activities together and increasing campus density, more people will walk within campus.

Housing is one of the most important keys to campus transportation. In many areas, housing near campus is considered desirable, leading to increasing values that may price out students, staff, and faculty from the ability to reside near the school. The result is that more and more of these people live beyond walking distance (a half mile), beyond biking distance (about two miles), or in outlying areas that are often not well-served by campus. Building student and faculty housing on or near campus is one way to reverse this trend. In areas of particularly high housing values, providing housing also may increase the ability to attract good faculty and students.

Finally, a number of campuses such as the University of Maryland and University of North Carolina have developed land-use plans that emphasize the creation of friendly-feeling pedestrian cores. In some cases this requires removing existing parking lots and eliminating existing automobile access to core areas of campus. While this may be largely motivated by the desire to create a more beautiful campus, one result of this type of decision is a shift toward modes of travel other than the private automobile.

References

Daggett, J. and R. Gutkowski. 2002. *University Transportation Survey: Transportation in University Communities*, found at fcgov.com/uts.pdf. City of Fort Collins and Colorado State University, Fort Collins, CO.

Eagan, D., and J. Keniry. 1998. *Green Investment, Green Return: How Practical Conservation Projects Save Millions on America's Campuses.* National Wildlife Federation, Washington, DC.

Litman, T. 1999. *Parking Requirement Impacts on Housing Affordability*, found at www.vtpi.org/park-hou.pdf. Victoria Transport Policy Institute, Victoria, BC, Canada.

Nelson/Nygaard Associates. 2000. *City of Fort Collins University Area Strategic Transportation Study: Existing Conditions and Opportunities*, Colorado State University, Fort Collins, CO.

Tumlin, J. 1999. Nelson/Nygaard Associates, personal communication.

University of California–Santa Barbara. 2001. *University of California–Santa Barbara Parking and Transportation Committee 2001–2002 Rate Recommendation*, found at www.park.ucsb.edu/ptmemo.html.

U.S. EPA. 1998. *Technical Methods for Analyzing Pricing Measures to Reduce Transportation Emissions.* U.S. EPA Report No. 231-R-98-006, found at www.epa.gov/clariton/clhtml/publitle.html.

Chapter 7

Campus Case Studies

This chapter examines a wide variety of transportation demand management (TDM) applications in use at campuses across North America. The sample was chosen not as a comprehensive list, but rather as a balanced representation of locations and sizes. Each campus is pursuing interesting TDM
programs. While many strategies may be modified to fit diverse institutional applications, it is important for university planners and officials to
note the successful TDM approaches of universities with similar demographics and surroundings. This chapter progresses from large, urban-
centered universities such as the University of Washington, to schools in
smaller urban areas such as the University of Montana, to schools in more
rural settings such as Cornell University. We conclude the chapter with
Stanford University's unique program.

The U-PASS at the University of Washington–Seattle

The University of Washington is a large teaching and research institution
with an enrollment of more than 36,000 students and 23,000 employees.
Its 640-acre campus is centrally located in Seattle and includes a major
medical center and health sciences complex. Three transit agencies serve
the University District. More than 225,000 vehicles pass into the University
District each day.

The University of Washington's U-PASS program was initiated in 1991 in
cooperation with the City of Seattle and Metro Transit. Since its inception,
the U-PASS program has been recognized as one of the most comprehensive
and successful university TDM programs.

The U-PASS program was developed in large part as a response to a 1983
agreement with the City of Seattle to create a development and transportation master plan (TMP). The city wanted to ensure that campus expan-

sion would not increase regional traffic and parking demand in surrounding neighborhoods. The plan was intended to reduce peak-period traffic to the campus. The TMP would limit the university parking to their existing parking supply, or 12,300 spaces. Even though UW enacted the TMP during the 1980s, by 1989 it was obvious that a bigger step needed to be taken, as they were not going to meet the TMP's goals. The university was compelled to undertake earnest action to meet its commitment when it began a major expansion in 1989. If unmitigated, this expansion would have brought an estimated additional 10,000 cars a day and would have necessitated the construction of four new parking garages. The TMP was expanded to include the development of the U-PASS, which enabled the university to exceed its original traffic and parking mitigation goals. A year after the advent of the U-PASS, the State of Washington passed the Commute Trip Reduction Law in an effort to curb increasing congestion and pollution. This law requires large employers of one hundred or more people to take steps to reduce single-occupancy vehicle trips. The state law has served as an impetus to UW to continue building on its achievements. In 2001, the university again updated the TMP but maintained the goal of capping peak-hour traffic to campus at 1990 levels and maintaining the cap of a maximum of 12,300 parking spaces. The university has an agreement with the City of Seattle that sets performance standards, binding the university to meet targets limiting the amount of traffic coming to campus. Targets are set for the morning and afternoon peak periods, and for the 24-hour daily total traffic.

The U-PASS program's great success can be attributed to the simultaneous implementation of significant price increases for parking, while improving pedestrian, bike, and transit accessibility in and around campus. The pass provides for flexibility in mode choice so that university commuters feel free to use the transportation mode that suits their needs at any given time. Transportation planners resolved to avoid two major pitfalls often cited for failed alternative transportation programs: lack of convenience and system rigidity. The idea that emerged was similar to a health club membership. The universal transportation pass would allow unlimited access to a wide range of transportation mode choices for a low quarterly cost. Just as health club members demand a variety of fitness programs and facilities for their individualized desires and needs, so do commuters. The program

7.1
The U-PASS program
supports both transit
and pedestrian activity.
Courtesy of University of
Washington

also has been very innovative in its efforts to make it easy for people who use the U-PASS to also have easy access for occasional car trips to campus.

One of the steps the university took was significantly raising the price of parking at the inception of the program—increasing the cost of a quarterly parking permit by 50 percent, from $78 in 1990 to $108 in 1991. They have continued to raise the price since then, up to $196 in 2002. This has created a powerful financial incentive for the use of alternative modes. At the same time, the menu of options provided by the U-PASS has helped make these large pricing increases politically palatable to the campus community. The comprehensive transportation benefit package contained in the U-PASS includes the following options:

- *Transit.* U-PASS holders are entitled to unlimited access to all regular bus transit routes anytime, seven days a week. These transit agencies serve more than fifty routes throughout King and Snohomish counties, including thirty routes running through campus. Each bus is equipped with bike racks. Pass-holders also ride commuter train routes for no fare. In 2002, U-PASS-holders made 8.2 million trips by transit. Since the program began, the number of university affiliates (students, faculty, and staff) commuting by transit increased from 21 to 36 percent.
- *Carpools.* Carpools receive free parking permits if two or more participants per vehicle hold U-PASSes. UW has a creative approach, allowing carpool parking both by regular carpoolers who obtain carpool permits, and by "occasional carpoolers." The latter approach allows a set of U-PASS-holders to park free at any of eight designated locations around campus by showing the attendant the required number of U-PASSes. Since the program began, the number of individuals participating in carpools has increased by 57 percent.
- *Vanpools.* U-PASS-holders pay subsidized vanpool fares. The U-PASS program will cover the first $40 of the monthly vanpool fee for pass-holders who live ten miles or more from campus. Vanpool use has increased by a large percentage since the program began but still serves a very small number of people—there were 231 participants as of the 2001–2002 academic year.
- *Ride-match program.* The university offers two ride-matching ser-

vices for commuters trying to form car or vanpools. This program is available free to anyone who lives or works in the Puget Sound area.

- *Nightride shuttle.* This evening service, operating from dusk to 12:30 a.m. picks up passengers every 15 minutes and delivers them to their destination in neighborhoods within one mile of campus. Providing nighttime service enhances the TDM program by catering to daytime transit, bike, or pedestrian commuters who choose not to use those modes at night because of safety or convenience concerns. In addition UW Cares, a safety escort walking service, is available by telephone arrangement.

- *Bicycling.* The revenues from the U-PASS program help pay for improved bike facilities. Currently, bike racks on campus—40 percent of which are covered—accommodate 5,500 bikes. UW has 348 secure bike lockers, more than any other U.S. campus, that are paid for by a $50 annual fee. The Burke-Gilman paved trail runs directly through campus. The UW bicycling guide indicates bike routes to and from campus. Shower and locker facilities are provided in designated buildings for bike commuters. Nine percent of faculty, 5 percent of staff, and 4 percent of the student body commute by bicycle.

- *Reimbursed ride home.* Faculty and staff U-PASS-holders are eligible for an allowance of fifty taxi miles each quarter so long as they pay a 10 percent co-payment for each trip. This benefit guarantees that alternative transportation users won't be stuck on campus should they miss their regular ride home. This is offered in order to provide a level of comfort to pass-holders, but is actually used very seldom. In 2002, there were only 130 trips.

- *Flexcar.* The University of Washington has partnered with Flexcar to provide carsharing opportunities on campus. Flexcar has ten cars available on campus. Users pay a membership fee, and a user fee for each hour they check a car out. U-PASS-holders receive a discount on both the membership fee and the hourly charge. In 2002, 490 U-PASS members purchased a Flexcar membership, and four university departments purchased departmental memberships.

- *Flexible parking.* Employee U-PASS-holders who occasionally need to drive may purchase up to two daily parking passes per week at the discounted rate of $2.36 a day. For comparison, the normal price for a one-day parking permit is $8. This is an important incentive. Many people may be willing to use transit or other modes on a regular basis, but are reluctant to give up their parking permits because they need to drive once in a while. These discounted daily parking passes help resolve this problem. On average, 750 pass-holders use this option each day.

In addition, for faculty and staff who have parking permits, if they choose to give up their permit and begin using a commuting alternative, the university will hold their lot assignment for a six-month period. This means that the user has a chance to make sure that the alternative really works. This is also an important incentive, because otherwise permit holders may be unwilling to give up their parking spaces.

- *Shuttles.* The Health Sciences Express shuttles passengers between the local hospitals and the university for free. There is also a Disabled Persons Shuttle, or Dial-a-Ride, which is an on-demand shuttle service taking people with disabilities from one part of campus to another.
- *Merchant discounts.* All U-PASS-holders can receive discounts from about fifty university district merchants for goods and services by presenting their pass.

As of the 2001–2002 academic year, the U-PASS budget was about $11.3 million annually. The following revenue sources contribute to its budget:

- U-PASS sales: $5.6 million (50 percent)
- Parking fees: $4.1 million (37 percent)
- Parking fines: $0.7 million (7 percent)
- Other sources: $0.8 million (7 percent)

The majority of these funds, about $10 million, is spent on contracting bus service from the transit agencies.

In 2002, the pass cost $35 per quarter for students and $49 for faculty or staff. Students receive their U-PASS sticker each quarter with their registration confirmation. The quarterly fee is included in the tuition statement; students automatically pay unless they actively choose to opt out. Faculty and staff who have validated UW Husky cards may purchase a U-PASS at three campus commuter centers. They can purchase it on the spot or through a payroll deduction. A large percentage of the campus community chooses to buy the U-PASS. In 2002, more than 31,000 students—86 percent of the student body—purchased a pass, as did 9,800 faculty and staff. For comparison, there were 630 parking permits sold to students and 4,400 parking permits sold to staff.

In order to get the program off to a strong start in 1991, the university launched a promotional campaign in which the motto was U-PASS: For You and the U. The initial education campaign was critical in helping the new program gain acceptance and in overcoming resistance to the increase in parking fees. The information and marketing strategies included:

- A brochure promoting the U-PASS program was circulated among students, faculty, and staff. The material stressed that university commuters would benefit from lower prices, more transportation options, and a healthier environment.
- An advisory ballot was distributed to all 34,000 students to gather and assess their input. A sample of 1,250 employees also was surveyed. Comments were solicited from all faculty and staff on parking fee increases.
- UW sponsored a campuswide transportation fair in fall 1990 to promote the program.
- In November 1990, a campuswide forum debated the plan and encouraged students and employees to make their voices heard by returning their ballots.
- Campus groups, such as the Student Assembly, the Faculty Senate, and the graduate student government debated the program; all ended up passing resolutions supporting it.

The results of the ballots indicated an 88 percent approval rate among students and a 91 percent approval rate among employees. Sixty percent of the students favored an optional program rather than a mandatory fee with automatic coverage. Getting the students and staff to buy into the program before it was implemented was essential to its acceptance.

The university has taken many marketing steps to ensure its continued popularity and to monitor and evaluate its effectiveness. These include:

- Addition of a full-time information specialist position
- Widely distributed, comprehensive educational brochures
- Creation of three staffed commuter information centers and six information kiosks
- Joint marketing strategies with the transit agencies
- Development of an extensive, user-friendly Web site that outlines benefits, policies, and latest news items
- An annual transportation fair in the fall semester
- U-PASS newsletter
- Annual traffic, parking, and mode choice surveys
- Biennial telephone surveys

One other innovative marketing approach is the use of geographical information so that students and employees can be e-mailed information on specific transportation choices available to them based on their home address.

Impacts of the U-PASS

The U-PASS nearly met its goal of 75 percent participation within its first year. As of 2002, student participation was 85 percent, while faculty/staff participated at a rate of more than 65 percent. Transit ridership among students increased by 54 percent between 1989 and 1996, while faculty transit ridership increased by 82 percent during that same time period. General transit ridership increased by 60 percent. Much of the increase took place in the early years of the program, followed by incremental growth.

During the first three years, the transit agencies increased their bus service to campus by about 60,000 hours, an increase of 20 percent, as a result of increased ridership. The university and the transit agencies cooperated in splitting the costs of the additional service. By instituting lower cost vanpool services on other routes, the transit agencies were able to free up buses, thus avoiding additional capital expenditures.

Based on surveys conducted by the university, the mode share for commute trips to campus has shifted substantially since the creation of the program. Table 7.1 shows this change.

TABLE 7.1

THE SIGNIFICANT INCREASE IN THE PERCENTAGE OF TRAVELERS USING TRANSIT AND THE DECREASE IN
THE PERCENTAGE OF DRIVERS SINCE THE UNIVERSITY OF WASHINGTON STARTED THE U-PASS PROGRAM.
(COURTESY UNIVERSITY OF WASHINGTON)

Travel Mode	Faculty		Staff		Students		Weighted Average	
	1989	2002	1989	2002	1989	2002	1989	2002
Transit	11	24	25	36	21	39	21	36
Carpool/vanpool	11	16	15	15	9	9	10	11
Bicycle	9	9	6	5	9	4	8	5
Walk	7	6	6	4	31	31	23	22
Other	2	2	4	2	4	2	4	2
Drive alone	60	43	44	38	25	16	33	24

Because of the agreement between the city and the university, an annual traffic count measures both peak period and average daily traffic to campus. Table 7.2 shows the change from 1991 to 2002.

What this shows is peak-period traffic, which has been almost flat over an eleven-year period, despite the fact that there are 8,000 more people coming to campus each day than in 1991. The demand for single-occupant vehicle parking permits dropped as well. In 1990, there were 11,525 spaces available on campus; by 2002 this dropped to 11,400. Parking lot utilization dropped from 87 percent to an 85 percent occupancy rate in 2002. This data is remarkable given the university's expansion in the past decade. In addition, it runs counter to trends across the United States, where communities and universities are experiencing an increase in vehicle trips.

The U-PASS has earned the reputation of a model TDM program emulated across the country and even internationally. In evaluating the possibility of the University of British Columbia adopting a similar program, a policy report to the Vancouver City Council described it accurately: "The U-PASS is one of the most successful and comprehensive transportation demand management programs in the United States. It is an excellent example of 'carrots and sticks' working together to encourage people to travel less by car . . . in a way that makes sense to commuters. In Seattle, this program has resulted in significant shifts from car driving to transit riding

TABLE 7.2

THE NUMBER OF CAR TRIPS TO THE UNIVERSITY OF WASHINGTON REMAINED STABLE
DESPITE A DECADE OF CAMPUS GROWTH. (COURTESY UNIVERSITY OF WASHINGTON)

	1991	1999	2000	2001	2002
Trips to campus (7 a.m.–9 a.m.)	6,628	6,878	6,872	6,868	6,738
Trips from campus (3 p.m.–6 p.m.)	8,205	8,634	9,084	8,852	8,951
24-hour vehicle trips	56,316	59,667	61,879	62,344	60,010

as well as significant improvements to the transit system. It provides a model for universities, colleges and other large employers. It also provides innovative ways to provide transit financing."

University of British Columbia: A Comprehensive TDM Program

The University of British Columbia (UBC), Canada's third-largest university, is located five miles from downtown Vancouver. During the 2002–2003 school year, approximately 32,000 undergraduates and 7,000 graduates attended the university, a quarter of which resided on campus (UBC Public Affairs 2003). The 2001 Canadian census recorded more than 1.98 million people living in the Vancouver metropolitan area, with 545,671 people living within the City of Vancouver (Statistics Canada 2001).

TREK Program Centre

UBC created the Trip Reduction, Research, Education, and Knowledge (TREK) Program Centre in September 1997. As the University Transportation Planning Department, TREK is committed to improving transportation choices by promoting sustainable transportation at UBC. Their objective is to find convenient, cost-effective ways to travel to and from UBC without using a single-occupancy vehicle.

TREK has pursued the creation of a U-PASS program since late 1997. In February 2003, a record number of 15,502 students voted on the U-PASS referendum, with 69 percent in favor. The program will commence in September 2003 with a mandatory student fee of $20 (Canadian) per month. A $5 rebate will be given to students residing in UBC housing. The university, through the TREK budget, contributes a $3 subsidy per pass. The primary goal of the U-TREK card is to reduce the number of single-occupancy vehicle trips to campus every day. A secondary goal of the program is to make the one-day per week switch to non-single-occupancy vehicle travel cost neutral to drivers. Other Canadian universities with U-PASS programs include the University of Victoria (Vancouver, British Columbia), Queens University (Kingston, Ontario), University of Guelph (Guelph, Ontario), University of Western Ontario (London, Ontario), Trent University (Peterborough, Ontario), and the Southern Alberta Institute of Technology (Calgary, Alberta).

The central issue that stalled the implementation of the U-TREK program was the required increase in bus service. BC Transit (now TransLink) wanted the university to fund the $3 million increase in buses, service, and capital improvements necessary to implement U-TREK. The university hired a consultant to examine the finances and true costs of the bus service, and

TABLE 7.3

THE ESTIMATED VALUE OF THE SERVICES AVAILABLE TO STUDENTS AT THE UNIVERSITY OF BRITISH COLUMBIA THROUGH THE U-TREK PROGRAM. THE ACTUAL COST TO STUDENTS IS $20 PER MONTH. THE U-TREK CARD OFFERS A VARIETY OF SERVICES AT A SUBSTANTIALLY REDUCED RATE. (TABLE RE-CREATED FROM UNIVERSITY OF BRITISH COLUMBIA TRANSIT SERVICE PLAN DISCUSSION PAPER #8, TABLE 1.1.1)

Program Component	Comparable Monthly Value
Unlimited transit use	$63–$120
Campus shuttles	$10
Secure bicycle parking	$10
Bike products, services	$10
Showers, lockers	$10
Ridematching	——
Vanpool and carpool parking	$5–$8
Guaranteed ride home	$30
Airport shuttle	$5
Merchant discounts	$25
Total value	$168–$228

it continued to argue that the investment in U-TREK was a financial benefit for BC Transit. Promoting efficient, cost-effective service to students was investing in the next generation of transit users. A joint market survey identified the "price point" of the students to be $20 per month. Offers were made by BC Transit around $25 to $28 per month. One sticking point for the transit agency was the loss of revenue on all-purpose student trips. Surveys conducted on other campuses found that for every transit trip to or from campus taken by a student, two to four transit trips would be taken to other destinations. A close examination of UBC students found that for every trip made to or from campus via transit, fewer than one side trip on transit was made. In 1998, the Greater Vancouver Transportation Authority, or TransLink, was formed and absorbed BC Transit. The new CEO at TransLink helped to move the process along. In early 2003, TransLink made the final offer of $23 per month, and the university agreed to cover the cost difference to bring the student price down to $20. Both entities also agreed to pursue corporate sponsorship to help defray some of the increased service costs (Lovegrove 2003).

Transit Benefits

Apart from parking price increases and supply reductions, transit fare discounts are likely to be the largest single incentive for mode shifting within the U-TREK program. Implementing the U-TREK card will provide the following benefits to UBC students (all amounts in Canadian dollars):

- Unlimited three zone travel on TransLink Bus, SeaBus, and SkyTrain services for $20/month, reduced from $65/month
- 23,000 hours of increased service on bus routes serving UBC
- All-night Friday and Saturday service between downtown Vancouver and UBC as of summer 2003

UBC staff and faculty, as well as community members, have expressed great interest in joining the program and this option will be explored after the student component has begun.

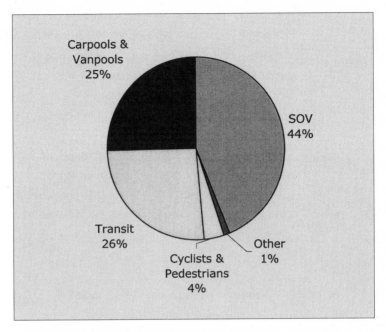

FIG. 7.1
The University of British Columbia modal split from 2002 shows the popularity of transit and HOVs.
Note: This modal split does not include on-campus residents. (Courtesy of UBC TREK Program Centre)

Carpool Program

To be eligible for the carpool program, a carpool must consist of at least three registered students, faculty, or staff of UBC who commute together an average of three times per week. Carpools receive preferential parking spots reserved until 9:30 a.m. (TREK 2003).

Bicycle Programs

In 1998, the Alma Mater Society (AMS—the UBC student government) Bike Co-Op entered the alternative transportation scene as a student-run organization dedicated to improving the environment for bikes and bikes for the environment. The Co-Op is best known for its fleet of more than 230 purple and yellow bikes. Campus housing donates abandoned bicycles removed from campus racks during the summer; bikes also are accepted from the community. Members who volunteer for three or more hours receive keys to the free bikes and can ride any bicycle on campus. Membership costs

$10 for UBC students and $20 for the general public. Membership bene-fits include a 10 percent discount on new parts and free maintenance clin-ics. The Co-Op runs a Build Your Own Bike program, a Bicycle 101 Repair course, and weekly maintenance classes on rotating topics. Inside the Stu-dent Union Building on the UBC campus is the Bike Kitchen, a full-service nonprofit bicycle shop owned by the Bike Co-Op (Alma Mater Society 2003).

UBC has an informal focus group of students, faculty, staff, and other stakeholders who bicycle to and from the university. This Bicycle User Group (BUG) provides feedback and suggestions to UBC organizations and officials as to how to best improve cycling facilities on and around the campus. With the implementation of the U-TREK program, the following benefits will be added:

- New covered bike parking at three locations
- Continued expansion of shower facilities
- Secure bike storage at the Forest Science Centre
- Expanded campus shuttle service (TREK 2003)

TREK teamed up with the company BikeCartAge to offer the "CanCart" Loaner Depot Program in June 2000. UBC faculty, staff, students, as well as the general public, can use a CanCart for hauling while walking or biking. Cart capacities range from 100 pounds up to 450 pounds. The CanCart can be taken upstairs and stored on the bus in the designated handicapped area. It attaches without tools to a bicycle seat. CanCarts are available free of charge at seven on-campus and four off-campus locations, including gro-cery stores and City Hall. The carts are usually loaned for a three-day period; the process requires a simple registration likened to that of a video rental. As of spring 2003, there were 160 carts available. The program began with only six carts and has expanded due to strong demand. Advertising space is available, and the mobile billboards generate revenue to support the program.

Federal and provincial funding purchased the equipment because of its contributions to the Canadian compliance with the Kyoto Protocol. TREK

7.2
The CanCart hitch
system in use at the
University of British
Columbia allows users
to quickly and easily
adjust to different
modes of travel.
Photo courtesy of UBC Trek
Program Centre

provides BikeCartAge with a warehouse for the carts and administrative equipment for the organization, while BikeCartAge provides the carts, helps manage cart depots, and trains students to manage carts and depots (Balyi 2003; BikeCartAge 2003).

Campus Fleet

TREK maintains two natural gas vans for use by campus departments, organizations, or AMS clubs. These vans double as an airport shuttle available during times of heavy traffic between the campus and airport, such as resident move-in and winter break. TREK also operates the van as a free grocery shuttle to carry campus residents to the grocery store at a designated time twice a week. TREK plans to convert the vans to a 15 percent hydrogen-methane mixture, with hopes to increase this percentage up to 30 percent (Lovegrove 2003).

Outreach Programs

Each month TREK honors a UBC community member with the Star TREKer Award. This award recognizes individuals who regularly use alternative transportation. Star TREKers are featured on the TREK Web site (TREK 2003). The TREK Web site (www.trek.ubc.ca) is one of the outstanding features of the TREK program. The Web site provides excellent details about all of the TREK programs. It allows access to status reports, TDM research, survey forms and responses, and numerous reports on various transportation projects. The Web site home page features a pie graph of the UBC modal split so a visitor can immediately get a feel for transportation habits at UBC. The Web site offers all the necessary information about any transportation choice within a few links that follow a logical, efficient path.

UBC Strategic Transportation Plan

The Strategic Transportation Plan (STP) was developed to honor commitments outlined in the Official Community Plan (OCP) for Vancouver and UBC. The plan was developed to respond to growing concerns about growth and the resulting pollution and transportation congestion. The OCP sets

TABLE 7.4

FALL 2002 CONDITIONS VS. FALL 2002 TARGETS AT THE UNIVERSITY OF BRITISH COLUMBIA (UBC). UBC WAS ABLE TO MEET AND/OR EXCEED SEVERAL OF ITS 2002 TARGETS, BUT DID NOT REDUCE SINGLE-OCCUPANCY VEHICLE TRIPS TO THE DESIRED LEVEL. (TABLE RE-CREATED FROM TABLE 8.1 OF *STP 2002 STATUS REPORT*, P. 56.)

Mode	Fall 2002 Actual		Fall 2002 Targets	
	Trips	Mode %	Trips	Mode %
Single-occupant vehicles	48,400	42.6%	42,800	34.8%
Carpool and vanpools	29,100	25.6%	46,200	37.6%
Transit	29,700	26.2%	26,500	21.5%
Bicycles	3,300	2.9%	4,900	4.0%
Pedestrians	1,600	1.4%	1,800	1.5%
Heavy trucks	400	0.4%	300 max.	0.2%
Motorcycle, other	1,000	0.9%	500	0.4%
Total person trips	113,500	100%	123,000	100%
Total vehicles	64,900		62,900*	

*Estimated based on target SOV and HOV targets

objectives for land use and transportation, and guidelines for evaluating future planning and development decisions upon the principles of economics, ecology, and community. The OCP was developed through the cooperation of the City of Vancouver, BC Transit, UBC, and others. More than eighteen months of consultation with more than 5,000 stakeholders produced 55 strategies aimed to reduce single-occupancy vehicle reliance on and around the UBC campus.

The OCP set the following TDM goals:

- Develop and implement, as a top priority, a comprehensive and integrated transportation management strategy (known as the STP)
- Reduce 24-hour single-occupancy vehicle traffic volumes to and from UBC by 20 percent below 1997 levels by November 2002
- Increase 24-hour ridership on public transit to UBC by 20 percent above 1997 levels by November 2002
- Reduce the impact of heavy truck traffic to and from campus by improving coordination of goods and service vehicle movements and by requiring UBC-related trucks to use the City of Vancouver's truck routes
- Implement an accessible, safe, environmentally friendly, and cost-effective campus shuttle system

As of fall 2002, TREK has achieved three of the four primary goals set out in the STP. Transit use has increased to more than 26,500 trips, the trip rate per capita has decreased, and travel times have shifted away from peak periods. Although UBC vehicle trips increased 7 percent from fall 1997 to fall 2002, the campus population grew by 16 percent. SOV trips decreased 9 percent per capita over the last five years, which represents positive measurable progress toward the 20 percent target reduction goal in total SOV trips. One major incentive for non-SOV use was the decrease in campus parking. UBC reduced its parking supply from 0.37 parking stalls per student in 1997 down to 0.30 stalls per student in 2002. Still left to accomplish is the reduction of single-occupancy vehicle trips below 42,800 person trips per day. The implementation of the U-TREK card remains the primary methodology employed to further improve and accomplish the goals of the STP.

The most significant change observed in the *Fall 2002 STP Status Report* was the increase in transit ridership. Transit service to and from UBC increased 30 percent from 1997 to 2002, and ridership in turn increased 56 percent. The biggest disappointment was the nearly 20 percent decline in carpool and vanpool participation, with a 31 percent reduction per capita. This leaves carpool and vanpool participation 37 percent below the targeted levels. According to several focus groups conducted by UBC, many HOV participants switched over to transit. The increased flexibility of transit service versus ridesharing was the primary reason cited for the conversion. TREK concluded that while it will continue to promote ridesharing benefits and services, increasing transit service would be a more efficient investment. The focus groups identified two primary reasons why single-occupancy vehicle decreases have not been as large as anticipated. First, the cost of round-trip transit is greater than the cost of daily parking on campus. Campus parking costs $3 to $3.50 per day. In contrast, round-trip transit costs $4 to $8. One of the objectives of the STP is to fully index parking prices with the cost of round-trip transit service. To index the two prices would require a 25 percent increase in parking rates, which would offset any reductions in parking demand. The other reason for increasing single-occupancy vehicle trips cited by the focus group was the parking system of monthly parking permits. Once a single-occupancy vehicle commuter purchases a monthly parking permit, there is no marginal cost of parking on subsequent days. Rather, drivers are encouraged to drive to maximize the benefits of their permit purchase.

In September 2001, UBC altered start times for morning classes in an effort to spread peak travel demand over a longer timeframe. During peak times, many UBC buses were full, forcing drivers to pass up riders due to lack of space. This signaled a latent demand for bus service. Morning classes had all previously begun at 8:30 a.m. Classes were distributed between start times of 8:00 a.m., 8:30 a.m., and 9:00 a.m., with two thirds of the students arriving at 9:00 a.m., one third at 8:00 a.m., and faculty and staff maintaining the 8:30 a.m. start time. Analysis of transit ridership before and after the adjustment indicates that at least 12 percent of the ridership increase was due to the schedule change. This means that UBC buses are now able to carry 12 percent more people because of the dispersion of the peak travel demand load. TransLink saved an estimated $1 to $2 million by not having to add more buses to handle the additional ridership.

Bicycle ridership at UBC increased 22 percent from 1997 to 2002, and 5 percent per capita. This increase was 33 percent below targeted levels. The failure of bicycle ridership to attain target goals may be accounted for by the increase in transit service. Support for this conclusion comes from the University of Victoria. When the University of Victoria implemented its U-PASS program, it saw an immediate 37 percent decrease in bicycle trips. Pedestrian trips also have increased since 1997, but represent only 1.4 percent of the transportation modal share in 2002. Including campus residents into the modal split raises the pedestrian–bicycle modal share to 25 to 30 percent.

TREK Budget

The TREK Program Centre receives $200,000 from the university capital budget. This funds capital improvement projects, some of which receive supplementary funding through TREK partnerships with other campus departments. The $700,000 operating budget comes from parking revenues. TREK employs fifteen students part-time during the school year and full-time through the summer. The fall 2003 implementation of U-TREK will double the TREK budget, but TREK is responsible for providing the $3 university subsidy for the program. The university hopes to recover some of this cost by selling greenhouse gas credits, raising parking prices, and recommending service efficiencies to TransLink. (Greenhouse gas credits arise from the Canadian Government's commitment to reduce carbon emissions by 6 percent below 1990 levels by 2008. A benchmark emissions standard is set for institutions; these institutions may choose to lower their emissions to meet the standard, or to purchase credits from those institutions below the benchmark.) The subsidy is rather large compared to other universities with a U-PASS program. At the University of Washington, the U-PASS program is funded completely by the students; the University of Victoria contributes a $1 subsidy per student per month for its U-PASS program (Lovegrove 2003; UBC 2003).

The University of California–Davis: The Bicycle and Beyond

Davis, California, is described as "a university-oriented city with a progressive, vigorous community noted for its small-town style, energy conservation, environmental programs, parks, preservation of trees, red double-decker London buses, bicycles, and the quality of its educational institutions." The City of Davis has been deemed one of the healthiest American communities in which to live and retire: in 1995 the Bicycle Federation of America declared Davis to be America's Best Cycling City.

The number of cyclists on the road in the mid-1960s prompted city officials to design safer and more efficient accommodations for bicycles. The city installed bike lanes on the already wide outer lanes of all arterial streets, as well as bike paths dispersed throughout the city. Davis pioneered bike lanes on streets, convincing the California legislature to make them legal, and creating a model for other cities to follow. The university responded by connecting campus with city paths, closing off the campus core to cars, and adding high-visibility bike parking at virtually every campus building.

Today Davis has 48.8 miles of bike lanes and 49 miles of bike paths. Eighty percent of all collector and arterial streets within the city have bike lanes and/or adjacent bike paths, the highest ratio in any U.S. city. As of 2002, the city has grown to more than 62,000 residents, and the university to 29,000 students, with roughly 11,000 nonstudent employees. Estimates place the number of bikes in the city and the university at 53,000. The abundance of bike lanes, relatively flat terrain, and mild weather contribute to the bicycle's modal share of 20 to 25 percent of daily trips.

Bike-only light cycles at major intersections are an innovative feature of the Davis bike culture. Davis experimented with the bicycle signal head in 1990 and has since expanded its use to other intersections. The signal head displays red, yellow, and green bike icons that give bicyclists their own turn cycle. Davis petitioned a change in California law to permit the installation of the signal heads, which were modeled after similar devices in the Netherlands, England, Germany, and China (City of Davis 2002, 2003; Bustos 2003).

Bicycles on Campus

The bicycle's central role in the City of Davis carries over to the university. A 1996 campus survey showed that 60 percent of the student population

7.3
Davis cyclists receive
their own turn cycle
through a bicycle
signal head.
Courtesy of David
Takemoto-Weerts

either biked or walked to campus, and 20 percent of faculty and staff walked or biked, averaging 15,000 to 18,000 bikes on campus each day.

Fourteen miles of campus bike paths combined with a wide array of bike services maintain and promote a safe and pleasant mode of transportation. Students receive discounts or rebates on locks, cables, lights, reflectors, and helmets. Operating revenue comes mainly from the sale of bike licenses and bike auctions. Semiannual auctions of more than 300 bikes abandoned on racks provide discounted bicycles to students. Bike registration costs $8 for three years; renewal is only $4. The operating budget for bicycle services is roughly $40,000 to $50,000 per year. Additional funds are available from parking fines and forfeitures, as well as federal, state, and local grants.

A full-time coordinator runs the bicycle program with 10 part-time student employees. Students patrol the campus in an electric pickup truck to enforce registration and parking compliance as well as collect abandoned bikes. Transportation and Parking Services (TAPS) employs a full-time bicycle enforcement officer who, in conjunction with Campus Police, enforces traffic and equipment regulations. Unlawful bicyclists may choose

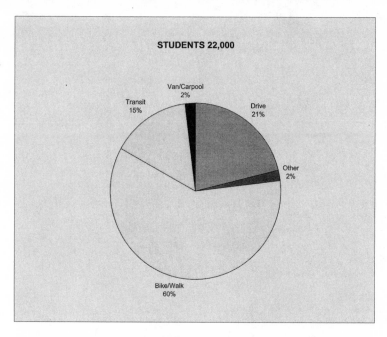

STUDENTS 22,000

Van/Carpool 2%
Transit 15%
Drive 21%
Other 2%
Bike/Walk 60%

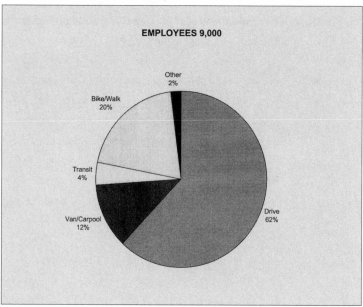

EMPLOYEES 9,000

Other 2%
Bike/Walk 20%
Transit 4%
Van/Carpool 12%
Drive 62%

FIG. 7.2
This 1996 Davis modal split shows that walking and biking are the dominant mode of travel at the University of California–Davis campus with 22,000 students. (Courtesy David Takemoto-Weerts)

to attend bicycle traffic school to reduce ticket fines from $81 down to $10. TAPS and the Cowell Student Health Center's BikeRight Program sponsor bicycle education classes to complement the safety, repair, and maintenance classes also offered on campus. The Associated Students of UC–Davis (ASUCD) Bike Barn is a full-service repair shop on campus, with do-it-yourself tools available on loan. The university provides thirty-six bicycle lockers that can be rented for $20 per quarter. These lockers, offered with shower facilities, are primarily used by commuters, but are not in high demand. The university also provides summer bike storage for students and employees.

Beginning in the summer of 2001, TAPS began offering temporary parking permits to faculty and staff cyclists who did not own a parking permit. These permits allow twelve days of use over a six-month period for $6 per use. While a daily permit costs only $5 per day, these permits feature much closer parking to university facilities. Many faculty and staff complained at having to pay any cost at all. They believed that they should be rewarded for being dedicated cyclists. However, parking at Davis during inclement weather can be very difficult. Bicycle Services believes that offering faculty and staff bicyclists free temporary permits would encourage an onslaught of cyclists turned drivers during foul weather and would further exacerbate an already troublesome situation. This is also the driving force for excluding students from the program.

The university and the City of Davis maintain a very cooperative relationship on the bicycle front, working extensively on issues of engineering, encouragement, education, and advocacy. The city bicycle coordinator sits on the university bicycle committee. Davis and the university also have applied jointly for state and federal aid for bicycle improvement projects (Takemoto-Weerts 2003; University of California–Davis TAPS 2002).

Going Beyond the Bicycle

The success and recognition achieved by the bicycle programs at UC-Davis do not solve the entire transportation issue for the campus community. TAPS offers additional programs to accommodate those not too comfortable on two wheels.

TRANSITPOOL AND TRAINPOOL

TAPS offers the Transitpool program for university faculty, staff, and students. Each member must not possess a parking permit to enjoy the following benefits:

- Up to a 40 percent discount on the purchase of monthly, quarterly, and half-quarter transit passes
- Emergency ride home service
- Complimentary daily pool parking permit: two uses/month or six uses/quarter
- Pretax payroll deduction of transit costs for qualifying employees

In 2002, TAPS began a pilot Trainpool program. Each participant receives a subsidy of up to $18 per month to ride Amtrak trains at a reduced rate. Amtrak offers a commuting option for Davis employees who live in San Jose or Sacramento. Participation includes all the benefits of the Transitpool program (University of California–Davis TAPS 2002).

UNITRANS

Unitrans provides transit service for the university and the City of Davis. Student initiatives fostered the operation, which began in 1968, and service to the general public became available in 1972, coupled with funding from the City of Davis. Interested in both high-profile and high-capacity service, students purchased London double-decker buses for the original fleet. Unitrans remains a student-run organization, employing 175 students (150 drivers) and only 13 full-time staff as of 2002.

During the 1980s, students passed a referendum raising student registration fees by $13 in exchange for no-fare Unitrans service. A valid sticker on a current registration card allows students to ride with no-fare; as of 2002, students pay $24.50 per quarter for the bus program. Unitrans also provides no-fare service to anyone possessing a legitimate UC-Davis parking permit and City of Davis employees with proper ID. Unitrans operates fourteen routes, providing 2.5 million trips annually, and on the average weekday carries nearly 15,000 people.

Future improvements for Unitrans include the phasing out of high-

7.4

These bright red London double-decker buses continue to provide extra capacity and publicity for Unitrans.

Courtesy of Unitrans

emission older buses, expanding service to accommodate increasing student enrollment, providing higher frequency service to growing neighborhoods, and providing real-time scheduling information for riders. Unitrans operates on an annual budget of roughly $2.5 million, with labor constituting approximately 70 percent of costs, followed by 10 percent for fuel and 20 percent for materials. Student transit fees generate 57 percent, or just over $1.5 million in revenue. Other sources include Davis Transportation Development Act funds (18 percent), Yolo County TDA funds (1 percent), federal operating funds (14 percent), university contribution (3 percent), fare and bus pass sales (4 percent), and ads and miscellaneous (4 percent) (ASUCD 2002; Palmere 2002).

CARPOOL AND VANPOOLS

Students, faculty, and staff residing outside the Davis area may participate in the registered carpool program. Carpools pay a substantially reduced price for campus parking and receive preferential parking in their choice of specific lots when arriving before 9:30 a.m. The university also offers incentives for vanpool use, including reduced parking rates, reserved parking, temporary individual parking permits, and some subsidy (UCD TAPS 2002).

Future Efforts

The University of California–Davis is participating in an innovative Smart Mobility Model Project to develop and test new approaches to transportation planning. The project is a collaborative effort among the UC–Davis campus, the California Department of Transportation (Caltrans), UC–Wide Partners for Advanced Transit and Highways, and Institute of Transportation Studies at UC–Davis and UC–Berkeley. The goal of Smart Mobility is "to optimize individual mobility through improved connectivity among modes, enhanced techniques to link land-use planning and transportation system design, and advanced information and clean fuel technologies." The project began in 2002 with an intensive research effort to determine the impact of expanding existing services and to quantify the need for new options.

After developing an understanding of the factors affecting transportation patterns in the Sacramento/Davis area and the problems facing residents, Smart Mobility will propose one to three demonstration projects. These projects might include smart bus stops and shuttle services with real-time information, niche applications for electric bikes and small electric cars, e-commerce opportunities, and carsharing. The next two years will be devoted to the implementation of these demonstrations and research into their practicability, including their usefulness in the context of local planning decisions. The university hopes to determine the feasibility of applying innovative mobility services and technologies to the upcoming University of California–Davis Long Range Development Plan. Other alternative transportation improvements the university hopes to implement include awarding prizes and financial incentives to dedicated alternative transportation participants, and participating in efforts to create a universal bus pass for the entire region.

While the University of California–Davis has made great strides in reducing parking demand, it continues to face a parking shortage. To compensate for rising parking pressures and the loss of more than 850 spaces to new construction and renovation, the university will build a 1,500-space parking structure by 2005. TAPS began a four-year phased parking rate increase in 2002 to offset the debt obligation of the structure and to avoid short-term rate spikes (University of California–Davis LRAP 2002) (Table 7.5).

TABLE 7.5
THE UNIVERSITY OF CALIFORNIA–DAVIS WILL PHASE IN PARKING RATE INCREASES
TO HELP PAY FOR THE NEW PARKING STRUCTURE. (COURTESY OF UC-DAVIS TAPS)

Fiscal year	"A" permit	"C" permit	Visitor Rate
2002–2003	$3.00	$2.00	$1.00
2003–2004	3.00	2.00	0.00
2004–2005	4.00	3.00	0.00
2005–2006	5.00	5.00	0.00
Totals	$15.00	$12.00	$1.00

The University of North Carolina at Chapel Hill: Restoring Campus Green Space

The Research Triangle in the Raleigh-Durham-Chapel Hill metropolitan area serves as a case study where a large population, rather heavily dependent on the automobile, illustrates innovative approaches to car parking on its several university campuses. Our focus is on the University of North Carolina–Chapel Hill (UNC), which has a large medical complex in the midst of its academic campus.

The multifaceted effort to reduce single-occupancy cars coming to the UNC campus is an example of what is possible to alleviate the car parking dilemma of an expanding student body, a growing campus physical plant, and an enlarging university-based medical facility. Included among the attempted remedies: no freshman cars permitted on campus, free local bus passes, free shuttle bus service between Duke University in Durham and the University of North Carolina in Chapel Hill, access to the state-run North Carolina heavy-rail passenger service, a campus plan that reduces surface parking, a campus car rental for short-term use, and photo identification of cars using the large structured parking near the medical complex.

UNC has 25,000 students and 17,000 parking spaces. Between 2004 and 2014 the expansion of the physical plant is projected to be 4 million square feet. The new development plan has a modest 1,500 parking places, which means a smaller percentage of people will be able to drive to campus and park.

The UNC Parking Plan states that 77 percent of employees drive to campus today; in the near future as buildings are developed, only 55 percent of these people will be able to drive alone to campus. As Carlos Balsas has written, "campus planners have struggled to provide access and mobility without destroying campus qualities as communities" (Balsas 2003). UNC is a good example of this struggle.

A Campus Master Plan, approved in 2001, ushers in a new transportation policy designed to make the UNC campus more pedestrian- and bike-friendly. Transit service also will be increased. In the first eight months of 2002, the Chapel Hill bus system usage increased 38 percent after a free bus program was implemented. New student housing built on campus is another strategy to reduce car trips. Four new residence halls with 960 students and another 1,000 units of undergraduate housing are in the works. Soon 300 units of family housing are planned within walking distance of classrooms.

Today most campus parking is in surface lots, but the Campus Master Plan seeks to change this practice. Twenty acres of land currently paved for surface lots will be converted into ten acres of landscaped green space and bike/ped paths and ten acres will have new buildings where high-rise and midrise residence halls will house academic uses on lower floors. Visitors and patients at the UNC hospitals and campus clinics will use most new parking places. Future parking decks will be consolidated below the acres of a green campus. Campus planners state this will bring back the "livability" of a campus plan prepared in 1920 before the automobile became dominant on the campus of the oldest public university (established 1793) in the United States.

Greening a campus by consolidating parking structures underground does not satisfy everyone. The Daily Tar Heel campus newspaper reports that some people believe that new parking decks "would not [be] popular with commuters . . . who would want to pay higher rates for a deck so far from the center of campus?" (Corriher 2003) Some Chapel Hill City Council

7.5a

(ABOVE LEFT)
The University of
North Carolina plans
to convert ten acres
of parking into green
space, which will
surround this bell
tower.

Photo by Spenser Havlick

7.5b

(ABOVE RIGHT)
Parking places will
be underground to
preserve campus
beauty.

Photo by Spenser Havlick

members are worried that the proposed decks might increase traffic coming into the campus, which runs counter to the Campus Master Plan.

UNC plans to link the increased parking fees necessary to pay for these parking decks to employee income. The plan, according to a report in *The Daily Tar Heel* says that "students and employees earning less than $50,000 would see an annual parking permit fee increase of 5 percent. Employees earning between $50,000 and $100,000 a year would see a 10 percent increase annually, and those earning more than $100,000 a year would see an increase up to 20 percent. Some refinements, such as smaller salary gap brackets and an upper limit to annual increases may be considered." (*The Daily Tar Heel* 2003)

In 2004, the University of North Carolina will introduce a new technology that will photograph vehicles entering and leaving a large parking deck located near the UNC hospital. This deck provides parking for visitors and patients to the hospitals, but parking officials report many problems with stored student vehicles. Again, from *The Daily Tar Heel*: "The new technology will free up spaces for hospital users by tracking how long a particular car stays in the lot, thus cutting down on vehicle storage in temporary parking. This will help parking officials identify who is parking in the lot without cause, such as freshmen (who are not allowed to have vehicles on campus)" (Corriher 2003).

Students and faculty who come to the UNC campus without a car will be able to borrow cars in a campus rental program in fall 2003. Zipcar, the Boston-based rental car company, will have four Volkswagen Beetles with UNC logos. The program is designed for transit commuters and those who use UNC's Park and Ride lots. The goal of the short-term rental program is to encourage people not to bring their single-occupancy vehicles to campus. The program membership fee is approximately $35, which includes insurance coverage when the Zipcar is in use. The cars qualify for designated, preferential parking spaces. Potential users can register and reserve vehicles on a Web site. Several universities, including Harvard and the Massachusetts Institute of Technology, have implemented the Zipcar program.

A comprehensive system of on-street and off-street bikeways and striped bike lanes serve the Chapel Hill–Carrboro area. In addition, the regional American Tobacco Trail connects Durham, Raleigh, and Chapel Hill with a bike/ped system. New extensions, bus bike racks, sidewalks, and bike routes are ongoing additions in annual capital improvement budgets in the Research Triangle region, of which the University of North Carolina is an integral part.

Another effort to reduce the number of cars parked on the UNC campus and to reduce traffic congestion is the Commuter Alternatives Program (CAP). This program encourages all forms of alternative transportation including bicycling, walking, transit, park and ride, carpool, and vanpool. The program is free and requires the participant to commute to school or work and not hold a single-occupancy vehicle permit. Some of the benefits for participants include a book of nine one-day temporary permits good for one day per month, October through July: access to emergency daytime ride service for students and employees who live within the Carrboro and Chapel Hill city limits; all CAP members are eligible for prize drawings and gift coupons for use with local merchants. Carpool, vanpool, and deluxe carpool (four or more employees) users qualify for CAP benefits. Park and Ride members receive decal permits for each vehicle registered. More details are available at www.dps.unc.edu/alternatives/commuterprogram.htm.

The Robertson Scholars shuttle bus, which operates a free service between Duke University and the UNC campus centers, has two purposes. One is to promote better collaboration between the universities (course credits can be exchanged) and the other is to reduce auto trips. Duke tends to have higher credit hour tuition than UNC, which adds to the popularity of the shuttle.

Duke University also has an innovative financial aid policy on vehicles. The aid policy deducts 35 percent of an aid student's car value from the aid package if the car is less than five years old or costs more than $3,000. The editorial page of Duke's newspaper, *The Chronicle*, goes on to say "The philosophy ... makes sense. If the University is paying for part of a student's education, it has every right to ensure that the student is not cheating the system by possessing a valuable asset that could be liquidated—this policy ensures that Duke gets the most value it can out of its financial aid dollars to help all students receiving assistance" (*The Chronicle* 2003).

The North Carolina Research Triangle area, anchored by large medical and research universities, primarily University of North Carolina in Chapel Hill and Duke University in Durham, has a formidable transportation and parking challenge. Valiant efforts are under way at UNC to consolidate and reduce future parking underground, to return the campus to greenery, to provide additional walkways and bikeways, and to reduce single-occupancy vehicle trips to campus. Transit, biking, and other alternate modes, bolstered by marketing, are expected to cushion the loss of future parking.

The University of Montana at Missoula: Student-Led Efforts in a Small-Town Setting

The University of Montana–Missoula demonstrates that a modest-sized university (11,800 students), in a small to modest-sized city (80,000), can create an excellent alternative transportation program. What makes this

case study especially inspiring is the realization that the people in the spacious state of Montana have a strong dependence on the use of single-occupant cars and pick-up trucks. And yet this state university has a serious effort under way to reduce excessive auto use. In Montana popular destinations, population centers, major employment centers, and recreational sites are widely dispersed. The automobile is the most feasible transportation option for all motorists, including those of college age.

How does it happen that this public university, in a relatively small university town, in a state where the automobile is dominant out of necessity, can have a collection of very innovative practices? What UM has put in place could be the envy of many larger universities with relatively larger problems of traffic congestion, parking shortages, and other car-related problems. We can explain the University of Montana recipe for success with three factors:

- Student leadership
- Inspired, talented management programs for automobile alternatives
- Concern by the town and the university to reduce air pollution and congestion

Traffic growth in Missoula and at the university in the 1980s and 1990s coupled with the increase in air pollution from cars and the nearby forest product industry, prompted the formation of a University Transportation Task Force. It was composed of students, faculty, and city personnel. Significant inversion conditions during the school year, primarily in the winter, exacerbated the atmospheric pollution problems in Missoula's Clark Fork and Bitterroot valleys. Even though the administration of the University of Montana did not rank excessive student car use as a priority issue, student leaders on the University Transportation Task Force did believe car-related issues were a problem. They took the findings of the task force to the student body, the University of Montana Association of Students, for a student referendum to establish an Office of Transportation. The 1999 vote was successful and a $4 per semester fee was approved by the students to create alternatives to the single-occupancy vehicle. The fee was raised to $6 in 2000 and to $8 in 2003.

Nancy McKiddy, director of the Associated Students of the University of Montana Office of Transportation (ASUM), lists some of the services and programs of ongoing activities:

- Biodiesel campus bus fueled by campus kitchen grease that provides shuttle service to outlying parking lots. The service has fifteen-minute headway, it is free, and it has increased ridership 65 percent between 2001 and 2002.
- The Grisss Ride provides late-night bus service from points around Missoula and the U of M campus. The name is inspired by the university's grizzly bear mascot, the sss standing for safety, sustainability, and security.
- The Bike Checkout Program with sixty bikes available for a two- to three-day period serves the university student body as a transit supplement. The program operates much like a library book check-out system. A student ID card is used to check out a bike. It has been very popular with international students and others who don't wish, or can't afford, to purchase a new bike.
- A No Interest Bike Loan Program, one of the first in the United States, is a cooperative arrangement between the campus credit union and the U of M Office of Transportation. Up to $400 is loaned to a student for a bike purchase with no interest. The two stipulations are that the

7.9
Cornell University's TDM
program has preserved
the charm and
pedestrian ambience of
the Ithaca, New York,
campus.
Courtesy of Cornell University
Transportation Demand
Management Program

applicant must pay a down payment of 10 percent and must obtain a Missoula bicycle license. Up to forty bikes a year have been purchased with the program.

- New campus bike racks have been designed and installed with a U of M logo.

- A carpool Web site has been created to help connect students and faculty who wish to reduce single-occupancy vehicle trips to recreational destinations, conferences, or rideshares from homebound trips. This site is interactive and serves as an electronic message board to reduce car trips.

In addition to University of Montana innovations, Phil Smith, program manager of the City of Missoula pedestrian/bike program, adds to the list of achievements done by Missoula or in partnership with the university. Missoula provides free bus service to students under a flat fee contractual arrangement ($135,000 per year) with the U of M. The city has built new bike/ped bridges over the river and an overpass over local railroad yards in order to connect north–south destinations for students and townspeople.

More than thirty miles of street and off-street bikeways help make Missoula and its university campus more bicycle friendly.

The largest U of M alternate transportation event of the year is the Green Griz Week, also known as the Bike/Walk/Bus Week, which is in its twelfth year. Radio announcements, newspaper ads, posters, and a comprehensive Web site publicize the weeklong event of seventy activities. The ASUM Office of Transportation and KBGA radio sponsor the event, which encourages people to commute to the campus without driving all week. Volunteers hand out free raffle tickets as nonmotorists enter the campus. At the end of the week, a large festival takes place with music and food and dozens of gift certificates, prizes, and awards. Ten thousand raffle ticket holders participate.

Phil Smith coordinates city activities in the Missoula that run simultaneously with the campus car reduction celebration. Teachers and parents organize "walking school buses" for elementary schoolchildren. Nine different historic neighborhood walking tours are available, and all Missoula transit buses are free during the Bike/Walk/Bus Week. Commuter Challenge races are held among downtown businesses and community organizations where motorists "race" to a destination against nonmotorist commuters. The city markets its Missoula in Motion program for other travel solutions such as carpooling, telecommuting, guaranteed ride home, transit schedules, and the like at www.missoulainmotion.com.

Cornell University: Tackling Faculty and Staff Commuting in a Small-Town Environment

In the late 1980s Cornell University in Ithaca, New York, was experiencing tremendous growth in vehicle traffic and parking shortages that demanded an innovative solution. Interestingly, the problem lay more with faculty and staff commuters than with students, whose demand for parking remained stable. University leaders did not wish to follow the standard model of simply constructing more parking spaces and roads to accommodate the single-occupant cars driven by its 9,000 employees every day. They decided this option was simply too expensive and would actually exacerbate problems by encouraging traffic growth. Expanding automobile infrastructure also would diminish the quality of the pedestrian environment

and negatively impact campus green space. Concerned about the environment and economics, Cornell embarked on another path—the development
of a Transportation Demand Management (TDM) program. Implemented in
1991, the TDMP established an incentive program with one condition for
membership: Participants needed to give up their individual parking permit.

While some of the elements of Cornell's program are similar to those
of other schools profiled, there are several important distinctions. Cornell
has perhaps the most extensive TDM program of any major institution
located in a small town (Ithaca has about 30,000 residents). Their program
is also unique because it started with a major focus on faculty and staff
trips, rather than on student trips. And it has had a stronger focus and more
success with ridesharing than has been the campus norm.

One element is the OmniRIDE transit pass program. In a cooperative
effort with city and county transit agencies, Cornell distributes bus pass
stickers that affix to the employee identification card. Cornell pays the fare
for all campus, city, or county buses within Tompkins County and subsidizes
the purchase of monthly bus passes for out-of-county commuters. Unlike
the universal bus pass programs at other profiled universities, this is available free to employees but not students. OmniRIDErs also receive a free
book of one-day perimeter parking permits for each six-month period.
Employees pay nothing for the OmniRIDE stickers: The sole condition is they
cannot order a semester parking permit. Students could purchase a pass for
$75 per semester in 2002.

The various transit agencies in Ithaca were consolidated in a joint venture to simplify operations and fare structures. The new service is called
TCAT. Prior to this, the university had its own transit agency, as did the City
of Ithaca, and Tompkins County. The spirit of cooperation engendered by the
OmniRIDE program provided the impetus to consolidate the three separate
transit systems. Faculty and staff who do not join OmniRIDE can ride
any TCAT bus in TCAT's zone one, the area immediately surrounding campus Monday through Friday by simply flashing their Cornell ID card when
boarding.

Ridesharing is a key element of the TDMP. Commuters who set up carpools are entitled to discounts or even rebates on parking fees, depending
on how many are in the car and which lots they choose. Members need to

turn in their individual parking permit and obtain one group permit with all participating vehicles listed on it. The fee for the permit is split among all the carpoolers; for large enough carpools there is a rebate payment that is split among the members. Large carpools also receive preferential reserved parking locations. Depending on the parking location and the number of carpoolers, the cost for the carpool permit varies. For example, in the core of campus an individual permit cost more than $600/year in 2002; a two-person carpool shared a fee of $350, and a four-person carpool paid no fee and got reserved space. In one parking zone a four-person carpool received a rebate payment of $320. Cornell maintains a Web-based rideshare board to help carpoolers find partners.

Cornell offers a thirty-day trial period for carpoolers and OmniRIDE participants to try the programs during which the person may quit the program and have a parking permit returned. It also offers a broad range of supplementary services to make it easier for individuals to give up their parking permits, including an emergency ride home program, occasional parking privileges, night safety shuttles, and a campus to downtown express lunchtime bus service.

Cornell has one no-fee satellite parking lot for occasional commuters or those who would be economically disadvantaged by paying fees. A Cornell shuttle bus provides rides to campus. Cornell also established a Parking Hardship Review Board that gives partial or full grants to those who cannot afford parking fees and cannot use alternatives or the free satellite lot. Emergency medical technicians, volunteer firefighters, or commuters with dependent care responsibilities who depend on having a car on campus for quick exits can get half-price parking permits.

Student parking fees were kept below employee rates for many years, but in 2002 Cornell made the decision to raise student rates to provide incentives for environmentally sustainable commuting and to discourage single-occupant vehicle use. The new student parking permit price was raised to $600, a level exceeded only by the highest faculty/staff rate. Even with the higher rate, there is still a substantial subsidy for student parking. In an interesting approach, continuing students who enrolled prior to the rate increase were grandfathered in at the previous rates.

Impacts of TDMP

Cornell University is extremely enthusiastic about the outcome of its TDMP. In just one year, the program resulted in a 26 percent decline in the number of vehicles being brought to campus each day. The actual financial savings as a result of the program were far greater than anticipated. The Office of Transportation Services summarized its interpretation of the financial savings in a 1996 report (Lieb 1996):

> Our somewhat enthusiastic original projections from 1991 called for a first-year savings of $53,504: our actual was greater by an order of magnitude: $635,634. Our projected cumulative savings by the end of 1993–94 were $1.2 million; our actual savings were just shy of $4 million. The differences that led to this dramatic difference... can be explained by three changes: the university transitioned from 20 year to 10 year debt, the cost of providing TDMP turned out to be roughly one-third the original projection (although participation was double); and we built fewer spaces.
>
> We know that in the first year the number of single occupant vehicles brought to campus dropped by 2,500... caveats aside, we can say with a measure of confidence by the end of 1997–98 TDMP saved the university a total of nearly $17 million. Extrapolated out of a modest $68,290 per year increase, by 2002–03 (the year that the first parking garage would have been paid off), the university will have saved nearly $36 million since the inception of TDMP.

As of 2002, thirty-seven percent of faculty and staff participated in the TDMP program.

University of New Hampshire: Creating Change at a Rural Campus

The rural town of Durham, New Hampshire, houses the University of New Hampshire (UNH) and its 10,500 students. Durham is in the southeastern corner of New Hampshire near the Maine border. It is located one hour from both Boston and Portland, and 20 minutes from the New Hampshire and Maine seacoasts. This town of 12,660 people has only two signalized intersections in its 25.5 sq. miles (Town of Durham 2002). Because of the rural character of this area, the automobile is the dominant transportation mode. However, a long-term institutional commitment to sustainability combined with related environmental concerns and core campus parking congestion have led the campus toward a new transportation approach.

UNH Bicycle Programs

The Office of Sustainability Programs (OSP) has played a crucial role in transportation planning in general and the student and faculty bicycle programs at UNH in particular. The goal of the OSP is to develop a University-wide education program that links the principles of sustainability to university life. Established in 1997, the OSP is a collaborative effort between students, faculty, and staff, as well as international, regional, and local partners. The community bike programs are part of the Climate Education Initiative (CEI), a universitywide effort that integrates the ethics, science, technology, and policies of greenhouse gas reductions into its teaching, research, campus policies, and outreach. There are five bicycle hubs throughout the campus that feature bicycle pumps, Allen wrenches, and adjustable wrenches for minor bicycle repairs. A student ID or state driver's license is necessary for checkout.

In April 2000, the OSP initiated the Yellow bike co-operative. For a $5 annual membership fee, UNH students were given a key to use any yellow bike on campus and within the Town of Durham. Roughly 75 bicycles were purchased from the Bedford Recycling Center over the program's three years. In April 2002, the Commuter Bicycle Pilot Program, or Cat Cycles, evolved from the Yellow Bike program. The Yellow bikes were difficult to maintain because uniform parts could not be used on all the different models; disappearing bicycles were also a problem. The Cat Cycles program provides any university member with free access to a Cat bike (named after the UNH Wildcats). These single-speed cruisers, equipped with a lock and cargo basket, can be checked out for up to a week. Any of the nine new bicycles are checked out at the Visitor Service Center. The program arose as a partnership between the OSP and UNH Transportation Services, and is now overseen and administered through Transportation Services.

The OSP began operating a Blue Bike program for campus departments in April 2002. The OSP helps departments purchase bicycles similar to the Cat bikes, but for use only by the department. These bikes can be used to run errands, attend meetings, and make deliveries. As of spring 2003, six departments had participated in the program (University of New Hampshire OSP 2003).

Transit and Carpools

University of New Hampshire Transportation Services operates the two transit systems that serve the UNH campus—the Wildcat Transit and the Campus Connector. Wildcat Transit connects the campus with the cities of Dover and Portsmouth, and the Town of Newmarket, while the Campus Connector connects the outer campus with the campus core. The Campus Connector is fare-free for all passengers, and Wildcat Transit is fare-free to university students, faculty, and staff with a university ID (UNH Transportation Services 2002).

UNH commenced a special parking program for carpool users in fall 2002. Fifty spaces in a lot adjacent to the campus core were set aside as an incentive to save resources and parking spaces. The program offers no direct financial benefits to the users in terms of parking prices; at least two members of the carpool must purchase parking permits. Faculty and staff display both permits to access the spaces, while student carpools must obtain a special permit tag from the Parking Office to supplement their student parking decals. There are 125 commuter students registered as a carpool, and the lot is generally 80 to 90 percent full, with about 5 to 10 percent of the spaces being occupied illegally. One of the benefits of this permit system is that when circumstances prevent carpooling, drivers retain their commuter permit to access a single-occupancy vehicle parking space. The program expanded to 70 spaces in fall 2003 (Pesci 2003).

The Costs of Parking

Several local businesses in Durham rent their facilities for student, faculty, and staff parking. The annual parking rates charged for these lots range from $400 to $600. In contrast, a UNH faculty, staff, or commuter permit cost $32 in 2002. Commuter permits are limited to students living more than one mile from campus. There has been a long-standing freshman parking ban on campus and some discussion of extending the ban to the sophomore level. However, the increasing fragmentation of student schedules makes it unlikely that the ban will occur anytime soon. For now, the university is encouraging more students to find employment on campus or along transit routes. UNH also is working with the student body to identify popular areas of student employment that are not currently served by transit (Pesci 2003).

UNH transportation staff has identified the following points in an assessment of its transportation system:

- UNH parking fees do not reflect the differential cost and market value of core campus proximity and peak demand times. The difference between the cost/value and the price of parking permits constitutes a subsidy.
- UNH's subsidized parking system has resulted in increased demand for parking that has exhausted a parking surplus that was intended to last for another ten years. This pattern of subsidized parking fueling growing demand is consistent with the experience of other campuses.
- UNH's generous parking subsidy is contradictory to the most basic tenets of a TDM program.
- UNH's subsidized parking system has resulted in a high volume of traffic on local and regional roads due to the number of vehicles—particularly single-occupancy vehicles—coming to the campus each day.
- As an institution of higher education committed to sustainability (the balancing of economic viability with ecological health and human well-being), UNH must make its management practices consistent with its values and educational mission (University of New Hampshire OSP 1999).

UNH Transportation Policy Committee (TPC) 2003: Final Report and Recommendations

The recommendations made by the TPC in its final report to the UNH president in February 2003 are based on "the collective fundamental belief that the current status of parking and transportation at UNH is structurally irrational and unacceptable and must change." The current transportation system limits mobility across all modes, causes unnecessary street congestion, decreases productivity, enhances campus frustration, poses pedestrian safety deficiencies, and negatively impacts air quality.

The report recognizes the automobile as the dominant mode of

TABLE 7.6

FISCAL YEAR 2002 ESTIMATED ANNUAL COST OF A PARKING SPACE AT THE UNIVERSITY
OF NEW HAMPSHIRE. OPERATIONAL AND CAPITAL COSTS OF A PARKING SPACE GREATLY
EXCEEDED THE RATES CHARGED TO USERS, PROMPTING THE UNIVERSITY TO OVERHAUL ITS
RATE STRUCTURE. (COURTESY OF UNIVERSITY OF NEW HAMPSHIRE CAMPUS PLANNING)

Direct Operational Costs	Cost per Space
Snow plowing	$1.50
Stripe and paint	$1.20
Reclaim pavement and curbs	$1.20
Equipment replacement	$0.75
Treat and clean basins	$0.50
Repair asphalt and cracks	$1.35
Administrative overhead—facilities	$0.50
Basis of facilities charge, FY 2002 ($45,000)	**$7.00**
Indirect operational costs	
Safety phones	$2.50
Lighting	$8.00
Police patrol	$7.00
Parking enforcement	$71.50
Indirect operational costs subtotal	**$89.00**
Capital costs	
Projected $2,000/space amortized over 10 years	$200.00
Total	**$296.00**

transportation for the campus in the present as well as the future. UNH has
not formally gathered modal split data for the campus to quantify the
extent of automobile dominance. The expectation of continued automobile
dominance is based upon the rural setting of UNH and the wide geographic
distribution of its faculty, staff, and students. The committee founded its
recommendations on the general university consensus that under current
pricing and current driving behavior, the campus has a parking deficit of
600 spaces during peak demand. Over the next five years, the university will
lose just over 100 spaces, driving the deficit upwards of 700 spaces. During
fall 2002, the TPC completed the first phase of a parking feasibility study for
an 800-space lot. Construction costs are estimated at $20,000 to $28,000

per net additional parking space. Estimated annual operational costs are $300 to $400 per space. The university is in the process of studying the price-sensitivity demand for such a structure.

The TPC used the results of a spring 2001 survey of the UNH population to shape their recommendations. Fifty percent of respondents were not opposed to increasing the cost of parking fees to as much as $400 per year, if the additional funds were "dedicated exclusively to the expansion or improvement of the parking and transportation systems in fiscally sound, effective, user-friendly and environmentally friendly manners."

To more effectively manage demand and to provide funding for the future parking structure, UNH will implement a two-tiered parking price system no earlier than July 2004. Currently lots are designated to faculty, staff, commuters, and residents, restricting drivers to a limited number of parking options. Under the proposed system, there will be a huge increase in publicly equal access lots, a big selling point for the student body. Three zones were created based upon walking distances to the campus core.

The faculty union poses a large stumbling block to the implementation of the proposed rate increases. The price of parking is tied to the faculty union contract and the union must approve any changes. In June 2003, the UNH president turned the recommendations into policy. However, the policy will not affect students and nonunion employees until the faculty union accepts the changes.

Long-Range TDM Goals

The TPC recognized a link between class location, student demographics, and transportation patterns. There are three main academic buildings that consistently account for one third, and sometimes up to one half, of the off-campus student class enrollments. The TPC encourages a long-term goal of relocating the larger classes that are dominated by commuter students away from the campus core and off to the west, where more parking is available. Another long-term goal is an incentive system to more evenly distribute the peak transportation load across the week through a more even distribution of class enrollments. The transportation infrastructure exceeds capacity on Tuesday/Thursday, while excess supply is available on Friday. The TPC also would like to link the location of new academic space to

TABLE 7.7
COMPARISON OF UNIVERSITY OF NEW HAMPSHIRE 2002 PARKING PERMIT STRUCTURE WITH PROPOSED
CHANGES. PARKING PRICES WILL DRAMATICALLY RISE TO DECREASE THE UNIVERSITY'S PARKING SUBSIDY.
(COURTESY OF UNIVERSITY OF NEW HAMPSHIRE TRANSPORTATION SERVICES)

Location	2002–2003 Faculty, Staff, and Commuter Student	Proposed Unreserved Rate	Current Resident Rate	Proposed Resident Rate
Zone 1 (core)	$32	$200 ($140)	$300	$600
Zone 2 (perimeter)	$32	$125 ($88)	$300	$600
Zone 3 (remote)	$32	$50 ($35)	N/A	$250 ($175)

transportation in the university master plan. On the housing side, Transportation Services would like to decrease the current ratio of 0.8 to 0.9 parking spaces per bed to 0.7 parking spaces per bed. A goal of the campus master plan is to increase the percentage of students living on campus from the current 55 percent to a potential 60 to 65 percent (Pesci 2003; University of New Hampshire Transportation Services 2003).

Funding

Starting in fall 2003, students will pay a mandatory $35 transportation fee specifically for nonparking improvements. The transit systems will receive $350,000; the remaining sum will fund improvements to the Amtrak station, the bicycle programs and infrastructure, and a night safety program. Students will have a direct voice in how the funding is distributed (Pesci 2003).

Transportation Planning at Stanford

Stanford University added 2 million square feet of new building space during the 1990s, a 20 percent increase, without increasing peak period auto trips to campus. The story of how this happened provides an instructive example of foresight and planning.

Jeffrey Tumlin, Stanford's transportation programs manager from 1991–1997, described the techniques they used to grow without increasing traffic. Interestingly, the driving force was not environmental concerns—it was bottom line economics. His office was faced with a difficult financial situation in the early 1990s—the campus was growing, new buildings were being built over surface parking lots, and the only way to significantly increase the parking supply was building parking structures. But parking structures are expensive. Each net new parking space can cost more than $30,000, which translated into long-term costs of $150 per month per space every month for the lifetime of the structure. This was ten times what people were used to paying for parking and the campus population was unlikely to accept such an increase.

Another factor facing Stanford was concern from the surrounding community about the impact of Stanford's growth on traffic. This translated into hard-fought political battles on each new building. Stanford was able to negotiate an innovative agreement with Santa Clara County. Under this agreement, they would have the ability to add a substantial amount of new building space, without having to go through a major process on each individual building, in return for agreeing to meet a set of performance standards. The key standards were a cap on peak-period automobile trips to the campus. This is monitored by actual cordon counts, conducted under the county's supervision but paid for by Stanford. If the conditions were not met, Stanford would be required to pay for the cost of expanding key intersection roadways in the surrounding communities—creating a strong financial incentive for the university to meet the goals. The general use permit can be found at http://gup.stanford.edu/otherdocs/final_GUP_conditions.pdf.

The key insight Tumlin had: It was cheaper to pay people not to drive to campus than to build new parking structures. Stanford began a program of paying any employee who did not purchase a parking permit during the year $90, which has since grown to $160. This modest financial incentive convinced many employees to look for other ways to get to campus. They also slowly raised parking rates, increasing them by about 15 percent annually but still holding them well below the actual cost of providing parking.

At the same time they dramatically expanded the alternate ways to get to campus. They invested $4 million in improving bicycle facilities, and got 900 more people to shift from cars to bikes—a cost of $4,400 per person. Compared to the $18 million or more they would have had to spend on parking structures for the same number of people, they considered this a good deal. They also turned a main road through campus into a bike/transit mall, and dramatically increased transit service to campus. One of the unique aspects of this process was the conscious evaluation of economic efficiency as a key element of the planning process.

Stanford also helped develop the idea of on campus car rentals. In Tumlin's words: "Most students use their cars only sporadically, once or twice a week at most. At Stanford, we calculated that if we charged the full cost of parking to students, it would be cheaper for students to rent a car for three quarters of the weekends of the entire academic year than to store a car on campus. Unfortunately, most rental car agencies do not rent to people under 21. To overcome this problem, we contracted with a local rental car agency and leased them low-cost campus space in exchange for renting to all students and maintaining student-appropriate hours. They also agreed to provide bulk rental car discount books that could be sold to students or their parents in lieu of purchasing a vehicle."

The other key investment was to build housing that allowed faculty, staff, and students to live on campus. This was driven by the very high housing costs in the area but has the side benefit of reducing transportation demand. Tumlin said, "By far the most cost-effective way to reduce transportation demand is to house people where they work or go to school. Stanford has built thousands of student and faculty housing units over the last ten years."

References

Associated Students of University of California–Davis. 2002. *Unitrans*, retrieved November 16, found at unitrans.ucdavis.edu.

Balsas, C. 2003. Sustainable Transportation Planning on College Campuses. *Transport Policy* 10:35–49.

Balyi, S. 2003. Personal communication with Steve Balyi, Marketing and Communications Manager, University of British Columbia TREK Program Centre, April 2.

BikeCartAge. 2003. *BikeCartAge Mission and Products*, retrieved April 2, found at www.bikecartage.com.

Bustos, T. 2003. Personal communication with Timothy Bustos, Bicycle/Pedestrian Coordinator, City of Davis, California, March 5.

City of Davis. 2002. *Comprehensive Bicycle Plan*, City of Davis California, retrieved November 17, found at www.ci.davis.ca.us/pw/pdfs/01bikeplan.pdf.

City of Davis. 2003. *City Profile,* City of Davis, California, retrieved January 20, found at www.ci.davis.ca.us/aboutdavis/cityprofile.

Cornell Commuter and Parking Services. 2003. Web site, found at www.transportation. cornell.edu/Commuter_and_Parking_Services.

Corriher, B. 2003. Proposed Decks May See Some Resistance. *The Daily Tar Heel,* January 10, pp. 1–4.

Editorial. 2002. An Affordable Education. *The Chronicle,* March 29, p. 23.

Editorial board. 2003. The Wrong Actions. *The Daily Tar Heel,* January 13, pp. 8–9.

Lieb, D. 1996. *Commuting Solutions,* Cornell University Office of Transportation Services.

Lovegrove, G. 2003. Personal communication with Gordon Lovegrove, Director of Transportation Planning, University of British Columbia TREK Program Centre, April 17–18.

McKiddy, N. 2003. Personal phone interview with Nancy McKiddy, Director of the Associated Students of the University of Montana Office of Transportation, April 3.

Pesci, S. 2003. Personal communication with Stephen Pesci, Special Projects Manager, University of New Hampshire Planning and Transportation Services, May 5.

Statistics Canada. 2003. *Canadian Census 2001—Community Profiles,* retrieved April 16, 2003, found at www12.statcan.ca/english/Profil01/PlaceSearchForm1.cfm.

Takemoto-Weerts, D. 2003. Personal communication with David Takemoto-Weerts, Bicycle Coordinator, University of California–Davis, February 7.

Toor, W., and F. Poinsatte. 1999. *Finding a New Way: Campus Transportation for the 21st Century,* University of Colorado, found at www.colorado.edu/ecenter, Boulder, CO, pp. 46–50.

Town of Durham. 2002. *Town of Durham Information,* Durham, New Hampshire, retrieved May 2, found at www.ci.durham.nh.us/COMMUNITY/towninfo.html.

University of British Columbia. 2003. *Fall 2002 STP Status Report,* retrieved March 18, found at www.trek.ubc.ca/research/stp/status.html.

University of British Columbia Alma Mater Society. 2003. *AMS Bike Cooperative,* retrieved April 9, found at www.ams.ubc.ca/clubs/bikecoop.

University of British Columbia Public Affairs. 2003. *Facts and Figures 2002–2003,* retrieved March 18, found at www.publicaffairs.ubc.ca/ubcfacts/#housing.

University of British Columbia TREK Program Centre. 2003. *Programs and Research,* retrieved March 13, found at www.trek.ubc.ca.

University of California–Davis. 2002. *Long Range Access Plan 2002–2005,* retrieved January 24, found at www.taps.ucdavis.edu/LRPMASTR.htm.

University of California–Davis. 2002. *Transportation and Parking Services,* retrieved December 6, found at www.taps.ucdavis.edu.

University of New Hampshire Office of Sustainability Programs. 1999. *Trip Report and Recommendations on Sustainable Transportation in Campus Communities,* retrieved May 14, found at www.sustainableunh.edu/promise/actions/trip_report.htm.

University of New Hampshire Office of Sustainability Programs. 2003. *Community Bicycle Programs*, retrieved May 12, found at www.sustainableunh.unh.edu/climate_ed/bike_programs/index.html.

University of New Hampshire Transportation Services. 2002. *Parking Permit Prices,* retrieved April 18, found at www.unh.edu/transportation/parking/prices.htm.

University of New Hampshire Transportation Services. 2003. *Transportation Policy Committee Final Report and Recommendations to the President*, retrieved April 28, found at www.unh.edu/transportation/TPC/index.htm.

University of Washington. 2002. *U-PASS Annual Report*, found at www.washington.edu/upass/news_and_reports/upass_reports/annualreport2002.pdf.

University of Washington. 2002. 2003. *Transportation Management Plan*, found at www.washington.edu/community/cmp/cmpfinal/07_TMP_FP.pdf.

Chapter 8

Greening the Campus Fleet

While a university may implement policies that affect how students, faculty, and staff arrive at and depart from campus, the university cannot overlook the image it conveys in the policies concerning its campus fleet vehicles. Alternatively fueled vehicles do not alleviate parking and traffic congestion in and around campus, but their use can improve air quality, mitigate climate change, and increase domestic energy security. While several fuels offer drastically reduced tailpipe emissions, production emissions and energy use must be considered before advocating a fuel's environmental benefits. A study conducted by the Energy Information Agency and the Environmental Protection Agency (EPA) compared the lifecycle greenhouse gas emissions—tailpipe and refinery—of various fuels per mile traveled. The data showed that methanol and ethanol produced more greenhouse gas emissions than gasoline vehicles, while CNG and LPG emitted fewer greenhouse gas emissions than gasoline vehicles (NCSL 1999).

Colleges and universities offer a niche market for alternative fuel vehicles (AFVs) because campus fleets are often centrally fueled and their travel range is mainly limited to campus grounds. Campus maintenance vehicles and shuttle buses dominate AFV purchases because of their fixed routes or limited range. Many universities also serve as demonstration sites for AFV testing. For example, Toyota leased two "market-ready" hydrogen hybrid fuel cells to the University of California–Davis and the University of California–Irvine beginning in December 2002, starting a thirty-month program that will test six vehicles in total. Many manufacturers opt to partner with universities because of the research opportunities. This also presents excellent opportunities for students to be involved in the emerging technology of alternative fuels, as well as the university adaptation of such technology. Investments in alternative fuel infrastructure offer excellent opportunities for universities to partner with municipalities, local organizations, or state agencies to share facilities and expenses. Universities also have the opportunity to create incentives for students to purchase AFVs. These incentives can take the form of reserved parking spots, reduced parking rates, or utilization of the campus-fueling infrastructure. Students, faculty, and staff at the University of California–Santa Cruz can charge their vehicles free of charge at the campus's two electric charging stations (Scott 2003).

This chapter briefly overviews eight alternative fuels, examining fuel sources, available infrastructure, comparative costs, and potential emission reductions. Legislation mandates, financial incentives, and promotional efforts applicable to university fleets are discussed. A close look is taken at the roles of AFVs on several campuses as models for other campuses. Schools may purchase originally manufactured AFVs or convert conventional vehicles to alternative fuels. The latter may void the vehicle warranty, and thus is often undertaken only for older vehicles. Several schools, such as the University of Texas–San Antonio, purchase vehicles through a state contract. This policy does not eliminate AFV options, but may limit selection.

Legislation and Incentives

In 1992, Congress passed the Energy Policy Act (EPAct) to improve environmental quality and enhance our nation's energy security. Titles III–VII outline voluntary and regulatory approaches aimed at developing a self-sustaining alternative fuel market. The EPAct defines alternative fuels to include methanol, ethanol, and other alcohols; blends of 85 percent or more of alcohol with gasoline, natural gas, and liquid fuels domestically produced from natural gas; liquefied petroleum gas (propane); coal-derived liquid fuels; hydrogen; and electricity. The State and Alternative Fuel Provider Program requires state government and alternative fuel provider fleets to purchase AFVs as a percentage of their annual light duty vehicle (LDV) acquisitions. The program only applies to fleets with more than fifty LDVs in one of 125 designated metropolitan areas. As of 2001, 75 percent of LDV purchases were required to be AFVs. In 1998, the Energy Conservation Reauthorization Act amended the EPAct to allow federal, state, and local fleets bound under EPAct to satisfy up to 50 percent of their requirements through

TABLE 8.1

OVERVIEW OF NINE ALTERNATIVE FUEL TECHNOLOGY OPTIONS. (U.S. DEPARTMENT OF ENERGY AFDC 2003; PROPANE EDUCATION AND RESEARCH COUNCIL 2003; EPA 2002; NCSL 1999)

Fuel Type	Production	Availability	Emissions	Costs	Other Properties
Hybrid Electric Vehicles (HEVs)	· Conventional internal combustion engine combined with the battery and electric motor of an electric vehicle	· Three models available in 2003: Honda Insight, Honda Civic, and Toyota Prius · More than 62,000 sold through 2002 · Use conventional unleaded gasoline · Insight was the first to appear in 1999	· Fuel economy increases upwards of 68 mpg, leading to substantially reduced emissions · Prius reduces CO_2 by 50%, NOx, sulfates, and HC by 90%	· Around $20,000, slightly high for its class · Offers substantial fuel savings over lifetime (Insight could save $1,500 a year vs. other cars in its class · $2,000 tax credit for first year	· Forward momentum of braking recharges batteries, sometimes recharged by engine
Natural gas, as compressed natural gas (CNG) or liquefied natural gas (LNG)	· Mostly methane · Extracted from gas wells and from oil wells during crude oil drilling	· 130,000 vehicles in 2003 · 1 in 5 transit vehicles · Existing pipeline infrastructure · 1,300 refueling stations in spring 2002	· CO down 90 to 97% · CO_2 down 25% · NOx 35 to 60% · Little to no PM · Fewer toxic and carcinogenic pollutants	· 15 to 40% less than gasoline and diesel · High-pressure cylinders and fuel lines add $3,500–$6,000 to vehicle costs	· More than 85% produced domestically, rest imported from Canada · Methane is a potent greenhouse gas · Four times less power per volume than gasoline leads to more refueling
Propane, liquefied petroleum gas (LPG), or autogas	· Primarily propane mixed with propylene, butane, and ethane · By-product of natural gas processing and petroleum refining	· Largest worldwide market for alternative fuels · 350,000 LPG vehicles · 3,400 fueling stations	· CO down 30 to 90% · 50% fewer toxins and smog-forming emissions	· Most cost-effective alternative fuel when accounting for operating, ownership, and infrastructure costs · Same price per gallon as gasoline · Vehicles $3,000 to $4,000 more · Conversion to dual-fuel $1,000 to $2,000 · Lowest alternative fuel cost to modify infrastructure	· Higher octane can extend engine life two to three years · 90% of miles per gallon · 45% of U.S. LPG is derived from oil

Fuel Type	Production	Availability	Emissions	Costs	Other Properties
Methanol	· Manufactured from carbon-base feedstocks: natural gas, coal, biomass · Natural gas most economical	· 15,000 methanol FFVs · No longer available at public fueling stations · M100 vehicles no longer manufactured · Converted to MTBE and used as fuel additive since 1979. MTBE is now found to be groundwater contaminant	· M85 reduces hydrocarbons 30 to 40% · Reduces PM and NOx emissions · Formaldehyde released as direct by-product, but reduced indirect formation of formaldehyde	· Slightly lower per gallon than gasoline, but more per mile · Vehicles $300 to $500 more	· M100 can replace conventional diesel · Methanol vehicles offer more power and quicker acceleration · May be used to make hydrogen for fuel cells
Ethanol	· Produced from fermentation of sugar and starch crops such as barley, wheat, sugar beets, corn · 90% of U.S. production from corn	· Used in 10% blend to reduce CO emissions · FFVs run on E85 or E95, but can run on any blend · 150 fueling stations · More than 3 million FFVs sold	· CO down 40% · PM down 20% · NOx down 10% · Sulfate down 80% · Ozone-forming VOCs down 15% · May increase ethanol and acetaldehyde emissions (for E85)	· Priced same as midlevel unleaded gasoline in Midwest, slightly higher in other regions · No cost difference for mass-produced vehicles	· Creates jobs and generates revenue for central U.S. · Production competes with food · Questionable ability to meet large-scale demand · May be used to make hydrogen for fuel cells · Most buyers unaware of fueling options · 75 to 90% of vehicle range and 60% energy content of gasoline
Electricity	· Operate on battery storage of conventional electricity	· More than 4,000 vehicles in 2002 · 875 electric charging stations · Connecting vehicles to the existing grid is the only infrastructure impediment	· No tailpipe emissions · Can further degrade air quality when using coal-generated electricity · Environmental benefits may only be derived in areas of hydroelectric, natural gas, nuclear, solar, and wind generated electricity	· $15,000 to $40,000—up to two times the conventional cost · One-time tax credit up to $4,000 · Fuel $15/month compared to $50/month · Replace batteries every three to six years for up to $8,000	· Only 40 to 120 miles per charge · Charging 4 to 14 hours · Fewer moving parts require less maintenance · Large, heavy batteries minimize cargo and passenger space · Environmental concerns over battery disposal and storage

Fuel Type	Production	Availability	Emissions	Costs	Other Properties
Biodiesel	· Methyl esters produced from agricultural feed-stocks, primarily soybeans, or from waste products such as vegetable oil, cooking grease, and animal fat	· Used as diesel additive to replace sulfur · B20: 20% biodiesel and 80% petrodiesel · B100: pure biodiesel	· Lifecycle CO_2 emissions minimal to none · B20 reduces sulfate emissions 20%, CO 10%, PM 15%, hydrocarbons 10% · B100 reduces sulfate emissions 100%, CO 50%, PM 70%, HC 40% · B20 increases NOx emissions 2% and B100 9%	· B20 30 to 40 cents more per gallon · B100 sells for $1.95 to $3.00 per gallon · Engine modification little to none for minimal additional costs · May need to replace some hoses and seals more often	· Some concern over cold weather capabilities of B100 · Most users lower blend during the winter and/or use engine heating blocks and heated building storage
Hydrogen	· Worldwide, 48% produced from steam reforming of natural gas, 30% from oil (used mostly in refineries), 18% from coal, and 4% water electrolysis	· Most abundant gas in the universe · Can be transported 100 to 200 miles from refineries by truck · Must be cryogenically stored for long-distance	· Produces no tailpipe emissions when used in fuel cells · When burned in internal combustion engine, emits small amounts of CO, NOx, and HC, but no CO_2	· Extensive costs associated with installing an infrastructure for the production, storage, and transport of mass quantities · Some production methods cost more than the fuel it is replacing	· Safety concerns on-board vehicles and with mass distribution because of combustion properties
Hydrogen fuel cells	· Hydrogen combined with air (oxygen) to produce electricity	· Some demonstration products in use · All major automobile manufacturers involved in research · Used as primary source of power or as an auxiliary power to increase fuel efficiency	· Tailpipe emissions only heat and water, but must consider production emissions	· Fuel cell system expensive · See above costs of hydrogen	· Operate on higher efficiency level

All statistics refer to United States data unless otherwise noted. Actual emissions will vary with engine design. These numbers reflect potential reductions based on each fuel's inherently "cleaner" chemical properties and an engine that takes full advantage of those properties. Key: CO: carbon monoxide; CO_2: carbon dioxide; HC: hydrocarbons; PM: particulate matter; NOx: nitrogen oxides; VOCs: volatile organic compounds.

biodiesel. Fleets must purchase and use 450 gallons of pure biodiesel in a minimum of 20 percent blend, in a diesel vehicle weighing over 8,500 pounds, for one AFV credit. This amendment was also a likely stimulus for the biodiesel market. Biodiesel use among EPAct regulated state and alternative fuel provider fleets increased 67 percent between 2000 and 2001 (National Biodiesel Board 2003).

The EPAct provided federal tax deductions for the purchase of clean

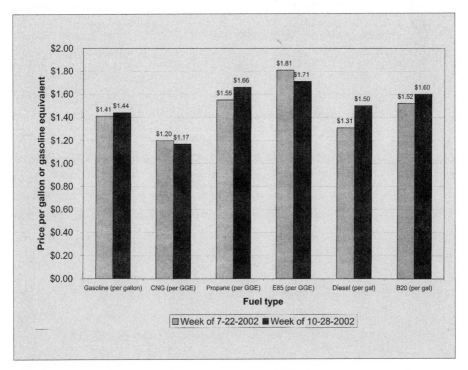

FIG. 8.1
U.S. fuel prices in late 2002. Although alternative fuel prices fluctuate by region and throughout the year, only CNG is consistently below the price of gasoline. (*Source:* U.S. Department of Energy *Clean Cities Alternative Fuel Pricing* report, December 2002)

fuel vehicles or the conversion of existing vehicles to clean-burning vehicles. These tax credits apply only to private colleges and universities because public universities are tax-exempt entities. The amount of tax deductions for qualified clean fuel vehicles is calculated from the gross vehicle weight, the type of vehicle, and the value of the vehicle's clean fuel vehicle property. The following are the maximum allowable deductions:

- Truck or van, gross vehicle weight of 10,000 pounds to 26,000 pounds: $5,000
- Truck or van, gross vehicle weight more than 26,000 pounds: $50,000
- Buses, with seating capacity of twenty or more adults: $50,000
- All other vehicles, excluding off-road vehicles: $2,000

Electric vehicles that qualify for the federal electric vehicle (EV) tax credit are not eligible for the above deductions. Vehicles powered primarily by an electric motor drawing current from batteries or other portable sources of electric current qualify for the electric vehicle tax credit. This includes all dedicated, plug-in-only EVs, and all series and some parallel HEVs. Qualifying EVs and HEVs can receive a credit of 10 percent of the cost of the vehicle (maximum $4,000). A tax deduction of up to $100,000 per location is available for qualified clean fuel refueling property or recharging property for EVs, provided the equipment is used in trade or business. Beginning in 2001, all Clean Fuel tax credits were reduced 25 percent per year until they are phased out by 2005. In addition to federal tax credits, states offer a variety of financial incentives in the form of tax credits, rebates, and allocated funds (DOE 2001; NCSL 1999).

The Clean Cities Program, established by the DOE, encourages voluntary private and public partnerships that increase the use of AFVs and build the supporting infrastructure. Many schools, such as the University of Pittsburgh, play an integral role in a city's ability to receive Clean Cities designation. Clean Cities focuses particularly on niche markets, such as those offered by campuses, where vehicles can easily share central fueling infrastructure. The DOE will provide funding through the State Energy Program to Clean Cities coalitions for the purchase of, and subsequent infrastructure for, vehicles operated on electricity, ethanol, propane, biodiesel, and natural gas (DOE 2003).

University Case Studies

Emory University

Emory University and its 11,600 students are located fifteen minutes east of downtown Atlanta. In the late 1990s, Emory embarked on its first alternate fuel venture with the purchase of electric utility carts, replacing pickup trucks. Community Services utilizes the carts to patrol parking facilities. (*Community Services* refers to the offices of parking, alternative transportation, police, and fire safety.) The university made a strong commitment to AFV purchases in October 2000 when Emory completed a road between its main campus and Clairmont campus. A 1,900-space parking structure,

8.1

To mitigate the
environmental
degradation of this new
road, Emory University
only permits travel by
foot, bike, or alternative
fuel vehicle.

Courtesy of Brian Shaw and
Emory University Alternative
Transportation

1,500 student beds, the Student Activity and Academic Center facilities, and a few other department facilities are located on the Clairmont campus. Because the road crossed through undeveloped forested land, several environmental concerns were raised regarding the project. The eventual compromise resulted in a road only navigable by foot, bike, or AFVs, with the exception of emergency services. Campus departments interested in using the roadway were forced to purchase AFVs. Housing, for example, purchased CNG vans for its trips back and forth. Gates are used to restrict the access of conventionally fueled vehicles.

Emory began operating ten buses in its campus shuttle fleet on CNG in 2000. The vehicles used the City of Atlanta fueling station. When the CNG fleet expanded to nineteen out of thirty-three buses in 2002, the university contracted with the Metropolitan Atlanta Rapid Transit Agency (MARTA) to fuel at one of its CNG stations (Shaw 2003). MARTA operates the third largest

CNG fleet among U.S. transit agencies, running 354 out of 702 buses on CNG (MARTA 2003). Emory has been awarded U.S. Department of Transportation Congestion Mitigation and Air Quality (CMAQ) funding to build a CNG fueling station on campus, but has not yet been able to receive the money. The Georgia state energy department helped secure this funding and will administer it when the money is available. Alternative transportation director Brian Shaw expects the station to eliminate the hesitation of university departments to purchase CNG vehicles.

Emory purchased five electric pick-up trucks from Georgia Power; Facilities Management uses three of the trucks as regular service vehicles, while Community Services uses the other two trucks for parking enforcement and other services. Emory, with the help of the Center for Transportation and Environment (Cte) and the state energy office, secured DOE funding for electric vehicles and infrastructure. Emory provided matching funds from its parking reserve fund. This fund is revenue generated by Parking Services that is set aside for deferred maintenance, debt maintenance, and special projects. Two Ford Th!nk neighbors were purchased for a campus carshare program administered by Cte. The Th!nk neighbor is an electric city car run on nickel-cadmium batteries; it can travel around fifty miles per charge, charges 80 percent in four hours, and reaches maximum speeds of 55 mph. The money also funded the construction of fifteen electric charging stations. The Clairmont structure was designed for additional electric capacity for future fueling stations. Cte also helped Emory secure a congressional earmark to purchase five electric buses for its shuttle fleet. Community Services purchased four Th!nk neighbors for escorts, special events, intracampus transportation, and other odds and ends. Unfortunately, Ford has abandoned its electric vehicle research to focus on fuel cell technology.

During the 2001–2002 school year, Emory Parking Services added a new category for alternate fuel vehicles. Electric, CNG, propane, and/or hybrid vehicles may park in specially designated parking spots in the parking decks. Parking rates remain the same as conventionally fueled vehicles, but spaces are reserved 24/7 in the parking deck of choice. The program was created in response to faculty members' push to be recognized for their clean air efforts. Emory does not market the program and has no plans to offer commuters a discounted rate; the university has chosen not to interfere with private purchasing decisions. Alternate fuel vehicle owners can obtain a special sticker for their parking permit to access spaces. Electric vehicles are the only ones permitted to park in front of charging stations (Shaw 2003; Turner 2002).

University of California–Davis

Unitrans is the student-operated transit service for the University of California–Davis and the City of Davis. Unitrans operates fourteen routes, provides 2.5 million trips annually, and on the average weekday carries nearly 15,000 people. In the late 1990s, Unitrans purchased fifteen dedicated CNG Orion buses and converted one of its London double-decker buses to CNG. Another double-decker bus was converted in 2003. As of 2003, twenty-seven buses out of the forty-four-bus fleet operated on CNG, accounting for 80 percent of annual miles. Unitrans reserves diesel buses for additional frequency needed to meet peak demand. Unitrans also is looking ahead to using biodiesel for its remaining diesel fleet and PuriNOx™. PuriNOx™ is a blend of diesel, water, and fuel additives that can reduce NOx emissions by 19 percent and particulate matter emissions by 54 percent. To fund its alternative fuel purchases and conversions, Unitrans matched CMAQ and Federal Transit Administration funds with student-generated revenue, and used funds from the local air quality management district (Palmere 2002; *Diesel News* 2002).

Unitrans has teamed up with the University of California–Davis Institute of Transportation Studies, City of Davis, Yolo County Transportation District, Air Products and Chemicals, Inc., NRG Tech, Fuel Cell Buyers Consortium, and Clean Air Now on the Hydrogen Bus Technology Validation Program. Two CNG Unitrans buses are being converted to operate on a hydrogen-CNG mixture that significantly reduces carbon-based and nitrous oxide emissions up to 90 percent. Three buses will run on the hydrogen-CNG mixture while two buses will operate on Proton Exchange Membrane fuel cells with compressed hydrogen. The hydrogen-CNG mixture will be 30 percent hydrogen by volume, a mixture that has been proven to reduce NOx emissions by a factor of 20 for light-duty vehicles. Increasing the hydrogen content further reduces NOx emissions, but sacrifices output power and can increase other pollutant levels. Yolo County Transportation District (YCTD)

8.2
The sixteen electric fueling stations at the University of California–Davis are primarily used by Fleet Services, but are also available for public use. Courtesy of UC–Davis Fleet Services

will operate buses in the Sacramento region and refuel at the Unitrans facility. The on-campus Unitrans fueling station will be modified to dispense hydrogen and the hydrogen-CNG mixture during summer 2003 and two buses were operational for fall 2003. Funding for the four-year, $12.3 million project has been provided in part by the State of California, the California Air Resources Board, YCTD, and the Federal Transit Administration. ITS-Davis's goals for 2005 include bringing 10 to 15 FCVs to Davis for campus and city demonstration, developing at least three hydrogen fueling stations, and designing and implementing California's hydrogen infrastructure. The University of California–Davis is studying the first-ever constructed liquid fuel cell bus, a 30-foot transit vehicle powered by a phosphoric acid fuel cell (Miller, M. 2003; UC-Davis ITS 2000).

There are 126 sedans, vans, and pick-up trucks that run on alternate fuels, representing nearly 17 percent of the 747-vehicle campus fleet. These vehicles are available for administrative use, but because of limited range, are used primarily by Facilities Services. There are sixty-five bi-fuel vehicles, sixteen dedicated CNG, thirty-eight methanol, five electric, and two hybrid electric vehicles. The UC–Davis fleet was the first in California to use bio-diesel, and B-20 is currently used for all eighty-five diesel vehicles. Fleet Services purchases 100 percent biodiesel for $1.91 per gallon, and mixes it with conventional diesel for its B-20 mixture. There are sixteen electric charging stations dispersed throughout campus; these stations are available for public use when fleet vehicles are not using them, accounting for roughly 30 percent of their use. Facilities Services also owns and operates a CNG fueling station. Facilities Services is a self-supporting business enterprise that funds its alternative fuel vehicles through its daily and monthly rate structure and modest funds provided by the local air quality district. Fleet Services will continue to purchase AFVs as 75 percent of their LDV acquisitions. As electric vehicle manufacturing has faded away, UC–Davis will move toward ethanol flexible fuel vehicles and CNG. Research also is being conducted to use the new hydrogen infrastructure for fuel cell automobiles as well as buses (Harris 2003).

James Madison University

James Madison University (JMU) is a state-supported university of 15,000 students, located on 400 acres in the urban area of Harrisonburg, Virginia. The JMU campus fleet, including leased vehicles from the State of Virginia, consists of 275 vehicles, about 20 percent of which operate on alternative fuels, predominantly bi-fuel CNG. Most of the CNG vehicles on campus are light-duty trucks. The university purchased ten ethanol vehicles for no additional cost, and pays only $50 more per vehicle for its four leased CNG vehicles. There is a CNG fueling station on campus, which also is used by some state agencies. JMU has had some difficulty getting parts for its CNG vehicles. Its oldest vehicles dated back to 1995, and as the technology has evolved, the new parts have become incompatible with the older models. Seven first-generation GM electric vehicles were purchased from Virginia Power six years ago. Five of the vehicles are still operable, while the other two are used for parts because of their outdated design. The electric vehicles are primarily passenger vehicles and some light-duty trucks for use exclusively on campus; a charging station for each vehicle was installed on campus after their purchase. Alternative fuel purchases began 7 to 8 years ago through proactive initiatives by Recycling Services to pursue other clean air issues. Recycling currently uses an electric vehicle for transportation, not for hauling. The other vehicles are used primarily as support service vehicles. JMU planned to purchase a hybrid passenger vehicle during summer 2003.

Facilities Management works closely on alternative fuel technology with the JMU College of Integrated Science and Technology (ISAT). The Facilities Management building is used as lab space by students for classes and senior research projects, and Facilities Management manager and alternative fuel coordinator Randy Poag splits his time teaching ISAT classes. Recent student research on the performance of a diesel engine using a biodiesel mixture laid the groundwork for the decision to begin using biodiesel for the campus fleet. As early as fall 2003, JMU planned to operate its recycling trucks on a 2 percent biodiesel mixture. JMU hopes to expand the mixture to its entire diesel fleet after the trial run, and hopes to increase to a 20 percent biodiesel mixture within 5 years. The 2 percent biodiesel mixture costs the university an additional 3 cents per gallon, while B-20 would cost an additional 24 cents per gallon. Small batches are produced on campus, but Facilities Management buys in bulk from a local distributor. They hope to negotiate with Food Services to use campus grease.

Facilities Management purchases vehicles through state contract. Fortunately, there are alternate fuel vehicles available through state contract. The vice-president of administration and finance has been very supportive of efforts and dispersing funds to upgrade fleet, which has reduced maintenance expenses. JMU hopes to more aggressively pursue AFV purchases through an expanded relationship with ISAT, the increased integration of CNG vehicles into the maintenance fleet in particular, and an educational campaign for university administration about the importance and applicability of AFVs on campus. JMU has been fortunate to spend very little university money on AFVs, receiving grants from the Virginia Department of Transportation and a National Parks grant to fund its purchases (Puffenbarger 2003; Puffenbarger et al. 2003).

University of Texas–San Antonio

The University of Texas–San Antonio (UTSA) purchases electric utility carts for its fleet because of their low costs, minimal maintenance demands, and durability. The utility carts are replacing trucks and vans for a fraction of the cost. The cart batteries need to be replaced every few years, which is the only major maintenance needed. UTSA also uses Daewoo Tiger ORVs as on-campus vehicles. Although run on conventional gasoline, these ORVs have excellent fuel economy and replace larger vehicles for lower costs. UTSA has a total of forty-five utility carts and ORVs. UTSA uses CNG vehicles in place of electric utility carts for its longer distance and hauling needs, such as mail delivery. UTSA has eighteen CNG, two LPG, and two ethanol vehicles, as well as an on-campus CNG fueling station. UTSA is eagerly anticipating the commercial availability of E-85 at San Antonio fueling stations, scheduled to occur sometime in 2004. The competitive price of E-85 has enticed UTSA to purchase E-85 compatible vehicles in preparation for the fuel availability. E-85 attracts UTSA more so than other alternative fuels because it offers a larger vehicle range, and its compatibility with conventional gasoline provides security from supply disruption. The Diamond Shamrock in San Antonio hopes to replace its diesel pumps with competitively priced biodiesel in the next 1 to 2 years. UTSA will fuel its diesel fleet with biodiesel when the fuel becomes available (Terry 2003).

University of New Hampshire

UNH is gradually switching its transit service and campus fleet from diesel or gasoline to CNG. The university currently maintains one CNG shuttle bus and two CNG Honda Civics. The university plans to install a fast-fill CNG fueling station on campus by spring 2004. The current slow-fill station takes up to seven hours to fill a tank; the fast-fill process can fill a bus tank in 20 minutes. Because this will be the only fast-fill station in northern New England, the fleet will be somewhat constricted in travel range. The facility will be shared with the Town of Durham for public works and school district vehicles. The university received $1.375 million in U.S. Department of Transportation CMAQ funding, as well as some discretionary money for the fueling station. All additional transit vehicles will be CNG. Some of the funding for the fueling station will be set aside to cover the incremental costs of purchasing a CNG vehicle instead of a standard fuel vehicle. Roughly $200,000 will be available for transit vehicles and $250,000 for nontransit vehicles. Any public entity is eligible to participate, although they may be required to provide matching funds. University departments are expected to use most of the funding, with some participation by the Town of Durham for emergency and school district vehicles (Pesci 2003).

University of Pittsburgh

In 1995, the University of Pittsburgh received funding for a three-year usage study of twenty 15-passenger natural gas vans. The Federal Highway Administration and the Pennsylvania Energy Office contributed $719,000 while Equitable Gas Company provided an additional $38,000. The vehicles were maintained by the University's Department of Parking and Transportation, and the School of Engineering conducted the research. The vehicles were purchased to comply with the EPAct of 1992 (*University Times* 1995).

Pitt utilized the CNG vehicles for vanpool routes, which were fueled while parked on campus by a specially trained staff member. The age and wear of the fleet prompted its retirement in 2002. Because no outside funding was secured for van purchasing, and high maintenance costs were associated with owning the vanpool fleet, the university chose to lease vehicles for the vanpool program. Alternative fuel vans were not available from the local fleet provider and thus the university's vanpool program has returned to gasoline vehicles (Miller, K. 2003).

University of Colorado–Boulder

In November 2002, engineering students at the University of Colorado designed and built a 60-gallon batch processor. The processor can produce 45 gallons of biodiesel. To build the processor, the students received a $1,000 grant from the Engineering Excellence Fund and $1,000 from the University of Colorado Environmental Center, and raised $1,500 through a fundraising event. Partnerships were established with Transportation Services and Dining Services. A pilot program was established to run one campus shuttle on B100 between the main campus and the student housing east of campus. The shuttle began operation in April 2003 and through mid-June had logged roughly 2,500 miles. The students are analyzing engine performance, wear, and emissions for the bus, and drivers are keeping daily performance logs.

In spring 2003, students passed a CU Biodiesel referendum allocating

8.3

The unveiling of the first B100 campus shuttle at the annual Alternative Transportation Fair at the University of Colorado.

Photo by Will Toor

$0.49 per student per semester to the new student group for the next four years. CU Biodiesel is a student and community group dedicated to providing petroleum alternatives to the University of Colorado and the Boulder community. This funding will help the organization establish a more permanent location to process cafeteria grease, as well as fund future expansions of the program. The group will build a 500 to 700 gallon processor to use all of the university and some of the community's waste oil. While the new processor is under construction during the 2003–2004 school year, CU Biodiesel will subsidize the incremental cost to the university to purchase biodiesel from a local provider. This allowed up to 75 percent of the shuttle fleet to operate on B100 and B20 in fall 2003. The student organization aims to establish the infrastructure for a student-run biodiesel production facility, and to produce enough biodiesel by 2005 to power all of the university's diesel vehicles, a demand of 50,000 gallons per year. In early 2003, the students processed 300 of the 400 gallons of waste hydrogenated canola oil produced by the university's cafeterias each month.

About 20 percent of each batch is glycerin, which the students are further refining into scented soaps. The group hopes soap sales will be a future source of funding. CU Biodiesel provides a step-by-step guide on how to implement a university biodiesel program on their Web site at www. cu-biodiesel.org. The project has sparked interest in biodiesel and alternative fuel research opportunities on campus, including a chemical engineering lab to study biodiesel production. CU Biodiesel is also in negotiation with a local fueling station to provide B20 and/or B100 on site (Azman 2002).

University of Montana

The BioBus at the University of Montana (UM) shuttles commuters to and from campus using a sliding scale mixture of biodiesel. The demonstration project has logged nearly 47,000 miles since its inception in September 2001. The pilot began operation with an older diesel bus in fall 2001 before its formal debut in February 2002 on a new bus. Student transportation fees purchased the bus and fund the program. In operating a new bus on biodiesel, UM did void the warranty, but strong student support for the program and administrative confidence in the bus's performance eliminated

BOX 8.1 | **MIDDLEBURY COLLEGE: SCHOOL BUS STREAKS ACROSS THE UNITED STATES.**
(BARKER 2003; CNN 2003)

After finals in May 2003, thirteen Middlebury students set off from Vermont to Conway, Washington, in a school bus powered by vegetable oil. The multipurpose trip spread the word about alternative fuels, toured rock climbing spots around the country, and provided many of the students with a ride home. The group also monitored the vegetable oil for fuel quality, fuel sourcing, acceleration, range, emissions, and long-range feasibility. The bus was equipped with two 55-gallon drums of reserve vegetable oil. Donations from restaurants and high schools kept the bus fueled along the 4,103-mile route. For the first half of the trip, the bus used conventional diesel to start up, which heated up and lowered the viscosity of the vegetable oil. Various biodiesel donations along the trip allowed the students to altogether eliminate the use of petroleum diesel for the second half of their journey. The project succeeded on the publicity front, with featured stories on CNN, CBS, Yahoo!.com, the *Chicago Tribune,* and the Associated Press. The trip was extended to Marin County, California, where the bus will be featured in the Transportation Exhibit of the Marin County Fair. The converted school bus will then be auctioned to a good home to continue its promotion of alternative fuels.

the warranty as an issue. The BioBus runs a three-mile route between the UM campus and Dornblaser Field Park and Ride. During spring semester 2003, UM consumed 1,100 gallons of biodiesel. The UM Office of Transportation commenced a late-night shuttle service that utilizes biodiesel for its five-mile route. UM uses B100 when the weather permits, and slides the blend down no lower than B20 when temperatures start to drop.

The Biobus project has outgrown its goal of utilizing all of the waste oil from dining services. The project has now expanded to canola oil and mustard seed oil grown by a local farmer co-operative to meet its demand. Dining Services has agreed to switch to healthier, more biodiesel-friendly canola oil for its fryers, despite a considerable cost increase. The biodiesel is processed by Sustainable Systems LLC, a local Missoula business and the parent company of Montana biodiesel. They are the first commercial biodiesel producer in the State of Montana, and currently operate a 10,000 gallons per month capacity plant. UM expressed interest in operating a shuttle bus with biodiesel around the same time that Montana biodiesel was trying to start up biodiesel production. Part of UM's willingness to pay $3 a gallon for biodiesel is their commitment to seeing the biodiesel producer get its feet off the ground. UM's commitment will help to drive down the cost in the near future. UM also was attracted to biodiesel because it required minimal initial costs and was a more renewable, closed-circle fuel. UM is looking to double its fleet in 2004 with the addition of two buses, both of which will run on biodiesel (McKiddy 2003; Miller, P. 2003).

University of Vermont

In spring 2001 University of Vermont (UVM) Transportation Services began a pilot project to operate one out of seven Campus Area Transportation System (CATS) buses on B-20. Concluding in summer 2002 that the biodiesel bus passed all operating standards, Transportation Services expanded the program to seven buses in fall 2002 and eight buses in 2003. A ninth bus was added for 2003–2004. The university purchases biodiesel from a local distributor for a 15 percent increase in fueling costs, and maintains a B20 mixture for the buses except when supply is limited. The program was initiated by an Environmental Studies senior thesis project, with support from the UVM Environmental Center. In 2004, four CATS buses will be retired and replaced with five CNG buses, and the campus mechanics shop will be modified to store CNG. A 2002 student independent study modeled future air emissions for the nine-bus CATS fleet under six different scenarios. Figure 8.2 shows the emission reductions possible through combinations of updating the campus fleet and implementing B20 and CNG vehicles.

While purchasing nine new model CNG buses would provide the greatest reduction in air emissions, it would be the most expensive option. The independent study concluded that the best financial and environmental program for the CATS fleet would be the periodic replacement of older vehicles combined with B20 use throughout the entire fleet (UVM 2003; Donovan 2002).

West Virginia University

In 1975, the Urban Mass Transit Administration of the U.S. Department of Transportation constructed the Personal Rapid Transit (PRT) system for West

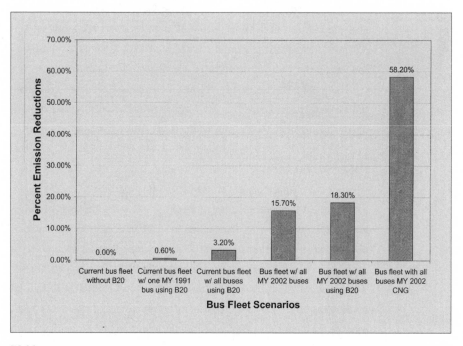

FIG. 8.2
Possible emission reductions were calculated for the University of Vermont Campus Area Transportation System shuttle fleet under six scenarios involving fleet upgrades and biodiesel blends. (Courtesy of Alison Donovan Hollingsworth)

8.4
An aerial view of the
Personal Rapid Transit
system at West Virginia
University.
Courtesy of West Virginia
University Photographic
Services

Virginia University (WVU) as a national transportation research laboratory. PRT is a system of computer-driven vehicles that move along a guided track powered by electric motors, similar to a monorail or light-rail system.

WVU was chosen as the host site for PRT because of the constant travel demand generated by its university community and the wide range of terrain and weather conditions in the region. WVU and its 23,000 students are situated between the Appalachian Mountains and the Monongahela River in Morgantown, a city of roughly 30,000 residents. As an older university located in a compact downtown area, WVU was unable to expand upon its main facility, and instead began the development of two remote campuses, which now hold about 50 percent of WVU facilities. PRT was seen as the best transportation option between the campuses because of the limited road access between the locations, the inability to expand existing roadways, and the desire to avoid the generated traffic congestion.

PRT boasts ridership levels of more than 15,000 students per day during the school year and has transported 56 million people more than 20 million miles since its inauguration in 1975. PRT can travel up to 30 mph and traverses the entire length of the system in under 12 minutes. The system operates seventy-three cars, which can each accommodate up to twenty passengers. The five stations of PRT connect the downtown WVU campus and downtown Morgantown with the Evansdale Residential Complex and the Medical Center Complex. The immense time-saving benefit of the system is the on-board vehicle switching capability of the cars, which allows passengers to bypass intermediate stations and proceed directly from origin to destination. PRT runs two operation modes—scheduled and on-demand. Some cars are dispatched on prearranged schedules while others are available on demand to waiting passengers within five minutes. The PRT cars run on rubber tires with a front guide axel that maintains constant contact with the guideway. PRT travels on elevated tracks roughly half of the time, and travels along the roadway the rest of the time. The electric motors operate primarily from coal-derived and some nuclear power.

The original PRT construction included three stations, forty-five vehicles, and $60 million in contracts. In 1978, the second phase of PRT extended the track system from two miles to four miles, added two stations, twenty-eight cars, and heated power rails to melt ice and snow. The federal government funded 80 percent of the project, while the remaining 20 percent was a combination of university, city, and county resources. Boeing Aerospace Co. designed the system and integrated a regularly scheduled maintenance program that has kept PRT in great operating condition. In 1992, the U.S. Department of Transportation allocated nearly $4 million to replace the heating system and a computer upgrade was performed for another $4 million.

Students, faculty, and staff access the system for no fare with their university ID, constituting roughly 93 percent of ridership. Students currently pay $60 for four months of service, which provides PRT with 50 to 60 percent of its total operating costs. WVU covers the remaining system expenses. Some faculty and staff receive the pass as part of their benefits package, while others pay the same rate as the students for service. This fee is subject to marginal increases every few years to compensate for inflationary operating costs. While WVU has benefited tremendously from the PRT system, the capital costs of the initial infrastructure prevent other universities and cities from following through with their desire to build a similar system. Even with a successful system and well-maintained infrastructure, WVU is struggling to find the $50 to $80 million needed to extend PRT two to three miles to the site of another satellite campus (Hendershot 2003).

Conclusion

This chapter provides detailed accounts of the implementation of alternative fuel vehicles at several campuses. Successful AFV programs in a variety of fuel types allow fleet managers to choose the most suitable fuel based on campus demands and regional availability. Many campuses receive federal and regional funding for their AFV purchases, which helps to establish the program and the infrastructure. Local and regional partnerships also play a large role in the development of infrastructure and the driving down of fuel costs. These partnerships increase outreach and educational opportunities, and in many areas support local economies.

While many campuses began their alternative fuel conversion to comply with the EPAct of 1992, many programs grew out of environmental stewardship and/or student initiatives. University campuses constitute a substantial market niche for AFVs because of their limited travel range, fixed routes, and central fueling stations. Campuses provide excellent research opportunities for the development and testing of alternative fuel technologies. The demonstrated success of alternative fuel vehicles upon university campuses will serve as a foundation for their widespread implementation.

References

Azman, A. 2002. Personal communication with Andrew Azman, Founder, CU Biodiesel, June 17.

Barker, D. 2003. Project Bio Bus Demonstrates Viability of Renewable Resources. *The Middlebury Campus,* May 5, retrieved June 3, found at www.projectbiobus.com/050703press.htm.

CNN Education. 2003. *Vegetable Oil Carries Kids Across Country,* retrieved June 3, found at www.cnn.com/2003/EDUCATION/05/21/vegetable.oil.bus.ap/index.html.

Diesel News. 2002. *PuriNOx Receives EPA Fuel Registration,* retrieved June 23, found at www.dieselnet.com/news/0210lubrizol.html.

Donovan, A. 2002. *UVM Fleet Emission Analysis,* retrieved June 17, found at www.uvm.edu/~bdiesel/BUSemissionsAnalysis.pdf.

EPA Office of Transportation and Air Quality. 2002. *Fact Sheets on Alternative Fuels,* retrieved June 23, found at www.epa.gov/otaq/consumer/fuels/altfuels/altfuels.htm#fact.

Harris, J. 2002. Personal communication with Jack Harris, Manager, Fleet Services, University of California–Davis, June 16 and November 7.

Hendershot, R. 2003. Personal communication with Robert Henderson, Manager, Personal Rapid Transit, West Virginia University, June 18.

MARTA. 2003. *MARTA Media Kit,* retrieved June 10, found at www.itsmarta.com/newsroom/martafacts.htm.

McKiddy, N. 2003. Personal communication with Nancy McKiddy, Director, Associated Students of the University of Montana Office of Transportation, June 18.

Miller, K. 2003. Personal communication with Kathleen Miller, TDM Administrator, University of Pittsburgh, June 3.

Miller, M. 2003. Personal communication with Marshall Miller, Institute of Transportation Studies, University of California–Davis, June 18.

Miller, P. 2003. Personal communication with Paul Miller, Sustainable Systems LLC, June 19.

National Biodiesel Board. 2003. *EPAct Summary,* retrieved June 5, found at www.biodiesel.org/pdf_files/EPACTSummary.PDF.

National Conference of State Legislatures. 1999. *Ground Transportation for the 21st Century.* ASME Press, New York.

Palmere, A. 2002. Personal communication with Anthony Palmere, Assistant General Manager, Unitrans, June 16 and November 6.

Pesci, S. 2003. Personal communication with Stephen Pesci, Special Projects Manager, University of New Hampshire Planning and Transportation Services, May 5.

Propane Education and Resource Council. 2003. *Fleet Economics of Propane*, retrieved June 13, found at www.propanecouncil.org/trade/fleet/economics.htm.

Puffenbarger, C. 2003. Personal communication with Carl Puffenbarger, Assistant Director of Sports Facilities, James Madison University, June 6.

Puffenbarger, C., et al. 2003. Personal communications with Carl Puffenbarger, Assistant Director of Support Services; Dr. Christie Brodrick, ISAT Professor; Randy Poag, Facilities Management AFV Coordinator and Lab Supervisor; Donnie Sites, Fleet Manager; Mike Kauffman, Transportation Manager, James Madison University, June 11.

Scott, W. 2003. Personal communication with Wes Scott, Director, Transportation and Parking Services, University of California–Santa Cruz, June 25.

Shaw, B. 2003. Personal communication with Brian Shaw, Director of Alternative Transportation, Emory University, June 9.

Terry, R. 2003. Personal communication with Roger Terry, Parking and Transportation Manager, Fleet Manager, University of Texas–San Antonio, June 9.

Turner, K. 2002. *University Senate Parking and Transportation Committee Annual Report 2001–2002*, retrieved June 4, found at www.emory.edu/SENATE/Senate/us_cmtes/traffic_ar_02.htm.

University of California–Davis Institute of Transportation Studies. 2000. *Hydrogen Bus Technology Validation Project*, retrieved June 16, found at www.its.ucdavis.edu/e-news/hydrogen.html.

University of Vermont Parking and Transportation Services. 2003. *Biodiesel Buses Project*, retrieved June 17, found at www.uvm.edu/~bdiesel.

University Times. 1995. Pitt to Study Natural Gas Vans. *University Times*, 27(23), July 20. Retrieved May 17, found at www.pitt.edu/utimes/issues/27/72095/14.html.

U.S. Department of Energy. 2003. *Clean Cities*, retrieved June 11, found at www.ccities.doe.gov/what_is.shtml.

U.S. Department of Energy. 2003. *Hydrogen, Fuel Cells, and Infrastructure Technologies Program*, retrieved June 18, found at www.eere.energy.gov/hydrogenandfuelcells.

U.S. Department of Energy Alternative Fuels Data Center. 2003. *Alternative Fuels–Information and Comparison*, retrieved June 16, found at www.afdc.doe.gov/altfuels.html.

U.S. Department of Energy Clean Cities. 2002. *Alternative Fuel Price Report*, retrieved June 24, found at www.afdc.doe.gov/documents/pricereport/pricereports.html.

U.S. Department of Energy Office of Transportation Technologies. 2001. *What Is EPAct? Fact Sheet*, retrieved May 21, found at www.ott.doe.gov/epact/pdfs/what_is_epact.pdf.

Chapter 9

Transportation Demand Management for Elementary and Secondary Schools

Those university students who adopt alternative means of transportation throughout their college careers are much more likely to continue to use alternative modes after they leave the university setting. Along the same lines, encouraging younger students to use alternate modes for traveling to and from school will result in a stronger inclination to consider universities and communities that provide pleasant and effective bus, bike, or pedestrian opportunities, helping to develop lifetime habits.

One significant difference between high school and university transportation is the role of the school bus. In the majority of school districts, transportation to and from the high school is provided by the school bus. Riding is not mandatory, but almost always exists as an option. However, the mere presence of school bus service does not necessarily alleviate parking pressures at the high school level. High school social mores tend to elevate those who own a car, or are friends with someone who does, far above those students who must rely on the yellow school bus. The school bus offers little in terms of flexibility, transporting a student only between school and home. Some students may opt to ride the public bus instead, particularly in the afternoon, to expand their destination options. Having a car—and especially a parking permit—distinguishes students from the lower classmen that ride the "loser cruiser." Affluent families perceive a student car as a necessity, alleviating the stress of chauffeuring the child. For the student, getting a license and a car is somewhat of a rite of passage and a badge of honor. But as parking pressures increase at high school campuses, "the make-or-break status symbol is less the license or the car than the parking permit, an increasingly scarce resource" (Gross 2003).

While the personal automobile may offer a gain in teenage social status, it comes at the cost of increased responsibility. According to New Milford,

Connecticut, high school principal Joanne Mendillo, "Driving to school has become such a distraction to the learning process that it's handicapping kids in a much, much greater way than people realize. . . . They are so convinced that they absolutely have to have the car at 16, that to work 40 hours a week to pay for it is not even a decision. It's just something that you do." This extra time at the job amounts to less time for homework and sleep. In 1992, New Milford High School began issuing permits only to students with at least fifteen credits toward graduation, essentially only seniors. When students were confronted about the repeal of their parking permits, they responded to an attack on their identity. Students accustomed to driving to school see the activity as a right, not a privilege. In some cases, the school district per-petuates the student reliance upon automobiles by not providing late buses to kids who participate in extracurricular activities (Judson 1992).

Typically only juniors and seniors are eligible to drive their own cars to school, since the driving age in the United States is generally 16 years of age. These students must compete with faculty and staff for school park-ing spaces. When parking pressures increase, some schools may choose to expand parking facilities to meet excess demand. There are several obstacles and disincentives to this approach. Many schools simply do not have available land. Often, cash-strapped school districts will be under pres-sure to spend money in the classrooms, rather than on parking lots. There is also the opportunity cost of using adjacent land for parking. The decision to install new parking competes with the decision to build more athletic fields, a larger auditorium, or campus green space. Many communities implore school districts to expand parking due to the overflow of students into sur-rounding residential neighborhoods. Residents complain when they are not able to find parking in front of their own homes and when student drivers are disrespectful of residential property. A residential parking permit (RPP) program can reduce the student overflow by limiting temporary parking to a few hours. Several successful applications of this approach are discussed in previous chapters.

Schools with limited parking capacity may choose to curtail student parking through a number of restrictions. Some schools bestow parking privileges only to seniors; other schools charge for parking on a semester or yearly basis. Nicolet High School in Glendale, Wisconsin, utilizes several

parking strategies. Only students who achieve above a C-plus average are eligible for parking. These students also must participate in a school- or community-based activity. Parking students must carpool, and parking costs $100 per semester as of 1999. Nicolet High School had 215 assigned parking spaces for its 640 juniors and seniors in 1999. In Woodinville, Washington, high school permit rates vary upon whether or not the student carpools. Carpooling students pay $30 while students who drive alone pay $60. Students sign up on waiting lists for the precious spots while half-empty school buses idle outside (Coles 1999). To reduce car trips to and from school, the Boulder, Colorado, Valley School District created the position of student transportation coordinator. The coordinator deals specifically with integrating alternate modes at the secondary level to reduce traffic congestion and improve air quality. This position is a unique partnership between the City of Boulder and the Boulder Valley School District.

This chapter explores the negative impacts of the recent trend to replace centrally located neighborhood schools with larger schools built on the periphery of the community. Lost in the transition are the ability of students to walk or bike to school and the role of the school as a community anchor. The chapter progresses into a series of case studies highlighting the different techniques used to reduce the auto-dependency of students at elementary and secondary school levels. The following four main themes arise when examining these techniques:

- High school programs combat the social impediments to alternative transportation, confronting the role of the personal automobile as a status symbol.

- Transportation curricula are introduced or enhanced. Designed to educate all levels of school children, these curricula follow the evolution of the transportation system, correlate air and water pollution with various transportation modes, and explore current and future transportation alternatives.
- Elementary and middle school programs focus upon increasing pedestrian and bicycle safety within school neighborhoods. An increase of student mobility is promoted for health purposes, with the positive externality of improving the environment.
- Partnerships between school districts, local organizations, and municipalities offer excellent opportunities to decrease the growing dependence of school children upon the automobile.

Poor Public Policies and the Age of "Mega-School Sprawl"

The National Trust for Historic Preservation believes that the small school you could walk to in a neighborhood where you knew your neighbors is being replaced by "mega-school sprawl"—giant educational facilities in remote locations to which no child can walk. The National Trust for Historic Preservation is a private nonprofit preservation organization that works to save diverse historic places and revitalize communities. In their report, *Historic Neighborhood Schools in the Age of Sprawl: Why Johnny Can't Walk to School,* the National Trust identifies public policies at fault for the increasingly common trend of schools "designed to serve as stand-alone educational facilities where community access is limited rather than encouraged." Central to this trend are acreage standards recommended to states by the Council of Educational Facility Planners International (CEFPI). CEFPI recommends a minimum area of ten acres for an elementary school, twenty acres for a middle school, and thirty acres for a high school. Additionally, each school should have one acre per 100 students. Acreage standards are not mandated and thus state compliance varies; New York requires only three acres for an elementary school while Minnesota mandates sixty acres for each high school. However, the majority of states rely upon these standards when evaluating school expansion to meet a growing population. The older, often historic schools average only two to eight acres and typically lie in densely developed neighborhoods with little room to offer for development. Acreage guidelines may be relaxed in large urban centers. However, in many small and midsize communities, acreage standards are used to defend the decision to build on large, often cheaper blocks of rural or undeveloped land around the periphery of the community.

Planning or zoning code exemptions, funding formulae, new building codes, and insufficient operating budgets contribute heavily to "school sprawl." Most renovation projects face a "two-thirds rule," where the renovation is preferred to new construction only if remodeling costs fall under two thirds of the cost of new construction. Because tight budgets force school boards to choose between new teachers and minor maintenance, older schools are often left to deteriorate in the expectation that voters will pass a new school referendum. A Massachusetts report found that state funding sources for school maintenance and repair have the "unintentional side effect of rewarding schools that allow their facilities to deteriorate." Real estate developers or property owners can influence local policy by donating land to school districts, thereby improving the value of new subdivisions and altering a community's growth patterns. The spread of families and neighborhoods to the outskirts of a community may warrant the construction of a peripheral school to meet the needs of an expanding community. However, it also may be argued that the numerous factors that move schools to peripheral areas preempt urban sprawl, that families follow the school. While researching planning and development activities in Lincoln, Nebraska, W. Cecil Steward, dean emeritus of the College of Architecture at the University of Nebraska, concluded that "the public school system ... is the most influential planning entity, either public or private, promoting the prototypical sprawl pattern of American cities." He refers to public school systems as "advance scouts for urban sprawl."

The National Trust calls on school administrators, public officials, and concerned citizens to reverse school sprawl policies and to establish policies that will preserve and upgrade historic neighborhood schools. The National Trust makes the following twelve recommendations:

- Put historic neighborhood schools on a level playing field with new schools. Eliminate funding biases that favor new construction over school renovation and good stewardship.

- Eliminate arbitrary acreage standards that undermine the ability of established communities to retain and upgrade (or replace on the same site, when necessary) historic and older schools that could continue to serve as centers of community.
- Avoid "mega-school sprawl"—massive schools in remote locations that stimulate sprawl development and are accessible only by car or bus.
- Develop procedures for accepting land donated by developers for new schools. Land in "sprawl locations" that are inappropriate for schools should be rejected.
- Encourage school districts to cooperate with other institutions (e.g., government agencies, nonprofits, churches, and private businesses) to share playgrounds, ball fields, and parking, as well as to provide transit services, when appropriate.
- Establish guidelines, training programs, and funding mechanisms to ensure adequate school building maintenance. Create disincentives for school districts to defer needed maintenance and allow buildings to fall into disrepair.
- Require feasibility studies comparing the costs of new schools with those of renovating existing schools before new schools are built and existing ones abandoned. Hire only architects with experience in rehabilitation work to conduct such studies. These studies also should consider the impact of a school's closing on existing neighborhoods, long-term transportation costs, and municipal service burdens. Finally, these studies must be presented to the public for comment before projects move forward. If they are presented only to the superintendent and school facilities committee, their use is limited.
- Reexamine exemptions given to local school districts from local planning, zoning, and growth management laws.
- Work to ensure that a minimum of 50 percent of the students can walk or bike to school in cities, towns, and suburbs. Promote Safe Routes to School legislation in all states.
- When a historic school cannot be preserved and reused, school districts and/or local governments should implement plans for the building's adaptive use or replacement so that it does not become a source of blight in the neighborhood.

- Promote "smart codes" legislation to encourage the rehabilitation and modernization of historic schools as well as other still-serviceable buildings.
- Provide education and training in school renovation techniques and options for school facility planners, contractors, private consultants, architects, school board members, municipal officials, and others.

Several states now recognize the role of older schools in American communities. These schools serve additional purposes as parks and green space, can enhance property values, and preserve the historic or older sections of towns. As of 2002, New York, Washington, Florida, and New Hampshire recommended less acreage than CEFPI standards. Maryland schools face no acreage standard and the state promotes reinvestment in existing schools. Indiana has lifted the acreage standard for historic schools. New Jersey adopted a rehabilitation code to decrease the costs of older school renovation. In Durham, North Carolina, neighbors of the George Watts Elementary School spent more than 120 hours working pro bono to create detailed engineering, architectural, and cost analyses of renovating the school. Residents discovered the renovation was feasible and cost-effective, repudiating the previous findings of a hired consulting firm and thereby preserving "the most cohesive element of the community." Communities in Idaho, Indiana, Wisconsin, and Minnesota also have pulled together to accomplish successful renovations of older neighborhood schools. A list of successful case studies and an appraisal guide for renovation projects can be found in The National Trust publication *A Community Guide to Saving Older Schools* (National Trust 2000).

The negative impacts of larger schools located in outlying areas have been growing concerns of citizens across the country. Despite a 70 percent rise in population between 1940 and 1990, the number of elementary and secondary schools declined from 200,000 to 62,000. In the last decade, the number of secondary schools hosting more than 1,500 students has doubled (LGC 2003). In November 1999, Duke University student Christopher Kouri prepared a report for the South Carolina Coastal Conservation League (SCCCL). *Wait for the Bus: How Low Country School Site Selection and Design Deter Walking to School and Contribute to Urban Sprawl* provides the factual

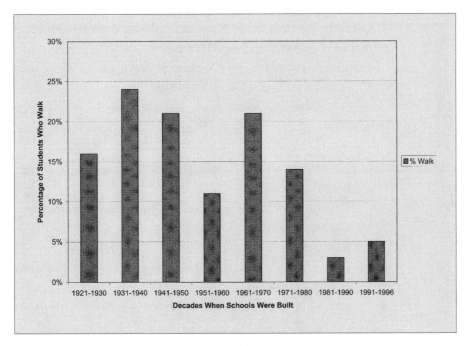

FIG. 9.1
South Carolina Low Country schools show fewer students walk to schools built in recent decades.
(Courtesy of South Carolina Coastal Conservation League)

data to substantiate citizens' concerns. Through a survey of 200 schools, the SCCCL found that school sites since 1971 have expanded 33 percent in acres per student, and schools built after 1983 were 41 percent larger on an acre per student basis. The South Carolina Department of Education enacted acreage requirements for all new construction in 1983. However, new schools built after 1983 were on average 60 percent larger than state acreage mandates. Looking for enormous sites, school officials placed new schools on rural or undeveloped land. These school sites impeded the students' ability to walk or bike to and from school. Schools built after 1983 achieved only 4 percent walking levels, while schools constructed prior to 1983 averaged 16 percent walking levels. Their location strains the ability of community members to use the playing fields, gymnasium, and other facilities during off hours.

Typically in South Carolina, the school district will not provide bus services to children within a 1.5-mile radius of the school. However, busy roads or other dangerous situations prompt the district to offer hazard busing to kids in the area. *Wait for the Bus* found an increase in every decade of the number of students receiving hazard busing. Schools built prior to 1971 offered hazard busing to only 6.3 percent of students, while in the 1990s, hazard busing serviced 28 percent of children.

Wait for the Bus cites five principal explanations correlating urban sprawl with the location of a new school:

- The edge of town boasts the only land compliant with high-acreage design requirements.
- School districts often accept "free" land from real estate developers who plan to build houses in an area.
- New school construction carries city services, such as water and sewer, into an undeveloped area, opening the door for residential and commercial developers.
- City government may face few restrictions in annexing a school outside city limits; nearby landowners may then join the municipality and possibly supersede rural development restrictions.
- Residents are drawn to a new school and development increases, altering the surrounding area.

In South Carolina, local districts maintain autonomous control over the selection process for a new school and are neither required to cooperate with planners and other government officials nor to coordinate the location with an existing community development plan. The SCCCL calls upon the State Department of Education to provide leadership, education, and technical assistance to local districts to better integrate school design with the needs of the community. The report advocates the reduction of acreage standards and a greater focus on the advantages of centrally located schools in preserving communities and mitigating sprawl. Local school districts are encouraged to include a local planner in the site selection process, to make full use of an existing road network to promote walking and biking, and to open school plans to comments from the local jurisdiction. To both local and state officials, the report recommends the incorporation of city buses into the school transportation plan, the channeling of more federal highway dollars toward increasing the safety of pedestrian and bicycle facilities in school neighborhoods, the preparation of a transportation cost-benefit analysis during the school planning process, and the maximization of existing parking facilities (Kouri 1999).

The Local Government Commission (LGC) argues that the deterioration of many schools in older neighborhoods is one of the principal drivers of families into the suburbs. The LGC is a nonprofit, nonpartisan membership organization composed of elected officials, city and county staff, and interested individuals who serve as a complement to the League of California Cities and the California State Association of Counties. LGC assists local governments in establishing and nurturing a healthier human and natural environment, a more sustainable economy, an actively engaged populace, and an equitable society. In 1997 and 2000, LGC organized two conferences to discuss the importance of smaller schools and promote the role of the school as a community anchor. "Healthy Schools, Quality Communities" and "Bringing Schools to the Community and the Community to the Schools" highlighted case studies of multiuse schools and the instrumental collaboration between cities, counties, and school administrations to develop successful schools in central locations. The leading examples include schools where the gymnasium doubles as an evening fitness center, schools whose playgrounds and yards are city parks, county libraries situated adjacent to high schools, and high schools whose auditoriums are used regularly by the community (LGC 2003).

The LGC partnered with the National Association of Realtors in 2001 to propose answers to the question: "How can we create neighborhood-based schools that have the potential to revitalize and stabilize communities?" The outcome of this collaboration is the study *New Schools for Older Neighborhoods: Strategies for Building Our Communities' Most Important Assets.* The study emphasizes three answers: maximize public resources through partnerships with city parks or organizations such as the YMCA; create more livable, walkable communities with less auto-dependency and sprawl; and attract and keep community members in older, often deteriorating neighborhoods. The publication highlights five communities that succeeded in locating new or improved schools in older neighborhoods through innovative approaches. For example, one school sold part of its land holdings to an apartment complex developer to raise funds for a massive renovation project. In Los Angeles, a deteriorated mall was chosen as the site for a new state-of-the-art school. The placement jumpstarted revitalization projects, and the school is the anchor of a new mixed-use neighborhood (LGC 2002).

Breaking Down Social and Safety Barriers

Beyond these big picture-planning decisions on school size and location, there are many strategies that can be used at individual school sites to manage transportation impacts. Some of these, such as managing parking supply and pricing, and providing student and employee transit passes, are very similar to the techniques used in higher education. Typically, school districts do not have the same level of transportation planning expertise and funding that are common within institutions of higher education, so many school districts have not explored these strategies. The information in the previous chapters of this book should be useful to these schools.

However, there are two other major differences between K–12 education and higher education. First, the cultural pressure to drive is much stronger at the secondary school level. Because of this difference, there are a number of programs that have developed to address these social barriers to alternative modes. In addition, there is a different set of safety concerns, particularly for younger children. Efforts to increase student use of nonmotorized transportation require more emphasis on providing safe routes than is required at the postsecondary level. In this subsection, we profile a number of efforts targeting both social and safety issues in schools.

A study conducted by a group of high school students in Boulder, Colorado, illustrates some of the social issues. Students in an AP statistics class at Boulder High School conducted a transportation survey of their peers in December 2001. The students confirmed that the automobile was the most popular mode of transportation both to and from campus. Of the students that usually drove to school, 49 percent carpooled, with the average carpool containing 2.9 people. Seventy-seven percent of students lived within 2.5 miles of the school and 76 percent spent less than twenty minutes traveling to school. By comparing transportation habits during the morning and afternoon commute, the students found a 10 percent increase in public bus use in the afternoon, and a 10 percent decrease in

TABLE 9.1

BOULDER, COLORADO, HIGH SCHOOL STUDENT TRANSPORTATION SURVEY RESULTS.
TWO HIGH SCHOOL TRAVEL SURVEYS DEMONSTRATE SIMILAR RESULTS, REVEALING THE
DOMINANCE OF THE AUTOMOBILE. (HILLIARD 2002A; MOODY ET AL. 2001)

Mode of Transportation	Boulder High School %	Fairview High School %
School bus	8	3.1
RTD public bus	24	24.5
Car	63	—
Driven by parent	—	35.9
Carpool w/student	—	25.4
Walk	2	7.2
Bike	2	3.6
Other	1	—

automobile use during the afternoon. Fifty-seven percent of students had
an extracurricular activity immediately after school. This afternoon shift
away from car use toward the public bus may correspond to the inability of
parents to pick up their kids during the midafternoon because of work commitments. The school day begins at roughly the same time as the common
workday, yet the dismissal of school usually occurs a few hours before the
workday ends.

Student analysis of the results drew two substantial conclusions. First,
the data "show that many kids living nearby school choose to drive to school
regardless of their close proximity." Secondly, "regardless of the distance one
lives from Boulder High School, if there is a car at the disposal of the student, he or she will typically drive to school when given the opportunity."
These conclusions are consistent with students' responses about how they
feel when riding the public bus. Given the choice of good, bad or neutral, 31
percent of students felt "bad" about riding the public bus and only 13 percent felt "good" (Moody et al. 2001).

Perhaps the most striking aspect of this survey is the comparison to
University of Colorado students. The University of Colorado main campus is
located in the same neighborhood as Boulder High School—the high school
campus is literally located a five-minute walk down a hill from the campus.
The two campuses can be accessed by the same bicycle paths and lanes and

TABLE 9.2

STUDENTS' TRANSPORTATION REASONING. FAIRVIEW HIGH SCHOOL STUDENTS
PROVIDE A WIDE ARRAY OF REASONS WHY TO DRIVE OR TO TAKE ALTERNATIVE
MODES TO SCHOOL. (HILLIARD 2002B)

Reasons for Driving to School	Reasons for Taking Alternate Modes
Long distance	Parents won't drive
Long bus trip	Likes independence
Need clean clothes	More time flexibility
Difficult to walk in high heels	Don't have to bum rides
Afraid of "helmet hair"	Convenient bus routes
Tight schedule	Avoid traffic and parking hassles
School starts too early	Comparable time travel
Flexibility for after school travel	High cost of driving

the same transit routes. Yet the mode share for college students is radically different than for high school students. For college student trips to campus, only 11 percent of trips are by car, 55 percent walk to school, 23 percent ride their bicycle, and 11 percent use transit (National Resource Center 2001). The largest difference is that high school students are an order of magnitude less likely to walk or bike. And this is in an area known as a mecca for outdoor activities such as bicycling.

Vancouver's off ramp Program

Better Environmentally Sound Transportation (BEST) of Vancouver, British Columbia, developed a pilot secondary school trip reduction program called off ramp. Existing programs that promote transportation alternatives in the workplace were adapted to be compatible with the specific needs of high school environments. off ramp has a long-term focus of developing strategies to get students walking, cycling, and taking transit more often. off ramp raises awareness of transportation issues, sponsors school events that offer the opportunity and incentives to try transportation alternatives, and works to dismantle barriers to sustainable transportation in high school communities.

Rather than merely preaching to students about the negative impacts of automobile use, off ramp trains student leaders to address and tackle the attitudes and circumstances limiting the use of alternative transportation among their peers. BEST's program manager worked with student leaders at fourteen urban and suburban schools while **off ramp** was first developed. The goal of **off ramp** is to train and support these students in developing activities to reduce the social impediments to alternative transportation in their local community. Youth leaders are taught (and peer-mentored) communication skills, group-building strategies, the steps of project development, and increased environmental awareness.

off ramp clubs try to lessen the perception that an automobile is necessary to "fit in." The student leaders are encouraged to tackle this issue any way they choose by adapting existing activity ideas and/or generating new ones. The variety and innovative nature of **off ramp** activities and strategies are limited only by the imagination of its student leaders. For instance, Vancouver's rainy winters have inspired cycling fashion shows to challenge the cliché that all cyclists wear spandex or dress like couriers. A scorecard was developed for spectators and judges to rate the style, comfort, water repellency, and safety of the outfits. There have been drama skits to overturn the dating myth that a car is a prerequisite to having a good time, and the "How Slow Can You Go?" bike race has raised the "cool factor" of cycling. Prizes and small giveaways have been randomly distributed to students traveling car-free at special events—hot chocolate for pedestrians in the morning, water or juice bottles for students at the bus stop.

Student leaders promote awareness and education in conjunction with domestic and international events. **off ramp** sponsors Car-Free Day (European Union), Walk to School Day (international), Cycle in the Rain Day (British Columbia), Earth Day (international), and Clean Air Day (Canada). Group bike rides have been organized to raise awareness and connect students with similar interests. School spirit can be augmented if schools compete against each other (or join together) through these bike rides; the administration has supported such activities by offering for the losing principal to wear the winning school's team jersey.

According to Arthur Orsini, founder of **off ramp**, "Stress is an increasing factor in the lives of teens. And for the young people drawn to **off ramp**, their commitment to environmental and social issues can intensify that burden. Increased awareness of climate change, greenhouse gas emissions, loss of

9.3

Creative events, such as the "How slow can you go?" bike race, draw positive attention to alternative transportation.

Courtesy of Arthur Orsini

farmland and the social costs of our car culture, while motivating and empowering in the long run, can ride heavy on young idealistic shoulders. In any program such as this, work must offer a balance of play and fun. **off ramp** addresses the issues in a playful empowering manner—such as skits, mock ads, or games of "Who Wants to be an Environmental Millionaire?" And fun in ways that do not strictly adhere to program goals, such as holding a meeting in an ice cream shop, going on a group bike ride, or learning theatre improvisation as a communication tool. And having some chocolates on hand doesn't hurt!"

The **off ramp** 2001 annual report demonstrates that the program's impacts extend beyond the student body. "Most teachers in our pilot schools believe in and apply the principles of **off ramp**. The posters, postcards, and buttons can be spotted on the walls of nearly every classroom. Some teachers even go so far as to sport **off ramp** wear or have their bicycles visibly stored in the classroom. From their participation in planning and carrying out events, it is obvious the teachers in **off ramp** schools are spreading the good word."

The **off ramp** pilot program received primary funding from the Climate Change Action Fund of the Canadian government, recognized for its efforts to raise awareness and encourage action about climate change through public education and outreach. Other local organizations provided additional funding. **off ramp** has designed a framework to expand its services across North America, offering training, program resources, and support to those interested in becoming a coordinator for schools in their area. **off ramp** envisions the part-time position to be suitable for an individual working for a school district, municipality, or regional environmental nongovernmental organization dedicated to education and sustainable transportation, and estimates program costs, excluding salary, to be roughly $13,500 for a four-school launch of the program. **off ramp** and BEST are in the process of cataloguing 101 of the coolest ideas and most successful strategies worldwide for youth to take action on sustainable transportation. Visit the **off ramp** Web site for more information at www.offramp.ca (Orsini 2002).

Transportation Curricula

Educating students about the impacts of their transportation choices upon our environment and health is critical to the development of smart commuters. Transportation curricula may be most effective when developed and enhanced over several levels of school. Transportation curricula may be taught in tandem with school curricula or used in organized group activities outside of the classroom. Many curricula are designed to educate students about transportation issues while furthering students' knowledge and skills in core subjects such as math, geography, science, writing, and social sciences. Transportation curricula will raise students' awareness of their transportation impacts and options, creating smart commuters who are more likely to seek out universities and communities with transportation options.

The 4-H Club—*Going Places, Making Choices*

The National 4-H Council developed an innovative curriculum for grades 9–12 that raises awareness about transportation, present and future personal mobility choices, and the impacts of those choices upon the environment. *Going Places, Making Choices* challenges youth to understand the interdependence between economic, environmental, social, and political concerns. Made possible by support from American Honda Motor Company, *Going Places, Making Choices* features five units focused on different aspects of transportation, each involving a hands-on project for the students:

- Unit 1: Students conduct community interviews and build a timeline linking community and transportation developments.
- Unit 2: Students record a personal travel assessment and evaluate the walking condition of their school neighborhood and community. Links are established between energy consumption and various modes of transportation.
- Unit 3: Model greenhouses demonstrate the impacts of greenhouse gases. Students learn about ozone depletion, climate change, and air pollution.
- Unit 4: Students learn to connect land use and transportation by creating a community. Students must reconcile community interests such as housing, business, recreation, and agriculture, with the natural constraints of the environment.
- Unit 5: Students perform a personal attitude and value assessment. The curriculum culminates in a community service project (National 4-H Council 2001).

Smart Moves

Climate Solutions, a branch of the Earth Island Institute, designed *Smart Moves for Washington [State] Schools,* a lesson guide with activity worksheets aimed at K–12 students. Climate Solutions aims to stop global warming at the earliest point possible by helping the Northwest become a leader in practical and profitable solutions. These classroom activities help students gain a better understanding of transportation choices, and how those choices affect their communities, future generations, and the environment. Elementary, middle, and high school classes have activities specifically tailored to their level of learning. A "Run-off Relay" simulates the interaction of stormwater to impervious surfaces, linking transportation to water quality. A trip log helps students calculate their CO_2 emissions, correlating air pollution with transportation choices. High school students brainstorm a TDM plan for their school and are encouraged to present their ideas to the administration. High school students also discuss the difficulties of design-ing a city and what has changed over time, culminating in the design of an ideal city (Climate Solutions 1999).

Extreme High School Clean Air Challenge

The American Lung Association of Sacramento-Emigrant Trails (ALASET) has hosted the Extreme High School Clean Air Challenge for more than eight years. The annual program reaches six to eight high schools to educate stu-dents about the detrimental health effects of poor air quality and moti-vate students to find ways to reduce air pollution. Major promotion efforts focused on walking or biking to school at least once a week, carpooling, organizing their schedule to reduce trips, and becoming familiar with low-emission vehicles. Prior to 2003, the program coordinated with the student government of each high school to plan the Challenge during a school day in May, which is Clean Air Month. The student government promoted the event and ALASET provided training through a one-day Youth Leadership Institute, which included expert talks in air quality and media outreach. A local band performed during lunch, clean air materials were distributed, zero-emission vehicles were displayed, and a bike was raffled off to those who arrived at campus via alternative transportation. The student govern-ments conducted a parking lot count pre-Challenge and one at the Chal-lenge event. Some schools decreased parking levels up to 30 percent.

The Extreme High School Clean Air Challenge adopted a new format for 2003. ALASET provides a fifty-minute assembly presentation with a mul-timedia format, interactive games, and prize giveaways. A local TV reporter, popular with teens, hosts the assembly. During the 2001–2002 school year, the presentation reached more than 13,000 students and faculty at nine high schools. Grants from the Sacramento Metropolitan Air Quality Man-agement District (AQMD), the Yolo-Solano AQMD, the Sacramento Munic-ipal Utility District, and the *Sacramento Bee* make the Challenge possible (ALASET 2002; Koster 2003).

Center for Appropriate Transport

The Center for Appropriate Transport (CAT) in Eugene, Oregon, is a nonprofit organization committed to community involvement in manufacturing, using, and advocating sustainable modes of transportation. CAT focuses on education and youth projects that provide kids with a hands-on transportation-based curriculum that is nearly nonexistent in public schools today. CAT programs challenge young people to gain real world manufacturing and business skills by allowing full-scale participation in all aspects of its programs. CAT operates a Bike Lab out of its Eugene Bicycle Works Shop that teaches kids bike maintenance and construction and the relation of the principles of physics and geometry to bicycle design and performance. Students also learn wheelchair repair and finish the session with a fully restored bicycle.

Another aspect of CAT is the Eugene Rack Works. This student-run business venture provides the Eugene–Springfield area with high-quality tubular bicycle racks manufactured by teens. CAT participants organize and provide valet bicycle parking at most of Eugene–Springfield's outdoor events. CAT also engineered a mobile school presentation to challenge students to brainstorm ways to decrease car dependency and share with students a diverse assortment of human-powered vehicles (CAT 2001).

Health and Safety Programs

In 1995, the Centers for Disease Control and Prevention (CDC) conducted a Nationwide Personal Transportation Survey of children ages 5 to 15. The survey found that only 13 percent of children walked or biked to school. Of the students who lived within one mile of the school, 31 percent walked. Less than 2 percent of students within two miles of school biked. While distance is the primary deterrent for walking or biking to school, concerns over traffic and crime are substantial factors in parents' decisions. Several techniques may be used in tandem to improve bicycle and pedestrian safety in school neighborhoods. Improved signage and stricter enforcement of road regulations will increase driver awareness in the area. Physical improvements to intersections, crosswalks, and sidewalks provide a safer infrastructure for school children. Finally, programs and curricula can teach children how to become safe and responsible bicyclists and pedestrians.

Linked to the decrease of students walking and biking to school is the rise of youth obesity. The percentage of overweight youth ages 6 to 11 has increased from 4 percent in 1963–1965 to 15 percent in 1999–2000. Similarly, the percentage of overweight youth ages 12 to 19 has increased from 5 percent in 1963–1965 to 15 percent in 1999–2000 (CDC 2002c). To increase physical activity among children, two of the national health objectives for 2010 call for increases in the number of children walking and biking to school (CDC 2002a). The following section highlights programs that improve the safety of walking and biking conditions around schools, and emphasizes the physical benefits of such activities.

"Kidswalk-to-School"

In order to encourage healthier transportation choices by parents and children, the CDC published *Kidswalk-to-School: A Guide to Promote Walking to School*. This publication aims to get children to walk or bike to school in groups accompanied by alternating neighborhood adults. This emphasizes daily physical activity and improved pedestrian safety and focuses the community on creating a healthier, safer, and more walkable environment. The CDC offers advice on theme days, contests, and other activities to attract

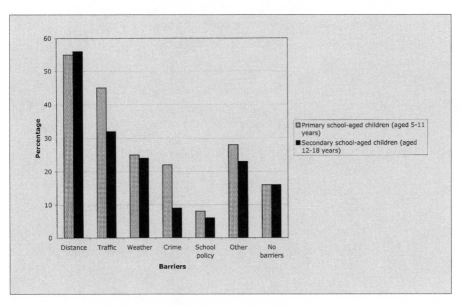

FIG. 9.2
The barriers to walking and biking for elementary and secondary schoolchildren can be numerous. Parents of elementary or secondary schoolchildren have slightly different concerns about their children walking or biking to school. (Centers for Disease Control and Prevention 2002a)

kidswalk-to-School

A Guide to Promote
Walking to School

WALK TO School It's COOL!

Department of Health and Human Services
Centers for Disease Control and Prevention

9.4
Neighborhoods are
encouraged to share
the responsibility of
walking or biking
children to and from
school.
Courtesy of the Centers
for Disease Control and
Prevention, Health
and Human Services
Department

students and adults to the program. It provides guidance on how to establish a program and how to form joint partnerships with community organizations, including public works, transportation, education, and health departments, PTAs, police forces, and politicians (CDC 2002b).

Safe Routes to School

The Safe Routes to School program began in Odense, Denmark, more than twenty years ago. The program succeeded in increasing the number of children walking and biking to and from school, as well as improving child safety. More than 60 percent of Odense school children now ride their bicycles to school, and the child pedestrian accident rate decreased by 80 percent in ten years. Prevalent programs have since been implemented in Austria, Germany, Belgium, and the United Kingdom. Sustrans, a sustainable transport charity of the United Kingdom, publishes an international newsletter about Safe Routes to Schools programs, dispensing information to more than fifty countries (Sustrans 2003).

Fourteen states in the United States have established Safe Routes to School programs, with efforts concentrated at the elementary and middle school levels. Parents have dominated the initiatives and have centered primarily on safety issues, but these efforts also serve to educate children about the health and environmental benefits of walking or biking to school. Neighborhood groups, traffic engineers, local officials, and in some cases state departments of transportation work together to make streets safer for pedestrians and bicyclists along school routes, while encouraging parents and their kids to take advantage of the many benefits of getting around on foot or by bike. The program found its U.S. roots in California in October 1999 when Federal Surface Transportation Safety funds were reserved specifically for Safe Routes. The first Safe Routes to School Bill directed $20 million per year for two years and was renewed in 2001 for another three years at $25 million a year. Marin County, California, saw a 57 percent increase in walking and biking to school in its first year (Davis 2003).

Safe Routes to School programs follow four intertwined models. The Dedicated Resource Model lays the foundation for the other models. It focuses upon policy actions to secure federal, state, or local funds for Safe Routes programs. The model also seeks transportation or safety funds that can be secured without legislation. The Engineering Model centers on providing safe facilities for pedestrians and cyclists in and around school neighborhoods. The model works to change motorist behavior primarily through alterations in street design and also through motorist education and marketing campaigns. Arlington, Virginia, and the Bronx, New York, provide excellent demonstrations of the Engineering Model.

The Enforcement Model highlights particularly dangerous areas of school zones and assigns police to the area. Police visit with children in the classroom and educate them on safe cycling and walking practices. The Enforcement Model is typically a short-term response that works best when integrated fully with the other models. The Encouragement/Education Model is the cheapest to develop and often employs neighborhood volunteers for special events and marketing campaigns. Common themes are walking school buses, group rides, contests, and special events. Monthly activities are encouraged to maximize the use of volunteers. The education aspect focuses primarily on child safety, and upon health and environmental awareness (Transportation Alternatives 2002). Kids play games like the Bicycle Safety Quiz Show and participate in Bicycle Safety Rodeos. The Frequent Rider Miles Program assigns points to each mile traveled by alternative mode. When each child accumulates a set number of points, their tally sheet is dropped into a raffle for gifts donated by local businesses.

The National Highway Safety and Traffic Administration (NHSTA) publication, Safe Routes to School: Practice and Promise, is a comprehensive survey of worldwide Safe Routes to School programs and similar efforts, including contact information. The report may be ordered free of charge from the NHTSA Web site: www.nhtsa.gov (Davis 2003).

Good Practices Guide

The Federal Highway Administration (FHWA) convened a group of bicycle safety experts and created the National Bicycle Safety Education Curriculum in 1998. The *Good Practices Guide for Bicycle Safety Education* serves as an informational resource for those planning or developing bike education programs. The guide highlights sixteen programs as case studies, fifteen in the United States and one in Canada. The various programs target children elementary through high school age, adults, and even the instructors themselves. The guide teaches how to find and secure program funding, gain publicity, partner with other organizations, perform self-assessments, and integrate the curriculum into the classroom when possible and appropriate. FHWA also maintains the Bicycle Safety Education Resource Center, which contains a database of specific training materials for each audience and a database guide that details the specific needs of eight identified audiences (FHWA 2002).

Earning by Learning

The Community Cycling Center, a nonprofit organization based in Eugene, Oregon, runs "Earning by Learning" clubs in low-income schools. The programs provide mostly middle-school kids with recycled bicycles and helmets upon the completion of a safety curriculum. "Earning by Learning" teaches kids how to use and maintain bicycles and develops their riding and mechanical skills, while improving self-esteem and teamwork. The clubs last for at least ten weeks, meeting after school for 1 1/2 to 2 hours per session. Session topics include the environmental and civic benefits of bicycles and recycling bicycles, helmet fitting, mechanical safety checks, obeying traffic rules, proper signaling and stopping, road and weather hazards, map reading, and proper parking. The clubs include short- and long-distance neighborhood rides to practice skills before graduation. As of 2003, Community Cycling Center had operated four bike safety clubs and an alumni group. The center runs a full-service bike shop that refurbishes donated bikes for the program and for sale. This shop generates revenue for operating costs outside the program. Various grant combinations from trusts and foundations provide the necessary funding for the programs. The administrative, personnel, and equipment costs of "Earning by Learning" were estimated at $9,800 to $11,800 for 2001 (Albright 2003; Community Cycling Center 2003).

Partnerships with Local Government

A number of communities have created cooperative efforts between the school district and the municipal government or transit agency. Such partnerships permit organizations to share resources and funding, resulting in their ability to exert a more powerful effort. There are many opportunities for communities to initiate such partnerships.

Portland Teen Transit Adventure

In November 2002, the City of Portland Transportation Options division organized the Portland Teen Transit Adventure to familiarize local youth with the mobility offered by local transportation networks, and to encourage the implementation of mass transit into their lives. Twenty-five kids ranging from age 12 to 18 were recruited from the local Boys and Girls clubs, and presented with am MTV Road Rules–style mission. Using only public transit, the teens were instructed to visit six local businesses and perform a task, in cooperation with the businesses. Stops included a bookstore, a bowling arena, a sushi restaurant, and a tour of a sports arena. For each completed task, the teams received a gift card or other prize. The young people were equipped with a bus schedule and a system map, and were allowed to ask only five yes or no questions throughout the day. In a survey after the adventure, the participants were excited to learn of the potential destinations that could be reached by using the system as a whole, rather than just riding the neighborhood bus. The Portland Transportation Options Division is part of the City of Portland Office of Transportation. Their goal is "to advance transportation options to promote livability and a safe, balanced transportation system." Their programs are mostly grant-funded, but also receive some tax dollars (Bower 2003).

Rogue Valley Transit District

The Rogue Valley Transit District concentrates a few TDM programs at the elementary and secondary school levels. The programs are funded through federal money channeled into Oregon and from marketing revenue from bus advertisements. "Gus Rides the Interactive Bus" carries about 5,000 students annually through the ins and outs of the public bus system. The fifty-minute session for K–6th grade students begins with a video and class presentation, and builds up to the children's ride on the public bus, where they can showcase their newfound knowledge of alternative transportation. The "Bicycle as Transportation" program can be modified for kids at all levels of K–12. About 1,000 students learn the curriculum each year through a fifty-minute classroom presentation. The program teaches kids four main ways bikes are better for getting around than cars: environment, exercise, money, and fun. The instructor and the kids brainstorm situations in which a car trip could be easily replaced with a bike trip and the session concludes with an overview of bicycle safety tips and rules of the road (Barnes 2003).

Roosevelt High School Way to Go

In spring 1999, the City of Seattle teamed up with the Seattle School District to run a pilot program at Roosevelt High School. The goal of the Way to Go program was to raise the awareness of future commuters about their alternative transportation options and to affect their current transportation choices. The City's Trip Reduction Initiative funded the project. Way to Go kicked off the last six weeks of the 1999–2000 school year with a transportation fair. In the fall, several yellow school bus routes were eliminated and the one hundred and seventy-five students along the discontinued routes were given free Metro bus passes. The school offered discounted Metro passes.to all students, installed covered bicycle parking, distributed educational materials, installed a lobby kiosk information center for alternative transportation, and held promotional events. Roosevelt High School recorded the following improvements:

- A nearly 200 percent increase in monthly sales of bus passes, rising from 25 a month to an average of 71 per month.
- Students with free passes picked them up 82 percent of the time vs. an average of 62 percent ridership on the school bus routes during the previous year.
- Thirty-nine percent of students said Way to Go made them more aware of the transportation choices available to them.
- Of the students previously driving alone, 15 percent stopped driving alone and 28 percent drove alone less.

During the second year of the program, more school bus routes were eliminated and the affected students received free Metro passes. One area school has implemented aspects of the Roosevelt project; the Seattle School District and the City of Seattle are working toward the expansion of the project into three selected schools. A Way to Go resource kit is available through www.seattle.gov/waytogo (Way to Go—Seattle 2002).

Contra Costa County SchoolPool Program

The SchoolPool program begins with the distribution of rideshare brochures to parents with school registration packets. Parents interested in carpooling register for free ridematch referral lists that provide the contact information of other interested parents from their child's school. Parents receive the initial lists within five days and receive updated lists during the next six weeks. If no available partners are found, each student may receive up to twenty free transit passes per school year to try public transit during the first two months of school. No school bus service and increased safety and traffic concerns around schools spurred the start of the SchoolPool Pilot Program in 1995. The program originally served five schools within one school district. By spring 2003, the program expanded to serve all of Contra Costa County, including more than 175 public and private schools in more than fifteen school districts. During the 1998–1999 school year, the program cost $65,000 for the 155 participating schools, had 1,204 nonsibling participants, and reduced more than 3.5 million vehicle miles. The program is administered by the Contra Costa Commute Alternative Network and made possible through sales tax revenue contributions from the Contra Costa Transportation Authority and Bay Area Air Quality Management District Transportation Fund for Clean Air monies (Osborn 2003; CCCAN 2000).

Boulder Valley School District Transportation Coordinator

The position of Student Transportation Coordinator is a partnership between the City of Boulder and the Boulder Valley School District. The city obtained federal funding through the Congestion Mitigation and Air Quality (CMAQ) program to pay for the first few years of the position. The coordinator works with the school community—students, staff, and parents—to find transportation options that reduce car trips to and from school. Landon Hilliard encourages and promotes bicycling, walking, and transit use to reduce traffic congestion and improve air quality. Local middle schools and high schools receive discounted rates on teen passes from the Regional Transportation District (RTD) when the school sells the passes. A standard teen pass purchased through RTD costs $21 per month, while passes sold at the school cost $10 per month (this reduction includes a subsidy from the City of Boulder). As of 2003, sixteen Boulder schools and five schools in neighboring Lafayette and Louisville sold teen passes on site. Hilliard is currently negotiating with schools and the regional transit provider to create an Eco-Pass program that allows school faculty and staff to purchase transit passes at a reduced rate. As of early 2003, two schools had signed up for the program and three more were ready to join (Hilliard 2003).

Conclusion

In August 2002, Fairview High School and the surrounding Boulder neighborhoods identified several parking and transportation issues of pressing concern, and compiled a list of potential solutions. The following set of strategies closely matches many of the approaches outlined in earlier chapters of this book:

- Improve bicycle parking
- Develop a formal carpool program
- Offer carpool incentives (e.g., priority parking, reduced parking fees)
- Provide free bike loans for lunchtime trips
- Make available discounted RTD bus passes
- Find ways to make the school bus a more attractive transportation option
- Expand school cafeteria and cuisine
- Raise parking fees
- Practice stricter enforcement of parking violations
- Appoint a FHS Student Transportation Coordinator to address transportation issues
- Build good will with neighbors through Adopt-a-Block idea
- Consult and work with student groups (student council, environmental club)
- Provide Eco-Pass for school staff
- Use Fairview newsletter and school papers for a transportation awareness campaign (Hilliard 2002b)

This demonstrates the applicability of many principles and programs described within this book to transportation issues in a variety of environments. Many of the programs detailed in this chapter can serve as foundations or models for programs in other communities. Program coordinators are eager to share ideas and provide guidance for communities initiating or enhancing programs. Students should be encouraged along the way to take an active role in improving or establishing TDM programs for their school and community. These efforts promote community involvement and leadership skills for students, while serving to improve the community. Many successful TDM programs at the university level evolved from concerned student leaders partnering with the administration to identify transportation solutions. Secondary school programs should not underestimate the value of student involvement. Community awareness at all levels is necessary to affect the large-scale planning decisions of school districts that may cause many of the transportation problems facing schools. University TDM programs provide several examples of successful approaches to managing transportation issues. By utilizing similar techniques at the secondary school level, schools produce smarter commuters who can build upon their experience and education to further enhance transportation choices within the university setting and within their community.

References

Albright, J. 2003. Personal communication with Jensi Albright, Administrative Assistant, Community Cycling Center, February 12.

American Lung Association of Sacramento-Emigrant Trails. 2002. *2001–2002 Annual Report*, Sacramento, CA.

Barnes, M. 2003. Personal communication with Matthew Barnes, TDM planner, Rogue Valley Transit District, Oregon, February 11.

Beaumont, C., and E. Pianca. 2000. *Historic Neighborhood Schools in the Age of Sprawl: Why Johnny Can't Walk to School*, National Trust for Historic Preservation, retrieved December 11, found at www.nationaltrust.org/issues/schoolsSum.pdf.

Bower, D. 2003. Personal communication with Dan Bower, Transportation Options Division, City of Portland, January 3 and 30.

Center for Appropriate Transport. 2001. *Education and Youth Projects*, retrieved February 12, found at www.efn.org/~cat.

Centers for Disease Control and Prevention. 2002a. Barriers to Children Walking and Biking to School—United States, 1999. *MMWR* 51:701–704.

Centers for Disease Control and Prevention. 2002b. *Kidswalk-to-School Resource Materials*, retrieved February 22, found at www.cdc.gov/nccdphp/dnpa/kidswalk/resources.htm.

Centers for Disease Control and Prevention. 2002c. *Prevalence of Overweight among Children and Adolescents: United States, 1999–2000*, retrieved June 2, found at www.cdc.gov/nchs/products/pubs/pubd/hestats/overwght99.htm.

Climate Solutions. 1999. *Smart Moves for Washington Schools*, retrieved December 12, found at www.climatesolutions.org/smartmoves/index.html.

Coles, A. 1999. High Schools Pressed for Space in Student Parking Lots. *Education Week* 6(October):7.

Community Cycling Center. 2003. *Bicycle Safety Clubs*, retrieved May 30, found at www.communitycyclingcenter.org/bikeclubs.html.

Contra Costa Commute Alternative Network. 2000. *SchoolPool: An A+ for Effort to Students Who Carpool*, retrieved July 22, found at www.cccan.org/publications.html.

Davis, C. 2003. Personal communication with Chris Davis, Safe Routes to School Instructor, Marin County, CA, February 12.

Federal Highway Administration, 2002. *Bicycle Safety Education Resource Center,* retrieved February 15, found at www.bicyclinginfo.org/ee/fhwa.html.

Gross, J. 2003. What's Big, Yellow, and Humiliating? *The New York Times* January 27, B1.

Hilliard, L. 2002a. *Transportation Mode Share at Fairview High School.* Boulder Valley School District, CO.

Hilliard, L. 2002b. *Transportation and Parking at Fairview High School: Issues and Solutions.* Boulder Valley School District, CO.

Hilliard, L. 2003. Personal communication with Landon Hilliard, Student Transportation Coordinator, Boulder Valley School District, CO, February 7.

Judson, G. 1992. Student Parking, at a Price. *The New York Times* May 24, A35.

Koster, N. 2003. Personal communication with Noelle Koster, Program Associate, American Lung Association of Sacramento-Emigrant Trails, February 11.

Kouri, C., 1999. *Wait for the Bus: How Low Country School Site Selection and Design Deter Walking to School and Contribute to Urban Sprawl.* South Carolina Coastal Conservation League, Charleston, SC.

Local Government Commission. 2002. *New Schools for Older Neighborhoods: Strategies for Building Our Communities' Most Important Assets,* retrieved January 4, found at www.lgc.org/transportation/schools.html.

Local Government Commission. 2003. *The Decreasing Role of Schools as Community Anchors,* retrieved January 4, found at www.lgc.org/transportation/schools.html.

Moody, M., A. Miller, C. Juhasz-Wood, J. Astley, M. Fraser, and K. Carnahan-Briggs. 2001. *Boulder High Transportation Survey.* Boulder High School AP Statistics Class, Boulder, CO.

National 4-H Council. 2001. *Going Places, Making Choices: Transportation and the Environment.* Chevy Chase, MD.

National Research Center and City of Boulder Audit & Evaluation Division. 2001. *Modal Shift in the Boulder Valley 1990 to 2000 (Travel Diary Report),* p. 12.

Orsini, A. 2002. Personal communication with Arthur Orsini, Director, **off ramp,** December 3.

Osborn, L. 2003. Personal communication with Lynn Osborn, Program Manager, Contra Costa Commute Alternative Network, March 24.

Sustrans. 2003. *United Kingdom Safe Routes to School,* retrieved May 23, found at www.saferoutestoschools.org.uk/html/what_srs.htm.

Transportation Alternatives. 2002. *The 2002 Summary of Safe Routes to School Programs in the United States,* retrieved May 30, found at www.transact.org/PDFs/sr_2002.pdf.

Way to Go—Seattle. 2002. *Roosevelt High School Way to Go Demonstration Project,* retrieved January 22, found at www.ci.seattle.wa.us/waytogo/schools.htm.

Chapter 10

Conclusions

For many years the authors have observed several common auto-related problems on dozens of college and university campuses. Over time we have seen what were once inconveniences become serious, and in some cases, chronic problems. They include parking shortages, traffic congestion, and inefficient campus land uses. The research that provides the foundation for this book included several hundred campus questionnaires, selected campus interviews, dozens of Web site searches, and many interviews with colleagues across the country.

The shortage of student and faculty parking is ubiquitous in North American institutions of higher education and in many secondary schools. Surface parking lots are in competition with other college facilities. The overspill of cars into neighborhoods creates vexing community relations. Student-generated traffic congestion and other forms of pollution accompany the surge of campus vehicles.

BOX 10.1   **TIPS FOR SMART CAMPUS TRANSPORTATION PLANNING**

A few of the lessons from institutions that have had some success:

- *Make sure to ask the right questions.* Do this when developing transportation plans and when hiring consultants to create these plans. A transportation plan should not simply examine how much parking to supply, but also should look at how to provide access to campus at the lowest cost and environmental impact.
- *Make sure that your administrative structure supports your transportation goals.* If all you have is a parking department, consider creating a broader transportation department.
- *Pursue partnerships with local governments and with transit agencies.* Even if there is a history of conflict, there are many opportunities to improve access to campus while also addressing the needs of surrounding communities.

Our primary interest was to discover schools that had identified car-related challenges and had implemented programs, facilities, and other innovations to reduce the negative impacts of car dominance. Our findings show how campus parking and vehicle use can be managed in a way that reduces the unwanted side effects of too many cars on campus. We have identified transit systems and bus pass programs that lure student motorists into more efficient and sustainable modes of travel. Transportation demand management programs including incentives for nonmotorized mobility make campuses more pedestrian- and bicycle-friendly places to work and study. Smart parking management allows some campuses to avoid investments in new parking structures.

We have highlighted eight academic campus case studies where unique experiments and models are providing an alternative to the single-occupancy (student) vehicle. Some schools, including high schools, have made remarkable progress in reducing auto trips to campus. Nevertheless, much needs to be done with improved campus transportation plans, greener fleets, universal transit passes, and financial incentives in order to create more sustainable, healthier campus communities.

Instead of offering our findings as "conclusions," we prefer to suggest the experiments for improving transportation options at the ivory tower are "works in progress." Some colleges have started TDM programs, or a "Bike to Campus" week, or a bicycle service center, or a campus biodiesel bus very

- *If your campus does not yet have a transit pass program, seriously consider creating one.* They are among the simplest and most popular steps a campus can take to start managing demand.
- *Don't be afraid to use the power of the market.* If there is excess demand for parking, consider raising the price.
- *Take nonmotorized travel seriously.* The short trip lengths and young healthy populations at many campuses allow for high mode shares. These types of trips are the cheapest to serve and have the least environmental impact.
- *Harness the power of students.* Many of the programs mentioned in this article were initiated or funded by students, whether through student government action or by direct vote of the student body.

recently and the degree of success or effectiveness is not yet clear. Other schools have undoubtedly pioneered in transportation innovations that we have not identified. But we hope what has been presented here will serve as a start for college communities that strive to be more car-free and more pleasant and livable places.

We have seen that universities have many opportunities to simultaneously save money, reduce the environmental impact of transportation to and from campus, and improve community relations. Because parking has not typically been priced at the true marginal cost of new parking supply, good economic analysis of transportation options for university communities will generally show that an economically efficient transportation policy will rely less on parking and more on transportation alternatives compared to most universities' current practice. This is one of those happy cases where the bottom line supports sound environmental policy.

We also have seen that there are a wide variety of strategies that are available to meet the needs of different types of institutions. Most of this book has focused on the broad set of approaches a university can take to influence the transportation behavior of students, employees, and visitors. The most important determinants are the supply and price of parking, the land-use plans that determine the length and type of trips, the financial incentives to drive alone or travel in other ways, the level of transit service available, and the ease of bicycle use. The decisions planners make in these arenas will have a very significant impact on the transportation choices of students, faculty and staff, and visitors. University communities are at the leading edge in transportation innovation, developing new approaches that may have broad application, from central cities to suburban corporate campuses.

Appendix

Research Contacts

We contacted the following institutions of higher education in our research for this book.

Aalborg University (Denmark)
Adams State College (Colorado)
Aims Community College (Colorado)
Amherst College (Massachusetts)
Amsterdam University
Appalachian State College (North Carolina)
Arapahoe Community College (Colorado)
Arizona State University
Beloit College (Wisconsin)
Berkeley College (New Jersey)
Berkely College (New York)
Boise State University
Bond University (Australia)
Borough of Manhattan Community College
Boston University
Briarwood College (Connecticut)
Bristol University (United Kingdom)
Bronx Community College
Bryn Mawr College (Pennsylvania)
California Polytechnic State University
California State University–Bakersfield
California State University–Chico
California State University–Dominguez Hills
California State University–Fullerton
California State University–Haywood
California State University–Long Beach
California State University–Monterey Bay
Cambridge University (United Kingdom)
Carleton College (Minnesota)
Carnegie Mellon University (Pennsylvania)
Cascadia Community College (Washington)
Central Oregon Community College
Cincinnati State Technical and Community College
City College of San Francisco

Clackamas Community College (Oregon)
Claremont Graduate University (California)
Clemson University (Georgia)
Colby College (Maine)
Colgate University (New York)
College of William & Mary (Virginia)
Colorado Christian University
Colorado College
Colorado Mountain College–Breckenridge
Colorado Mountain College–Steamboat
Colorado Mountain College–Vail
Colorado Northwestern Community College
Colorado School of Mines
Columbia State Community College (Tennessee)
Columbia University
Community College of Rhode Island
Community College of Spokane
Contra Costa Community College (California)
Copenhagen University
Cornell University (New York)
Danville Community College (Illinois)
Diablo Valley College (California)
Duke University (North Carolina)
Eastern Michigan State University
Edmonds Community College (Washington)
El Centro College (Texas)
Emory University (Georgia)
Estrella Mountain Community College (Arizona)
Evergreen Valley College (California)
Fond du Lac Tribal and Community College (Minnesota)

Foothill–De Anza Community College (California)
Fort Lewis College (Colorado)
Freiburg University (Germany)
Fresno City College
Fresno Pacific University
Fresno State University
Front Range Community College (Colorado)
George Mason University (Virginia)
Georgia Institute of Technology
Georgia Southern University
Golden Gate University
Griffith University (Australia)
Grinnell College (Iowa)
Hampshire College (Massachusetts)
Harold Washington Community College (Chicago)
Harvard University
Harvey Mudd College (California)
Haverford College (Pennsylvania)
Holyoke Community College (Maryland)
Hostos Community College (New York)
Houston Community College
Howard Community College (Maryland)
Humboldt State University (California)
Humboldt University (Germany)
Iowa State University
Jackson Community College (Mississippi)
James Cook University (Australia)
Kellogg Community College (Michigan)
Kennedy-King College (Chicago)
Kings College (United Kingdom)
Kings University (Canada)
Kingsborough Community College (New York)
La Guardia Community College (New York)
Lackawanna Junior College (Pennsylvania)
Lansing Community College
LaTrobe University (Australia)
Lewis & Clark College (Oregon)
Louisiana State University
Loyola University (New Orleans)
Malcolm X College (Chicago)
Marquette University
Massachusetts Institute of Technology
McGill University (Canada)
Mercer County Community College (New Jersey)
Mesa State College (Colorado)
Metropolitan State University (Denver)
Middlebury College (Vermont)
Monash University (Australia)

Montana State University
Mount Holyoke College (Massachusetts)
Mount Hood Community College (Oregon)
Mount Royal College (Canada)
Murdoch University (Australia)
North Carolina State University
North Virginia Community College
Northern Arizona University
Northwestern University
Oakton Community College (Illinois)
Occidental College (California)
Odense University (Denmark)
Ohio State University
Oregon State University
Pennsylvania State University
Pepperdine University
Peralta College (California)
Pomona College (California)
Potomac Community College (West Virginia)
Princeton University
Purdue University
Queensborough Community College (New York)
Raritan Community College (New Jersey)
Reed College (Oregon)
Regis University (Colorado)
Rensselaer Polytechnic Institute (New York)
Ricks College (Idaho)
Rose State College (Oklahoma)
Sacramento State University
Salt Lake Community College
San Jose City College
Santa Barbara City College
Santa Clara University
Santa Rosa Junior College
Seattle Central Community College
Shelton State Community College (Alabama)
Shoreline Community College (Seattle)
Simon Fraser University (British Columbia, Canada)
Smith College (Massachusetts)
Sonoma State University
South Puget Sound Community College
Southern Illinois University
Southern University (Baton Rouge)
St. Louis Community College
St. Olaf College (Minnesota)
Stanford University
Swarthmore College (Pennsylvania)
Syracuse University

Texas A&M University
Texas Southmost College
Texas State Technical College
Truckee Meadows Community College
(Nevada)
Tulane University (Louisiana)
University College of Utrecht (Netherlands)
University of Alaska
University of Alberta
University of Arizona
University of Bohn (Germany)
University of British Columbia
University of Calgary
University of California–Berkeley
University of California–Davis
University of California–Irvine
University of California–Los Angeles
University of California–San Diego
University of California–Santa Barbara
University of California–Santa Cruz
University of Canberra (Australia)
University of Colorado–Boulder
University of Colorado–Colorado Springs
University of Connecticut
University of Denver
University of Edinburough
University of Florida
University of Georgia
University of Hawaii
University of Illinois–Urbana-Champaign
University of Kansas
University of Kentucky
University of Leiden (Netherlands)
University of London
University of Maryland
University of Massachusetts–Amherst
University of Miami
University of Michigan–Ann Arbor
University of Minnesota
University of Montana
University of Nebraska
University of Nevada–Las Vegas

University of New Hampshire
University of New Mexico
University of New South Wales (Australia)
University of North Carolina–Charlotte
University of North Carolina–Wilmington
University of Northern Colorado
University of Notre Dame
University of Oregon
University of Pittsburgh
University of Portland
University of Quebec
University of Rhode Island
University of Southern Colorado
University of Texas
University of Texas Medical Branch
University of Texas–San Antonio
University of the Pacific (California)
University of Vermont
University of Victoria
University of Washington–Seattle
University of West Los Angeles
University of Wisconsin–Green Bay
University of Wisconsin–Madison
University of Wisconsin–Milwaukee
University of Wyoming
Utah State University
Valley Forge Military Academy
(Pennsylvania)
Vanderbilt University (Tennessee)
Virginia Tech University
Warren Wilson College (North Carolina)
Wayne County Community College
(Michigan)
Wayne State University (Michigan)
West Virginia University
Western Michigan University
Western State College (Colorado)
Western Washington State University
Whittier College (California)
Wor-Wic Community College (Maryland)
Yale University

INDEX

Italicized letters *b, f, t,* and *p* refer to boxes figures, tables, and photos

Island Press Board of Directors